The Enneagram in Love & Work

Also by Helen Palmer
The Enneagram: Understanding Yourself and the Others in Your Life

THE ENNEAGRAM

in Love & Work

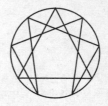

Understanding Your
Intimate & Business Relationships

Helen Palmer

■ HarperSanFrancisco
An Imprint of HarperCollins Publishers

To my husband, Christopher, and our son, Josh,
for so many good years together

THE ENNEAGRAM IN LOVE & WORK: *Understanding Your Intimate &*
Business Relationships. Copyright © 1995 by The Center for the Investigation
and Training of Intuition. All rights reserved. Printed in the United States of
America. No part of this book may be used or reproduced in any manner
whatsoever without written permission except in the case of brief quotations
embodied in critical articles and reviews. For information address Harper-
Collins Publishers, 10 East 53rd Street, New York, NY 10022.

HarperCollins Web Site: http://www.harpercollins.com

HarperCollins ®, 📖 ®, and HarperSanFrancisco™ are trademarks of
HarperCollins Publishers Inc.

Text design by Margery Cantor

FIRST HarperCollins PAPERBACK EDITION PUBLISHED IN 1995

Library of Congress Cataloging-in-Publication Data
Palmer, Helen.
The enneagram in love & work : understanding your intimate & business
relationships / Helen Palmer.
ISBN 0–06–250679–X (cloth)
ISBN 0–06–250721–4 (pbk.)
ISBN 0–06–250808–3 (intl. pbk.)
1. Enneagram.   I. Title.   II. Title: Enneagram in love & work.
BF698.3.E54P35   1993   92–56417
155.2'6—dc20

95 96 97 98 99 ❖ RRD(H) 10 9 8 7 6 5 4 3 2 1

Contents

Acknowledgments

I owe a great debt to the thousands of people who have been willing to speak on Enneagram panels and to share their insights and self-observations. I wish to acknowledge their embodiment of the nine types and to thank them for teaching us about themselves. Thank God for people who have been willing to work.

I want to thank my strong core of students who have been with this material for more than twenty years. Special thanks to Debra Olsen, the hub of our small universe, who has kept us focused at difficult times.

My heartfelt thanks also go to Jim Fox of the HarperCollins legal department for defending my right to open the Enneagram of personality types to the public. He, along with my editor John Loudon, has been a true friend of the work. I thank John from the very bottom of my heart for his editorial guidance and exquisite patience in bringing this book forward. I also wish to acknowledge Ani Camichian of HarperSanFrancisco, who believed in me more than I believed in myself. Finally, I want to thank production editor Mimi Kusch, copyeditor Holly Elliott, and designer Margery Cantor for their extraordinary efforts.

Foreword

Helen Palmer's contributions to the Enneagram require a special commentary. While it is true that she has elucidated the personality types in an original way, and added her own particular emphasis to the study of type, it is not these obvious contributions for which she should be recognized.

The first time I saw the Enneagram being taught, it was presented in an oral-tradition format, a method that Helen has been developing for more than twenty years. The memory of that initial class still remains with me and it is therefore with pleasure and confidence that I introduce her book about the Enneagram types and their interactions.

For starters, Helen is largely responsible for developing what is now becoming known as the Enneagram oral tradition. The approach is based on Claudio Naranjo's earlier exploration of personality type using interview techniques. This is not simply the passing of information from generation to generation by the spoken word, although the tradition encompasses this; it is representatives of the types themselves presenting their own stories, often in panel format. In this way we hear directly the self-observations, understandings, mental preoccupations, and strengths and weaknesses of each type. The oral tradition is, in my opinion, superior to any other way of teaching and learning the Enneagram material. It brings the system to life, which allows people to identify their own type more readily, to appreciate differences, and to deepen self-understanding.

The oral tradition is a stunning method with which to convey sensitive psychological insight. Yet it also happens to be the ideal framework in which to demonstrate Helen's elucidation of each type's recurrent way of organizing attention. This focus on the role of attention, and the consequent awareness that different organizations of attention can produce, will endure over time as part of the theoretical core of the system. It was her insight into the way that we are each bound by a habitual organization of attention that first attracted me to the Enneagram. This can be called the molecular level of the way that personality works, since attention defines what we can perceive and what information gets left out as we collect and sort the data presented to our senses. When grasped, this fundamental understanding allows us all to realize that we are simply incomplete rather than right or wrong.

Beyond the oral tradition and personality's underpinning in attention lies Helen's lucid work concerning the direct relationship between original essence and each type's system of awareness. In this view, personality can become a friend, instead of an enemy, of essence, a source of energy to use for personal development and in claiming the higher aspects of our type. In this book she further shows how the energy of each personality is manifested in particular one-to-one, social, and self-preservation behaviors.

I have taught with Helen in the Enneagram Professional Training Program since 1988. We have worked on the integration of personality with essence for both ourselves and those who attend the workshops, for ultimately we must live as best we can in both the realm of personality and the realms of essential self. Just as the personality can provide a path back to the essence of all beings, so too can the energy of essence form a path forward to develop a healthy personal life. It is an honor to be associated with this pioneering approach to the material.

DAVID N. DANIELS, M.D.
Clinical Professor, Department of Psychiatry and
Behavioral Science, Stanford School of Medicine

I

Introduction

1

Personality Typing

FREUD WAS ONCE ASKED to define the elements of a fulfilling life; he is said to have answered, "to love and to work." His goals for the "talking cure" were therefore the pleasure of loving relationships and productivity.[1] A couple of generations later, Freud's hopes for humanity are just as apt. We do indeed devote most of our time and energy to matters of the heart and mind; and most of our joys and sorrows concern relationships and careers. We have come a long way, however, in observing the central differences among people and what can help them to love and work well.

The Enneagram in Love & Work describes nine different ways of relating in intimacy and business. Each viewpoint is determined by certain mental and emotional concerns. The nine types dovetail well with a wide range of current psychological thinking, but they describe normal and high-functioning people rather than pathological trends. No type is better than another, and each can be effective, but they interact in radically different ways.

The nine personalities are part of a human development model called the Enneagram. *Ennea* means "nine" in Greek, and *gram* means "model." In 1988 I wrote *The Enneagram: Understanding Yourself and the Others in Your Life.* That book is based on self-descriptions of the nine personality types, set in the model's framework of spiritual ideas. *The Enneagram in Love & Work* is intended as a companion. This book describes how the nine types interact in intimate and work-related settings. There is not much duplication of information between the two books. I have attempted to introduce some new material about the types, including a directory of the ways in which they typically relate to one another.

The best way to recognize your type is by listening to people who share your own point of view. When those who know their own type tell you how they love and work, you know you're either like them or you're not. For years I've taught the Enneagram using panels of speakers who represent their types. Listening to others describe themselves is by far the best way for people to understand themselves. It is better than any teacher's opinion, or any book.

The panelists speak as living authorities. They draw us into their lives by offering their private insights, their personal thoughts, and an authenticity of feeling that imprints their point of view on the listener's memory. The teacher's role is to develop a conversation in ways that respectfully demonstrate the key behavior patterns and the inner intentions of type.

Listening to live presentations is especially encouraging when secure people tell about the ways they've learned to work with themselves. A common prejudice still exists about self-observation. Many think of it as work for broken people rather than as a means for personal growth. This bias is grounded in our cultural belief system. If being able "to love and to work" is the key to living well,[2] why then would people who are already successful in life, who can already love and work exceptionally well, be interested in radical self-change? The answer lies in the stories of successful people who want more than a fulfilling career, more than a good sex life, and more than a healthy family. They have every reason to be entirely satisfied with themselves, but they are not. They are attracted to the Enneagram and tell their stories on panels because the Enneagram is one of the few personality systems that anchors type in spiritual life. The explosion of interest in Enneagram studies in recent years is due to this anchor. The system provides a link between personality type and higher consciousness.

The Soup of the Soup of the Soup

I knew that the Enneagram was making an impact when ads like this started to appear in local papers. It's hard to imagine a better grass-roots testimony to the practicality of the system.

East Bay Express, personals ad, June 1992

SOULMATE/BEST FRIEND? Vegetarian, athletic, romantic, affectionate, open-minded, intelligent, optimistic, liberal, unconventional, nonmaterialistic, attractive Amer-Asian male (26, 5'6") seeking life partner (tall, attractive, 26 to 30s) with same qualities. Drug-, smoke-, T.V.-, alcohol-free. Please write with photo.

RUBENSESQUE. Straight black female, 36, seeking conversation, companionship, and fun with black male who has wit and sanity.

ENNEAGRAM SIX, 44, seeks Enneagram Nine woman 40s, for shared vision, movement, warm fuzzies. Also shared interests: health, growth, wisdom, nature walks.

I was horrified about the ad. Can the Enneagram, with its profound capacity to evoke compassion for different types of people, be so easily trivialized? What about its vital spiritual aspect? Where are the ads like: "Enneagram Six, courageous and faithful, seeks Enneagram Nine to develop love and right action"? Where are the ads that say, "Male Six—seeking any suitable companion. The goal is spiritual liberation"?

There is a Sufi story that illustrates the situation. It concerns the dilution of teachings that were once hearty and nourishing. Dilution is actually a classic way for secret oral teachings to maintain secrecy from one generation to the next. They are hidden in public places and from time to time become available to large numbers of people. But only some find them palatable. The few absorb the message, trace the teaching to its source, and help to renew its vitality.

> A kinsman came to see the Mulla from somewhere deep in the country, bringing a duck as a gift. Delighted, Nasrudin had the bird cooked and shared it with his guest. Presently, however, one countryman after another started to call, each one the friend of the friend of the "man who brought you the duck." No further presents were forthcoming.
>
> At length the Mulla was exasperated. One day yet another stranger appeared. "I am the friend of the friend of the friend of the relative who brought you the duck." He sat down like all the rest, expecting a meal. Nasrudin handed him a bowl of hot water.
>
> "What is this?"
>
> "That is the soup of the soup of the soup of the duck that was brought by my relative."[3]

When too many come, the material gets watered down, losing its original vigor. Inevitably so few can be affected that the teaching loses popularity and is rejected as useless. It becomes obscure, sometimes for generations, not because it is untrue but because of the nature of the times.

Like seed that lies dormant during seasons of drought and cold, the perennial teachings disappear for long periods and are renewed when the human climate is right.

Following Freud's directive, the current climate offers many teachings that concern our ability to love and work well with one another. Most of these focus on the psychological traits that make people different from one another. Some describe the collective reality that all people share, but the Enneagram is one of the very few that join the unique and private world of personality with specific aspects of universal consciousness.[4]

The Enneagram's power lies in linking personality type to specific aspects of the human essence. Essence consists of the permanent, as contrasted to the accidental, elements of being. An awareness of essence has also been called higher consciousness or spiritual attainment. The higher aspects of type are actually spiritual qualities. They properly belong to the realm of the divine and are not to be confused with talents, creative leanings, and high-functioning psychological traits. Spiritual qualities are not the same as the clarity of mind and emotional generosity displayed by people who are psychologically mature.

These gifts of the spirit appear when awareness is shifted beyond the boundaries of thought and feeling. They cannot be grasped by analysis or emotion, because they are not of the same order of consciousness as psychological traits. There is a natural tendency to confuse aspects of essence with good psychological functioning, because to describe essence at all we have to name its many activities with words that describe ordinary events.

The Abhidhamma, the classic work on Buddhist psychology, is another ancient system that links type with spiritual life. The traits ascribed to the three Buddhist types correspond beautifully with the Enneagram's central triangle. The Greed type, like Enneagram Three, is motivated by gain. More money, more fame, more pleasure, and so on. The Hate type, like Enneagram Six, sees life as a battle. The Delusional type, like Enneagram Nine, tries to function without paying attention. In the Buddhist system, the three deluded views are counteracted by cultivating their opposite tendencies, which are Nonattachment, Compassion, and Mindfulness.[5]

The "Veil of Illusion"

Sacred psychology sees personality as a false-self system. The "true self" is spiritual in nature. It was overshadowed in early life when attention turned to meet the needs of survival. Over time we identified so strongly with the characteristics of our type, and came to rely so heavily on conditioned perceptions, that we forgot our true nature and "became" our personality, or false self.[6] The Enneagram is a psychology from sacred tradition that is based on nine personality types, which, from the perspective of the true, or spiritual, self, are nine illusions about life; and that illusion is the natural starting place for both psychological and spiritual growth.

> As for him who looks through eyeglasses, everything he sees seems to be the color that they are. And just as things appear smaller or larger according to the shape of the lenses, the passions and affectation of the soul make everything appear according to the passions that govern it.
>
> (Juan de Borya, *The Empresas Morales*, 1581)

2

Synopsis of the Nine Types

Pᴀʀᴛɴᴇʀsʜɪᴘ ᴅᴇᴍᴏɴsᴛʀᴀᴛᴇs ᴛʜᴇ ᴅɪғғᴇʀᴇɴᴄᴇs between us. Each of us can be telling the truth, yet each can have a different story to tell. We look at our marriage, a job, and our children from radically different angles, often without seeing a systematic bias. Extraordinarily precise, the Enneagram allows us to look deeply within our own character and to clarify relationships with clients, co-workers, family, and friends. That insight quickly turns to compassion when you compare your own bias with those of people who are unlike you. It stirs compassion to see through the eyes of others and to feel the pressure of their emotional life, because when you take on others' outlook, their perspective is right.

NINE POINTS OF VIEW

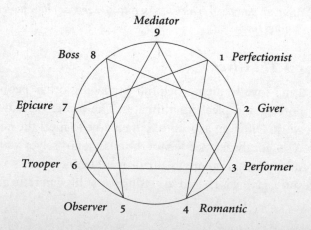

One ✦ The Perfectionist

Earning love by being perfect. Worrying about getting it right. Measuring up to the highest standards. Finding an ethical platform on which to build your life. Thinking centers on should, must, and ought to. We should have a faultless relationship. We must have a spotless record at work. At its best, the commitment to goodness serves as a humane guide to improvement. In self-defense, Ones often feel morally superior by finding fault with others.

FOCUS OF ATTENTION

- *Searching for perfection. Avoiding error and evil.*
- *Conscientious. High moral character.*
- *Think right. Should, must, and ought to.*
- *Do right. Emphasize the practical virtues: work, thrift, honesty, and effort.*
- *Be right. Severe internal critic. An internal judging voice.*
- *Compulsive work load can block out unacceptable feelings.*
- *Anger caused by unmet needs. Self-denial generates resentment. Not aware of own anger ("I'm just energetic today").*
- *Worry in decision making. Afraid to make a mistake.*
- *This focus of attention ensures an ethical and moral life. It can also lead to:*
  - *One-right-way thinking: right or wrong, black or white. No grays.*
  - *Superb powers of criticism. An intuitive sense of how perfect things could be.*

Two ✦ The Giver

Ensuring love by being helpful. Managing other people's lives. Supporting and pleasing intimates. The power behind the throne at work. Different aspects of self emerge to meet the needs of others. A self for the team, a self for the boss, many selves for private life. At its best, this giving is altruistic and generous. As a defensive gesture, giving is geared to getting something in return.

FOCUS OF ATTENTION

° *Gaining approval. Adapting to please others. Avoiding own needs.*

° *Pride in being needed. Being central in people's lives. Being indispensable.*

° *A sense of having many different selves to meet the needs of others.*

° *Confusion arises between the different selves. "Which one is really me?"*

° *Hard to recognize own needs. Needs are met by helping other people.*

° *Wanting freedom. Feeling confined by support given to others.*

° *Self-presentation alters to meet the needs of others. This way of paying attention can lead to:*

  ° *Empathic emotional connections or:*

  ° *Adaptation to the wishes of others as a way of gaining or retaining their love.*

Three ◆ The Performer

Winning love through achievement and image. Doing things with the family. High-powered and high-profile at work. Sensitive to status. Wanting to be first, to lead, to be seen. Emanating an impressive facade. Work is the area of interest; feelings are suspended while the job gets done. At its best, the performance orientation produces effective leadership. As a means of defense, image is tailored to bolster personal success.

FOCUS OF ATTENTION

° *Achievement, productiveness, and performance. Goals, tasks, and results.*

° *Competition and efficiency. Avoiding failure.*

° *Poor access to emotional life. Heart is in work.*

° *Convergent thinking. A multitrack mind focused on a single product or goal.*

- "I am what I do." Confusion between the real self and one's job or role.
- Learning to "do" feelings. Doing the look and learning the lines.
- Chameleon. Changing roles and changing image.
- This way of paying attention can maximize success. It also leads to:
  - Self-deception. Beginning to believe the public image.

Four ✦ The Romantic

Longing for love at a distance, feeling disappointed when love is near at hand. We used to be connected, now it doesn't feel right. We had it once. Where did it go? Lifelong searching for heart connection; attraction, hate, high drama, pain. Elegant lifestyles, unique presentation, a distinctive career, creative business views. At its best, the passionate quest leads to depth of feeling. As a posture, dramatic moods make Fours too precious for ordinary life.

FOCUS OF ATTENTION

- Wanting what is unavailable, far away, and hard to get. Avoiding the ordinary.
- Mood, manners, luxury, and good taste hedge low self-esteem.
- Attracted to the mood of melancholy. The flavor of longing.
- Disdaining ordinary life, the "flatness of ordinary feelings."
- Amping up ordinary life through loss, fantasy, artistic connection, and dramatic acts. Drama kings and queens.
- Push-pull relationships. Wanting the best of what is missing. Pushing it away when it's available again. This alternating focus reinforces:
  - Feelings of abandonment and loss, but also lends itself to:
  - Emotional sensitivity and depth. An ability to support others during pain and crisis.

Five ✦ The Observer

Detached from love and charged emotion. Needing privacy to discover what they feel. Separated from people in public, feeling more emotional when they're by themselves. Fives like protected work environments, no interruptions, limited windows of contact, and agendas announced in advance. At its best, the detached stance produces reliable, clear-minded analysis. As a psychological strategy, detachment minimizes contact.

FOCUS OF ATTENTION

° *Preoccupied with privacy and noninvolvement.*

° *Storing knowledge and the essentials of survival. Avoiding emptiness.*

° *Tightening the belt to maintain independence. Making do with less.*

° *Valuing emotional control. Preferring structured events, known agenda and time.*

° *Compartments. Keeping the departments of life separate from each other. Predetermined time slots for emotionally charged events.*

° *The power of knowing. Analytic systems and special information. Wanting the keys to the way the world works. Figuring out feelings.*

° *Confusing spiritual nonattachment with the need to detach from emotional pain.*

° *Watching life from the point of view of an outside observer. This way of paying attention can lead to:*

  ° *Feeling isolated from the events of one's own life or an ability to:*

  ° *Assume a detached point of view that is unaffected by fear or desire.*

Six ✦ The Trooper

Questioning love and a rosy future. Afraid to believe and be betrayed. Do you still want me? Will my work flourish? Is this certain? Should I doubt? Loyal in love, Troopers turn to their intimates for reassurance. Mistrusting authority, they ask hard questions at work. Well used, a questioning mind produces clarity of purpose. As a life stance, inner doubt interferes with progress.

FOCUS OF ATTENTION
- *Procrastinating. Thinking replaces doing. Avoiding action.*
- *High goals, often with a history of incompletion.*
- *Anxiety peaks with success. Success equals exposure to hostile forces.*
- *Amnesia about success and pleasure.*
- *Authority problems. Either submitting to or rebelling against authority.*
- *Suspecting other people's motives, especially authorities'.*
- *Identifying with underdog causes. Leading the opposition party.*
- *Afraid to recognize own anger. Afraid of other people's anger.*
- *Skepticism and doubt. Buddhist "doubting mind."*
- *A mental "Yes, but . . ." or "This may not work."*
- *Scanning the environment for clues to explain the inner sense of threat.*
- *This way of paying attention will confirm that:*
  - *The world is a threatening place, but also leads to:*
  - *Recognizing the motives and hidden agendas that influence relating.*

Seven ✦ The Epicure

Entitled to love and to be well regarded. Expecting projects to come out right. Love and work should be adventures. Wanting to lead a fabulous life. The best part of love is initial attraction. The best part of work is a brilliant idea. Brainstorming, planning, opening options. A positive future, an exciting career. At its best, the adventurous approach conveys its enthusiasm to others. As a self-serving tactic, the attraction to pleasure is a way to escape from pain.

FOCUS OF ATTENTION

- ° *Stimulation. New and interesting things to do. Wanting to stay high. Avoiding pain.*
- ° *Maintaining multiple options. Hedging commitment to a single course of action. Fearing limitation.*
- ° *Replacing deep or painful feelings with a pleasant alternative. Escaping to mental pleasure. Talking, planning, and intellectualizing.*
- ° *Charm as a first line of defense. Fearing types who move forward into friendly contact with people. Avoiding conflict by going through the cracks. Talking one's way out of trouble.*
- ° *A way of paying attention that relates and systematizes information so that commitments come with loopholes and options. This style of attention can lead to:*
  - ° *Rationalized escapism from a difficult or limiting commitment or:*
  - ° *The ability to find connections, parallels, and unusual fits. A talent for nonlinear synthesis of information.*

Eight ✦ The Boss

Expressing love through protection and power. Liking the truth that comes out in a fight. Pushing for contact. At ease with anger. Stand up for your people. Securing the bunker at work. Gravitating to positions of authority and control, Eights set the rules in love and business life. At its best, the take-charge stance develops leaders who use their power wisely. As a power stance, the best defense is a good offense.

FOCUS OF ATTENTION

- ° *Controlling possessions and personal space.*
- ° *Concerned about justice and power. Avoiding weakness.*
- ° *Excessive self-presentation—too much, too loud, too many.*
- ° *Impulse control. Needing to set limits.*
- ° *Difficulty in recognizing dependency needs and softer emotions.*

- *Boundary issues. Learning the difference between self-defense and aggression.*
- *Denying other points of view in favor of the "truth." Confusing objective truth with a subjective opinion that serves own agenda.*
- *An "all-or-nothing" style of attention, which tends to see the extremes of a situation. People seem to be either fair or unfair, either warriors or wimps, with no middle ground. This style of attention can lead to:*
  - *Unconsciously denying personal weakness or:*
  - *Exercising appropriate force in the service of others.*

Nine ✦ The Mediator

Merging with loved ones, losing boundaries. Taking on their point of view. Becoming stubborn instead of getting angry. Sitting on the fence. "I didn't say no, but I'm not sure I agree with you." Nines can relate to all sides of an argument, which derails their own agenda. "Yes" means "Yes, I'm reflecting your opinion." "Maybe" possibly could mean "No." At its best, the merging habit offers genuine support. As a protective measure, adopting many points of view cushions commitment to any one of them.

FOCUS OF ATTENTION
- *Replacing essential needs with unessential substitutes.*
- *Comforting self with unessential pleasures. Avoiding conflict.*
- *Ambivalence about personal decisions. "Do I agree or disagree?" Seeing all sides of the question. Decisions are easy when not personally loaded, for example, emergency actions or political opinions.*
- *Postponing change by repeating familiar solutions. Acting through habit. Ritualism. There's plenty of time. It can wait until tomorrow.*
- *Hard to initiate change. Easier to know what you don't want than what you do.*
- *Can't say no. Hard to separate. Hard to be the one to go.*
- *Damping physical energy and anger. Diverting energy to trivia. Delayed reaction time for anger. Passive aggression. Anger equals separation.*

- *Control by going stubborn. Do nothing. Wait it out. Control by using time. Wait some more.*
- *Paying attention to other people's agendas, which leads to:*
  - *Difficulty in forming a personal position, but also develops:*
  - *The ability to recognize and support what is essential to other people's lives.*

3

The Passions and Dynamics of the Types

SEVERAL BOOKS HAVE RECENTLY appeared that describe the nine Enneagram personality types in ways that conform to Western psychological thinking.[7] Each type is described in terms of a mental and emotional habit and the ways in which those habits are acted out. An older approach sees type as centered on one of the emotional passions that recur in sacred tradition. In this approach, the passion is the central axis that organizes the thoughts, feelings, and behavior patterns that are characteristic of type. Unlike ordinary emotions, which constantly change, the passion is the crux of an illusion, a compulsion, the linchpin that keeps the personality in place.

The emotional passion operates in tandem with fixed ideas about the world.[8] The total effect is powerful enough to create a "veil of illusion." We think we're seeing the full 360 degrees, but in fact our reality is determined by our bias. The Pride type Two, for example, sees that people are in need of help. The Lust type Eight sees that things are out of control. The Envy type Four sees that something is missing, and so on through all nine types. The good news is that we're skillful about dealing with our own sector of reality. The bad news is that we're boxed in.

The Passions of Sacred Tradition

Traditionally, there are seven biases or passions, plus two generic tendencies that all types hold in common, for a total of nine. The seven are widely known as Christianity's seven capital vices or deadly sins. George Ivanovich Gurdjieff (1872–1949), the pioneer of the Enneagram in the West, called the bias the chief feature of personality.[9] Knowing your bias, and those of the people to whom you relate, improves relationships immensely. This knowledge opens a clear view of loved ones as they are to themselves, without the bias of your own projections; and it puts a great many human difficulties into perspective. What once seemed to be arbitrary and harmful actions take on a new perspective. Arbitrary behavior can be entirely logical within a given framework; and the harm that people do is largely motivated by their own pain. Gurdjieff called the bias of personality Chief Feature.

Always the same motive moves Chief Feature. It tips the scales. It is like a bias in bowling, which prevents the ball going straight. Always Chief Feature makes us go off at a tangent. It arises from one or more of the seven deadly sins, but chiefly from self-love and vanity. One can discover it by becoming more conscious; and its discovery brings an increase of consciousness.[10]

Gurdjieff, a spiritual teacher of enormous personal magnetism, lived and taught during the period when Freudian ideas about the unconscious were barely being circulated. Stating that he learned the Enneagram from Sufi sources, he introduced the nine-pointed star diagram, including the internal flow pattern that unites the points in specific ways. The Enneagram diagram in use today became the signature of his work.[11]

Richard Rohr, a Catholic priest and Enneagram author, writes:

The juxtaposition of the passions with their positive alternatives has been prominent in the history of Christian spiritual-

ity. Geoffrey Chaucer (ca. 1340–1400), the greatest English poet before Shakespeare, offers an especially interesting list in the Parson's Tale from the Canterbury Tales. *Chaucer writes from the assumption that there is at least one specific virtue as an antidote to each capital sin. His ideas are very close to the Enneagram teaching, in that the corresponding pairs of his "sins" and "virtues" are practically identical.*

Chaucer designates a remedy, or healing virtue, for each "sin." Humility helps against pride, true love of God helps against envy, the remedy for anger is patience, laziness (sloth) is overcome through fortitude, avarice through compassion, gluttony through sobriety and moderation, lechery (lust) through chastity.[12]

Continuing the concept of passions as potential agents of spiritual liberation, the Christian poet Dante describes the seven areas of purgatory in practically the same language used in Enneagram studies today. Purgatory is the waiting place between earthly life and the heavenly realms, a place where sins are expiated in preparation for bliss, or permanent being.

Type	Dante (1265–1321), *The Divine Comedy, Purgatorio*		Oscar Ichazo, The Arica Training, 1970	
One	Anger	Meekness	Anger	Serenity
Two	Pride	Humility	Pride	Humility
Three			Deceit	Truthfulness
Four	Envy	Charity	Envy	Equanimity
Five	Avarice	Poverty	Avarice	Detachment
Six			Fear	Courage
Seven	Gluttony	Abstinence	Gluttony	Sobriety
Eight	Lust	Chastity	Excess	Innocence
Nine	Sloth	Zeal	Laziness	Action

Dante's articulation of the passions and their higher opposites from the *Purgatorio* section of *The Divine Comedy*[13] are placed next to the work of Oscar Ichazo, a seminal contemporary Enneagram teacher. Ichazo initially gave his version of the traditional passions at a training session held in Arica, Chile, in 1970. In a brilliant synthesis of traditional ideas, he applied Christianity's capital sins to Gurdjieff's nine-pointed star. Dante also described deceit and fear as states of consciousness, and Ichazo placed them on the Gurdjieff diagram, for a total of nine.[14]

Deceit and fear appear at what are called the shock points, or anchors, of the Enneagram's inner triangle.[15] Three and Six highlight the generic tendencies that all types of people hold in common. According to sacred tradition, the personality is a false-self system that developed in childhood and eventually overshadowed our "real," or spiritual, nature. Deceit involves identifying with the contents of our thoughts and feelings. Identification is a

THE PASSIONS AND ARROWS

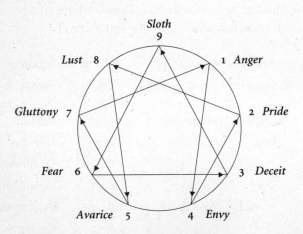

Arrows are added to Ichazo's placement of the traditional passions on Gurdjieff's nine-pointed star. (*Transpersonal Psychologies*, ed. Charles T. Tart [New York: Harper & Row, 1975; repr. El Cerrito, CA: Psychological Processes, 1983]).

psychological mechanism that is necessary for the formation of personality. We all identify with the characteristics of our type, but through identification we became deceived, or convinced, that our personality is our nature.

People who observe that identification with role and image is the chief feature of their psychological life place themselves at the Three point in the diagram. Their life stories highlight the dilemma of living through a false persona to gain approval and love. Their self-observations remind us that we all have replaced our true or spiritual nature with the characteristics of type.

Fear is the second "generic" quality that factors into the formation of type. Sacred tradition reminds us that children are born with physical trust and faith in the goodness of people. We all became frightened and guarded when that original security was invaded by distress and pain. People who identify with fearfulness as the major feature of their inner life place themselves at the Six point of the diagram. Their self-observations remind us of the fear that underlies the formation of type. They say that anxiety arises first in oneself and is then projected outward. They scan the environment to find an explanation for an inner sense of threat.

Projection is the major psychological defense mechanism for Six (paranoid style). It also plays its part in all biased perception. We all share the generic tendency to look outside of ourselves to explain why we feel the way we do. Our fear makes us project, or look outward, to find a reason for our distress.

The generic factor of fear in the formation of type is highlighted in the universal fear of change. It is very difficult to change a significant habit, even when we can watch ourselves act it out. We can have the benefit of support from people who love and encourage us, yet we still resist change. We stall. We are afraid. We vacillate. We doubt. We look at the problem from any number of angles. We tell ourselves that the problem is trivial. Most of all, we forget. Change threatens our personality. We are afraid to change our identity. To be defenseless makes us feel as vulnerable as children again.

Although they have traditionally been named in the negative, as vices, the passions are a primary source of energy for spiritual liberation. They are the raw material, the compost, the qualities of human nature that can be transformed to become aspects of divinity. It should also be pointed out that the Enneagram names only those nine facets of higher being that can be experienced by transforming negative emotional energies. Joy, for example, does not appear as one of the higher aspects of type; neither is there mention of emptiness or bliss. The model is focused on the passions as agents of change from ordinary to higher consciousness and deals only with the specific facets of being that are produced by transforming negative emotional energy.

The Arrows

A great deal of the power of the diagram lies in its shape. From the system of interlocking lines, predictions can be made about changes in personality during times of personal security as well as times of risk or stress. A secure situation, such as a good job or a promising relationship, causes us to relax our defenses. Risk mobilizes us for action. Following the flow pattern of the arrows, in risk situations one is likely to move with the arrow and adopt characteristics of the type ahead of one's own. In security one moves against the arrows into behavior patterns of the type behind.

Inner Centers of Perception

Gurdjieff embedded his thoughts about the passions (Chief Feature) in a model straight out of sacred tradition. His model describes humankind as three-brained beings. The three brains refer to three kinds of ordinary intelligence: mental, emotional, and physical. From this perspective, the incomprehensibly vast number of ways in which people can express themselves depends on only three kinds of awareness. There are exactly three input channels that support the utterly unique expression of an individual life, but the ways in which the input of thoughts, feelings, and sensation can be acted out are myriad.

The passion is emotional. It acts in concert with thoughts and physical sensation. To get beyond personality, thoughts and feelings are quieted and awareness shifted to a higher mental and emotional center. When successfully activated, the inner, or "higher," centers convey impressions from what is called objective reality, or essence. Objective perceptions are not distorted by the bias of type. They are not projections. They are views of the real. The activated inner centers are receptive to grace, or impressions conveyed from the realms of essence.

This perspective is entirely compatible with meditation practices that recommend the quieting of thought and emotions

GURDJIEFF'S THREE "BRAINS," OR CENTERS OF INTELLIGENCE

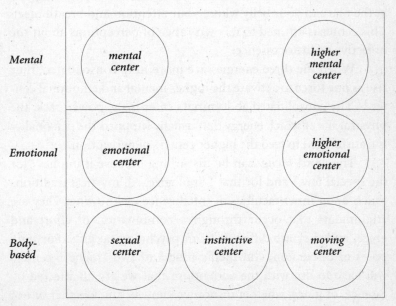

(Michael Waldberg, *Gurdjieff, An Approach to His Ideas* [London: Routledge & Kegan Paul, 1973], 112).

so that higher aspects of being can emerge. The deeper study of the Enneagram concerns "setting the personality aside" by quieting the mind and awakening the inner observer. When ordinary thoughts and emotions are quiet enough, the higher mental center (vision and knowing), and the higher emotional center (feeling and knowing), are receptive to grace.

Grace works on nature. The Enneagram approach prepares one's nature to receive the grace of higher forces in a way that accords with other spiritual traditions.

When the three physical energies are balanced and "collected," through meditation practice, they produce an intelligent awareness that is located in the belly.[16] The abdominal center is variously called the Hara (Zen Buddhism), the Kath (Sufism), and the TanTien (Taoism). Every mystical tradition has its own culturally correct description of the mental, emotional, and body-based centers. The abdominal center can be physically felt at the place in your belly where your attention and breath meet. This center is attuned to its own range of perceptions about the objective reality of essence.

When the three energies are more fully consolidated, they rise as one force to activate the higher mental and emotional center.[17] The consolidated abdominal center is the power pack, the physical site at which energy that usually supports the personality is transformed to feed the higher centers of perception.

The word *higher* can be disturbing because it implies "for the special few," and for that I apologize. All mystical traditions touch upon inner faculties of intelligence or knowing. They are attainments that occur through a combination of effort and grace, and they are different from psychological gifts. For purposes of discussion, Gurdjieff's model of two "higher" centers will have to do, with the addendum that we are all affected by essence, or grace, whether or not we know it, and whether or not we meditate.

SUBTYPE FOCUS OF ATTENTION

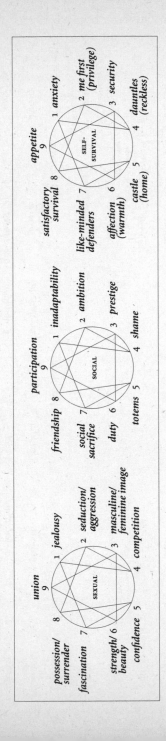

(Adapted from *Transpersonal Psychologies*, ed. Charles T. Tart [New York: Harper & Row, 1975; repr. El Cerrito, CA: Psychological Processes, 1983]).

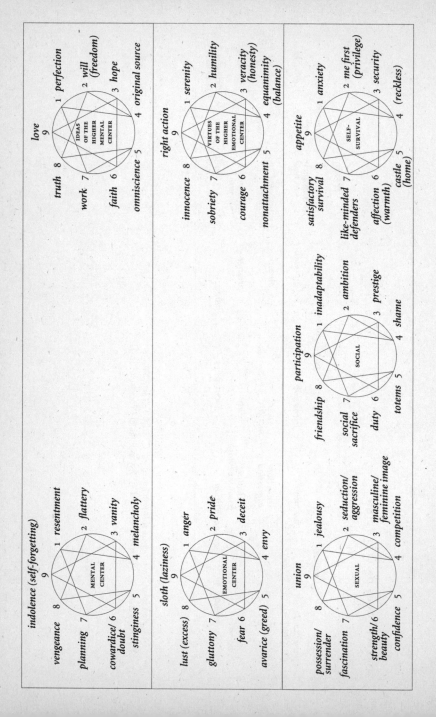

love
9

1 *perfection*

2 *will (freedom)*

3 *hope*

4 *original source*

IDEAS OF THE HIGHER MENTAL CENTER

truth 8

work 7

faith 6

omniscience 5

right action
9

1 *serenity*

2 *humility*

3 *veracity (honesty)*

4 *equanimity (balance)*

VIRTUES OF THE HIGHER EMOTIONAL CENTER

innocence 8

sobriety 7

courage 6

nonattachment 5

appetite
9

1 *anxiety*

2 *me first (privilege)*

3 *security*

4 *(reckless)*

SELF-SURVIVAL

satisfactory survival 8

like-minded defenders 7

affection (warmth) 6

castle (home) 5

participation
9

1 *inadaptability*

2 *ambition*

3 *prestige*

4 *shame*

SOCIAL

friendship 8

social sacrifice 7

duty 6

totems 5

indolence (self-forgetting)
9

1 *resentment*

2 *flattery*

3 *vanity*

4 *melancholy*

MENTAL CENTER

vengeance 8

planning 7

cowardice/ doubt 6

stinginess 5

sloth (laziness)
9

1 *anger*

2 *pride*

3 *deceit*

4 *envy*

EMOTIONAL CENTER

lust (excess) 8

gluttony 7

fear 6

avarice (greed) 5

union
9

1 *jealousy*

2 *seduction/ aggression*

3 *masculine/ feminine image*

4 *competition*

SEXUAL

possession/ surrender 8

fascination 7

strength/ beauty 6

confidence 5

Subtypes

The emotional passions are acted out in three different areas of life: self-survival, social, and one-to-one or sexual relationships. Survival concerns the ways in which people deal with self-preservation. The social arena governs relationships with groups and others. The sexual arena is focused on one-to-one relating.

Like the nine passions, the behaviors called "Enneagram subtypes" act as a hidden focus of personality type. Once it is discovered through self-observation, the subtype focus of attention is revealed as a behavior that is motivated by instinct (for survival, social relating, and sexual relating) dominated by the passion of type. The subtypes name a mental preoccupation in which the energies of the physical body (instincts) and the emotional energies of the passions are joined. Because the subtype focus of attention is an ordinary behavior, I have found them to be crucial pivots in the transformation of the nine passions into their higher opposites.

The diagram opposite shows how the passions of sacred tradition can be overlaid on Gurdjieff's core model of three "brains." Produced by Oscar Ichazo, these diagrams include Christianity's traditional higher opposite for each of the passions. Ichazo has also placed a mental preoccupation for each type and named its transformed higher opposite. He finalized the Enneagram model of human development in use today by assigning each of Gurdjieff's three vital energies or instincts to a specific domain of practical life, which he called the areas of self-preservation, sexual relating, and social relating.[18]

ENNEAGRAM OF PERSONALITY TYPES

(Adapted from *Transpersonal Psychologies*, ed. Charles T. Tart [New York: Harper & Row, 1975; repr. El Cerrito, CA: Psychological Processes, 1983]).

II

The Personality Types in Love & Work

1

One ⬡ *The Perfectionist*

PERSONALITY BIAS		ESSENCE QUALITIES
MENTAL	*resentment*	*perfection*
EMOTIONAL	*anger*	*serenity*
	SUBTYPE FOCUS	
	JEALOUSY	sexual
	INADAPTABILITY	social
	ANXIETY (WORRY)	self-survival

The One Bias

Worldview

The world is an imperfect place. I work toward perfection.

Spiritual Path

A preoccupation with error points to a search for *perfection*. From a spiritual perspective, the child felt *anger* at being separated from the perfect environment of essence. Anger is focused on violations of standards. The commitment to perfection is at stake. Anger disturbs the *serenity* of being held in a perfectly balanced flow of events. *Resentment* develops from seeing the difference between life as it is and how much better life could be. The Perfectionist strategy is a child's attempt to construct a perfect outer life both to cope with a critical world, and to protect the vulnerable sense of perfection. The search for perfection and a serene emotional life are both spiritual and psychological catalysts. The perfectionistic personality bias mimics the perfection of higher being.

Concerns

○ *Works toward perfection. Avoids error and evil.*

○ *Self-denial causes anger. Unmet needs generate resentment.*

○ *Finds an outlet for anger through correcting error and championing social causes.*

. ○ *Acts out anger in three key areas of life:*

> JEALOUSY *in sexual or one-to-one relationships.*
>
> NONADAPTABILITY, *adopting rigid, inflexible social opinions.*
>
> ANXIETY (WORRY) *about personal survival. "Am I good enough to make it?"*

○ *Looks for impeccable ethics as the mark of admirable character.*

○ *Conscientious. Monitors own actions.*

○ *Think right. Moralistic thoughts block real feelings. Should, must, ought to.*

○ *Do right. Admires the practical virtues: work, thrift, honesty, and effort.*

○ *Be right. Has severe mental critic that judges own actions. Harsh superego.*

○ *Feels guilt about not meeting high internal standards.*

○ *Dedicated worker. Work can block pleasure and shadow issues like anger.*

○ *Has difficulty reading the signals of anger. "I'm energetic today, not mad."*

○ *Self-criticism reverses in self-defense to become critical of others.*

○ *Worries about decisions. Afraid to make a mistake.*

○ *This focus of attention supports ethical behavior. It can also lead to:*

> ○ *One-right-way thinking, right or wrong, black or white. No grays.*

- ° *Has superb critical powers. Effective organizer and analyst.*
- ° *Leads by example. Ethical policymaker who tries to uphold standards.*

Personality Bias

We're all familiar with the One mind-set because we adopt it when our values are questioned. When it's a question of integrity, we, like Ones, search carefully for the correct approach. Once established in the right, we feel invincible. We're in service, mistakes seem less important than the purity of the intent. We are suddenly kind to ourselves, because we see the value of our own efforts. It is an honor to dedicate oneself to something good.

A life dedicated to perfection requires heroic effort. You can't help noticing when standards slip and no one else feels guilty. How can they ignore this? Have they no shame? The tension builds. Something has to be done. You start to see details slipping out of order. If others don't notice and you do, then you'll be held responsible. Your conscience goes wild when error is overlooked. "I saw. I knew. I'm guilty." You can't leave it alone. You feel compelled to fix it. You don't recognize the rising signals of anger. The tension feels entirely appropriate. Tension means that you're trying hard. You brace for greater effort.

If focusing on error becomes automatic, self-observation stops. All you know is that you're working desperately hard, that you see loose ends everywhere, and you can't rest until it's finished. The scope of the task enlarges. More details appear. It's late. It's out of control. Your mind flogs you for being tired and helpless. It's maddening that other people don't care. You don't realize how angry you are until you hear the jagged edge in your voice and feel the fury spiking through your body.

Anger leads to action. You can't hold back that shot of lightning. You know exactly what's wrong, because it's infuriating. Something perfect has been ruined. You can't keep quiet. You're too mad to care about overreacting. Attention locks on the right way to fix what's gone wrong, and anger fuels your conviction.

Ones grow by knowing what they want instead of what would be right. They grow by relaxing, by letting pleasure in. You have a choice when you can read the natural signals of anger and watch your mind begin to focus on error.

They can be helped in relationships by people who accept differences of opinion, who soften the one right way to perfection, and who are open to pleasure.

Subtype Focus:

Anger Affects Sexual, Social, and Survival Attitudes

Jealousy (Heat) in Sexual and One-to-One Relationships

Sexual jealousy is acted out in an angry, possessive way. Ones say it's a white-hot rage that seizes their guts if a relationship is threatened. A threat to sanctioned pleasure is maddening. "How dare you take what's rightfully mine?" Ones have such difficulty in recognizing what they want, and in allowing themselves to have pleasure, that any threat to gratification feels like losing a lifeline. You've earned the right to be loved. You deserve sexual pleasure. You're angry at being compared with a rival. You want to be made right again. If you had been perfect, there would be no contest.

This is permissible anger, based on the misconduct of associates or a mate. Jealousy quickly becomes obsessive. Your mind is besieged. You can't drop it. "This has to stop." You feel a compulsion to relieve the tension, an urgency to take action. You have to check up, you must go see, you have to know exactly who said what to whom. You want names and dates. You want confrontation. The rival shouldn't be here.

The focal point is fidelity, but jealousy extends far beyond a sexual agreement. You can be jealous of people who get promoted, whose ideas are taken seriously, who are popular figures at work. You need to feel right. You work hard at it and feel jealous when you're not validated. Saying "I deserve recognition" or "You should have paid attention to me" feels safer than "I want" or "I need." It is unthinkable to reach out openly and take what you want; but in cases of misconduct, "This has to be stopped" replaces the forbidden thought "I want to have."

Nonadaptability in the Social Sphere

Anger is acted out through correct causes and social ideals. Religious fervor and political conviction are prime outlets for wrath. Ones face each other across the barricades at public demonstrations, each supporting his or her side as the one right way. Your position in a group is defined by uncompromising opinions. You often choose friends who share the same beliefs. Social rigidity eliminates gray areas, shades of meaning, and loopholes where error might creep in. You've found the right ideological platform and are entrenched in the tenets of a perfect ideal. Now you're sure.

Once you take a position, it can be remarkably difficult to absorb new information. A decision should be either right or wrong. One error blows the whole decision apart. You'll have to review all the pieces again. You can't move without certainty. In extreme rigidity, the mind closes to alternatives. You can't take in new information because it could shake the foundation of a whole belief system.

The nonadaptable, or rigid, stance is particularly obvious in conflicts of orthodox ideas. The right-winger ranting about homosexuals in the gay district. The left-winger selling radical bumper stickers, who makes buyers feel guilty if they don't take one of each.

Anxiety (Worry) About Self-Survival

The conflict between doing what you want and doing what's right creates anxiety about survival. You want an exciting career but balk at the risk. All the unknowns spring to mind. All that risk of error. It looks like an either/or choice. You either find a safe career or take the time to find out what you want. You worry about selling out for safety, and you're terrified of a fatal mistake. Work decisions become monumental, because they trigger the inner tension between wants and shoulds. Wants are repressed. You don't know what you want, but you become unconsciously angry about having to sell out for economic security.

Ones can be stingy about what they have and what they earn. They are isolated by the belief that people do not willingly share. Love and support are therefore not freely given. They have to be earned with good behavior. To survive you must hold on to what you have. "What's yours is yours, and what's mine is mine." Everyone goes it alone in life. You support yourself and worry about having to support someone else. Worry and anger go hand in hand. Repressed needs flare up and are resentfully directed at people who don't have to worry about their livelihood. "Why do I have to go through this?" "Why don't you have to struggle?" "Life isn't fair."

Either/or thinking takes over. You can either be safe or be happy. You consider both sides of the decision. Procrastination sets in. The worry cycle starts. A bad choice could lead to catastrophe. "What if I pick the wrong profession? What if I can't make it? What if the job market fails?" It's not fair that hard work and sacrifice do not guarantee success. You can't decide, because there's a chance to go for the gold but you're terrified about survival. A slave to circumstance.

Focal Issues

Righteous Anger

You know that anger is building when Ones get physically rigid and superpolite. When anger spills, it will be well documented. Ones have to justify being angry. They also say that anger comes with total grievance recall. The mistakes of the past come bubbling back again. Forgiveness feels like pretending the incident never happened. If you forgive and forget, the same mistake could be repeated. It's wise to reassure a One. Admit the mistake again and put it in perspective. "That was then. This is now. But yes, I do remember."

The grudge list also provides a safe outlet. If Ones are angry about something that can't be expressed, an old source of irritation can reheat to become a discharge point. Reading the signals of forbidden feelings such as anger and sexual attraction can be a lifelong task for Ones. The feelings say: "I'm like a bottle with a cork in my mouth. Everything's jammed inside and I can't get it out, but I'm not angry." The thoughts say: "There's too much energy. I'm blanking-out. I have to leave." It helps to name the physical sensations. Start with the obvious. "Belly tight. Jaw clenched. Going blank." Then relax and collect yourself. These sensations may add up to anger.

Emotional Control

Ones weren't allowed to express "bad" emotions. Consequently they have a long-standing fear of going out of control. Suppressed feelings magnify in importance. In the eyes of a child, anger might rise to murderous heights. Any wave of strong emotion began to feel dangerous and was suppressed. Self-discipline and emotional control were highly valued.

Clamping down sacrifices emotional information. It's hard to know what you want, and you can't register the difference between a minor flash of anger and full-scale fury. Ones often find themselves bracing against their feelings. Simple relaxation exercises are enormously helpful, especially when they are coupled with an attention practice that allows feelings to surface into awareness.

Compulsive Tendencies (Doing Things Right)

Desires and needs would surely emerge if you took time to explore and to question. So you fill the time. Free time makes you anxious. There's never enough time. Time disappears in wall-to-wall activity. This Los Angeles contractor describes the rising tension that alerts him to his tendency.

> I know that I'm stressed when I get compulsive. I'm suddenly thinking about bolt sizes and codes, when I usually just use whatever bolts are in the kit. I might have to test several times to see if a perfectly tight screw is really tight enough. I know it's OK, but I have to go back and check, just in case. I even feel stupid about doing it, but I have to, or it might be wrong. I start rerunning the inspection codes, which I've already covered. Suddenly some small thing will be very important to check out, and I'm scared if I don't go do it. So I have to go see. I'm OK if I check, so I go do it. It's a relief to see that I did it right.

When Ones get focused, they're unstoppable. There's very little distraction outside the task at hand. The trick is to recognize the difference between working compulsively to block out anxiety and working because it's a pleasure.

The Inner Critic

We have all experienced persistent inner talking to ourselves when we're planning to do something risky or wrong, but this is only occasional. Ones describe their own internal thought statements as loud and intrusive: "A critical voice inside my head, that monitors my thoughts and feelings." It's like a superego run wild. The critic can be insulting and punishing. Ones say that they sometimes judge other people in sheer self-defense, to equalize the pressure. It's a relief to notice someone else's mistakes when your own mind is attacking you.

The critical tendency is known as Judging Mind (or Comparing Mind) in Buddhist meditation practice. The Judging

Mind state is particularly insidious, because it masquerades as giving good advice. Why question an inner voice that urges you to be a better person? Why question should, must, and ought to?

Judging Mind also leads to a cycle of mental comparisons. You compare your partner and yourself to other people. The thoughts say: "I wish my Sara was as smart as his Susie" or "I wish my lover was as cute as John." Comparing signals insecurity. You realize, with a jolt, that your mind is automatically judging. When you notice, check backward in time to discover what triggered insecurity.

Black-or-White Thinking

When error looms in the foreground, it replaces whole-picture thinking. Ones do not want a shadow in their relationships, because if attention locks on error, it obscures the worth of a good companion or the pleasure of a job well done. The relationship is either perfect or it's wrong. The job is either faultless or it's an embarrassment. A small omission can make an entire project seem mismanaged. It helps to remember the whole picture, to remember larger aims, because the error magnifies in importance. There's a compulsion to deal with it quickly. A 10 percent error fills 100 percent of the mind.

One Right Way

Black-or-white thinking makes yes-or-no decisions attractive. You want things to be clear, to minimize gray zones. You want the answer to be either right or wrong. Ambiguity signals dead stop. You don't want to be swamped by possibilities. Ones are not comfortable with multiple options. They do not like to make quick decisions, especially in a crosscurrent of information. Once a decision is made, they do not want to reformulate and open the question again. Ones can help themselves by attending to the logic and good intentions of different points of view.

Decision Making (What If It's Not Right?)

The conflict between what you want and what's "right" makes decisions difficult. A perfect choice would cover all the angles. The perfect job would be educational, fulfilling, constructive, and financially rewarding. The ideal mate would be approved of by your mother and all your friends. The preoccupation with correctness intensifies in logic-based decisions. It helps to factor your feelings into the equation, to decide in favor of wishes and dreams. Because it's hard to be totally certain, Ones are often pushed by deadlines. The process speeds up if "good enough" expectations and reasonable deadlines can be set. Not the highest, not the best, but good enough to get into motion.

Procrastination

Reworking the data "to be totally sure" doesn't seem like procrastination. The Perfectionist is mentally engaged, while action is on hold. Ones are trying to be clear, to make the best possible decision, but their meticulous and lengthy approach can make people feel frustrated and controlled. The usual reaction is annoyance. Others feel hung up while matters that are important to them are carefully dissected, and meeting after meeting is called.

Ones as Saints

Ones who do the right thing in their own eyes are not particularly self-critical. They don't get depressed, they don't feel guilty, and, feeling established in the right, they compare themselves favorably to others. In Enneagram classes, our students call them saints; they're perfectionists who've gotten the internal critic off their backs. Many of our saints are absolutely genuine. There is nothing make-believe about their goodness. They work well, their projects last, and they're genuinely loved by people.

Other Ones, feeling equally saintly, see no reason to question themselves. Their lifestyle, their family, their religion, or their career makes them feel morally superior. Good things happen to good people, and bad things happen to bad people. Since their way of life is good, they feel no need to criticize or to concern themselves about what other people think.

New Age Ones

Years ago, when I first taught the Enneagram, I saw a lot of old-fashioned Ones. They were definitely prim, and even those in their twenties seemed to belong to an older, more genteel generation. They were superpolite, concerned kids who managed to look totally straight in their old jeans and sneakers. Over time a new variety has emerged. They're Ones who were educated in a way that wasn't at all repressive. Now we're hearing that people "should" be sexual, that we "ought" to relax, that we're "supposed" to be creative, and that it's "right" to put pleasure on the schedule.

Trapdoor Ones

The trapdoor phenomenon is as old as human nature. It's a way to release emotional pressure by acting on forbidden needs. The trapdoor is a better designation than "going out the back door," which applies to people who cheat on their mates. Trapdoor Ones lead a double life, each of which satisfies different aspects of themselves.

A trapdoor is usually discovered during the twenties. It's very attractive when the pressure to conform is high. We still hear some pretty bizarre trapdoor tales, but the stories have lightened up in the last few years, which I take to be a sign of social progress. This one is from a young Boston bureaucrat, who writes: "The rules of one group always forbid something that's encouraged by another. If one department of my life doesn't know about the other, then I am obedient to both."

TRAPDOOR DOUBLE LIFE

A while back I saw a book of wonderful nude photographs. I was attracted to them, because the photographer clearly sought out models with less than perfect bodies. I'd always wanted to pose in the nude, but was afraid I wasn't perfect enough, so I hadn't done it. So I looked up this photographer and asked if I could model for him. There's a series of shots from that first session, in which I went from being obviously terrified and stiff as a board on camera, to being giggly, flirtatious, and clearly having the time of my life. Once I drowned the critic in a few glasses of wine, a whole new side of me emerged.

There's a delicious satisfaction about exposing my body without my face being seen, like sticking my tongue out at the world. None of the people whom I inwardly defy by posing will ever see my photographs, but I get the pleasure of proving that I'm not the drab, mousy creature I was brought up to be. They tried to make me into a good, sexless daughter with no secrets, and they failed.

A One Away from Home

Ones change radically when they're freed from responsibility. Like a kid whose homework is done, they can go out and play. The shift to security is far more dramatic than for other types of people. Ones are the Perfectionists of the Enneagram, and Sevens (the personality type they resemble when feeling relaxed and secure) are Epicures, the pleasure seekers of the system. A One away from home likes to play. Relationships flourish with scheduled vacations, in a way that they never could in a familiar setting. There's simply too much to do at home. You never get on top of it.

Pleasure

Paradoxically pleasure can make Ones anxious. Shoulds interfere with comfort. Responsibilities replace romance. Free time can make you worry. "The relationship will degenerate." "We'll get lazy. The work won't get done." It helps if a partner will initiate time off or model a more relaxed lifestyle. It's much easier to go along than to go first. When a Perfectionist realizes that work has replaced a promised pleasure, it helps to backtrack mentally, to remember what you wanted before shoulds blocked feeling out.

The backlash of pleasure is the Wrath of God. Lightning may strike. "I may lose control. Then the work will never get done." The mind begins to bargain with fate. "I'll only take an hour off." "I've earned the right to play." It helps to voice your worries out loud. Get a reality check. Talk to your partner. Check out your time, money, and deadline commitments. Minimize any actual risk that stands in the way of pleasure.

Security and Risk

DYNAMICS OF CHANGE FOR POINT ONE

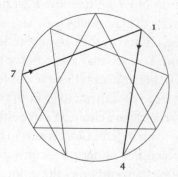

Security

In a secure life situation, the focal issues for Ones are less intensely felt. Judgmental thinking diminishes, it's easier to relax, it's easier to interrupt the flow of work and to have fun. Multiple options seem less threatening. "Let's do something different. Let's try something new." The shift to Seven happens naturally with a shift of scene. Ones are famous for being completely different when they're on vacation. They are undistracted by familiar responsibilities when they leave home. A more playful and relaxed aspect of being emerges that shows many of the characteristics attributed to point Seven. It's not that One "turns into" a Seven in security or "becomes" a Four under stress; it's that the preoccupations of the security and stress points are acted out from the perspective of a One. For example, when the Seven's fascination with exploring multiple options is acted out from the One perspective, it's more like seeing the good in different points of view rather than getting lost in plans and dreams.

The high side of the security point is reported to be like finding a guilt-free self. It's easier to know what you want and to just do it. Decisions are easily made and are based on wishes rather than shoulds. Life is simply a whole lot easier. The low side of the Seven position is reported as wanting everything and being very angry about years of self-deprivation. A kind of rebellious counterforce is set up in which the now-liberated One adopts a narcissistic worldview. There really isn't any need to struggle. That was in the past. Gluttony, the passion for Seven, is acted out through entitlement. You see that you deserve the best, without having to earn it. The better people deserve the very best from life.

Ones say that it can be difficult to be both critical and playful in the same day. It seems like a choice. You're either superresponsible or a flake. The main task for Ones seems to be integrating the security and risk reactions, rather than cultivating security over risk. A developed One then embodies the unique direction found at Four, coupled with the ease and experimentation of Seven and the rigor of One.

Risk

Early warning signs of stress show an intensification of the focal issues for Ones. The first reaction to stress is a tightening of a type's basic defenses. For Ones free time becomes anxiety provoking, work becomes compulsive, and pleasure is eliminated from the schedule. The inner critic becomes increasingly punitive. Emotional control tightens and anger rises. Right-or-wrong thinking intensifies, which adds to difficulty in decision making and the completion of important goals.

One is a classic Type A health risk if stress continues.[19] The spiritual message concerns adjusting effort, rather than rigidly following the one right way.

If stress continues, it becomes clear that the focal issues aren't equal to the task. In reaction to the now-ineffective One strategy, attention turns to the considerations of point Four. The One never "turns into" a Four, but the Four preoccupations are experienced from the vantage point of One.

Ones at Four typically fear that personal flaws will lead to abandonment and grief about not measuring up to high standards of excellence. In an emotional crash, Ones can become paralyzed by depression. Ones realize, with shock, that good behavior and overexertion do not guarantee success or happiness. The One is grief-stricken. "What else is there?" If the immobility of depression can be turned, Anger, the agent of change for Ones, swiftly follows. Now you're very angry that you had to struggle and it didn't work. It's not fair. There can be a concomitant reevaluation of the one right way. Maybe there's another, more effective and beneficial, life path. It helps to follow the anger trail to discover buried needs.

The high side of the stress reaction is the realization that buried emotional needs must factor into decisions. In Four what we "should" do is now far less important than finding out what we want to do. This may be a very positive moment in the One's emotional life. By following the Four agenda of moving deeply into sadness and pain, Ones in stress often examine questions of existence and meaning. "What are my authentic feelings for others, rather than what I ought to feel?" "What work would inspire me, rather than work I think I should do?" "What lifestyle would animate me rather than pacifying the inner critic?" These are forbidden questions for Ones. "What do I want, rather than what should I do?" Paradoxically a crucial positive change emerges under stress. Many Ones report that they discovered their true work and their true emotional nature during a period of loss, when they were forced by circumstance to dip deeply into the terrain of feeling.

The low side of Four is self-absorption ("Only I have suffered so") and depression ("Nothing has meaning"). There is the inevitable emergence of envy as the point Four passion. Envy is expressed with a One flavor, as feelings of personal worthlessness tied to self-comparison with successful, happy people.

One in Love

Living with Ones

- *Do remember details. Ones are detail conscious. They appreciate small gestures: being on time, remembering names, proper introductions.*
- *Speak respectfully. Make sure no one looks foolish. Ask for permission.*
- *Compliment thrift, effort, and dependability. Don't expect compliments in return.*
- *Cultivate your character. Set improvement goals. Don't flaunt your achievements.*
- *Admit error immediately. Admission clears the air and prevents resentment.*
- *Bring novelty and fun to relating. Ones tend to repeat the known.*
- *Avoid power struggles. Ones need to be right. There are at least two right ways.*
- *Maintain your own interests. Ones work long hours on their own.*
- *Humor is especially helpful. Worry vanishes with gentle humor.*

- *Ones perfect relationships. "What are our responsibilities?" "What are we learning?" "What does right relating mean?" Ethics of relating are reviewed.*

- *Scorched-earth policy. If the relationship develops a negative aspect, Ones think about calling the whole thing off. Relationships seem either black or white.*

- *Once committed and convinced, Ones dig in. Extremely loyal. Value a family.*

- *Guilt. Pleasure signals anxiety: lightning may strike if we're having fun.*

Intimacy

Paradoxically, although they are the Enneagram's critics, Ones shatter under criticism. Appearances matter a lot. "What do my parents think?" and "What will the neighbors say?" are recurrent themes. They read implied criticism into innocent remarks: "You look great tonight; what a nice outfit" can be read to mean, "I didn't look great on our last date. I should get rid of whatever I wore." Partners should preface criticism with praise and follow up with reassurances such as, "You've done a good job. We're almost there. There's one area that needs to be redone. By the way, are we still on for next Tuesday?"

Unexpected criticism is terrifying, because it implies that the inner critic has failed. Ones are vulnerable to critical catch-phrases that most people wouldn't take seriously. "Why didn't you finish?" or "Why is this so hard for you?" or "How come you can't?" feel like catch questions. Ambiguous phrases sound like a trap. Any implied criticism sets up immediate discomfort, which is quickly followed by a wish to improve, a justifying explanation, or a counteraccusation that points the finger at someone else. Fears of rejection are relieved by shifting blame elsewhere or judging back in self-defense.

If you live with a One, you have to relate to his or her critic. It can feel like living with two people. You learn to recognize the facial tension when the inner critic takes over; and you see how Ones sometimes measure their actions simply to pacify their own minds. Anger and criticality can be a call for help. Ones criticize in self-defense, to relieve the tension of being angry at themselves. They may need reassurance but feel guilty about having to ask. It helps to diffuse anger by seeing where Ones are deprived and giving them what they want.

By not asking, the One is immunized against rejection, but the partner feels bad about not guessing correctly. The One may be thinking, "Married people should act like X," "Lovers have X responsibilities to each other," "Everyone knows that friends should do X," but if this is not communicated, a partner can't respond. It's well for an attentive partner to reach out by inquiring, before the One concludes that he or she can't expect generosity in relationship.

Ones have to be educated to the fact that a spouse can have both good and bad points and still be a good person, that everyone has rough edges. Committed to perfection, Ones believe that a good relationship should consistently produce only good thoughts and feelings. "If I have any bad feelings, then I'm either in the wrong relationship or guilty about feeling unhappy." The way out is to appreciate the relationship as it is, to see the good in both struggle and success.

Perfectionists suffer for the faults of others. They feel responsible for a loved one's errors while at the same time feeling guilty because only a bad person would be angry or disillusioned or sad about their relationship. Therefore, whenever Ones slip into marginal dissatisfaction, they can become frantic about resolving the problem quickly. A spill on the carpet escalates to feeling guilty for judging the spiller. Ones are highly motivated to clean up the mess very quickly.

The following story from a young husband describes his sincere efforts to help his marriage by reasoning his anger away. His wife will see a tight, angry presence but will not know that he is

caught in his own mental cross fire. He wants to affirm her goodness, he wants to replace his negative thoughts with positive
thoughts, he wants to shut the critic up, and he can't express his
turmoil because it would look bad. His task has shifted from
his objective marital problems to pacifying his own inner critic.

> Anger is a bad sign to me. If I'm angry, it means that I
> don't love her anymore, and that I'm a phony for stay-
> ing. So I push the anger back and get depressed in-
> stead. [One moves to Four under stress.] Then I'm in a
> bind. It's wrong to stay, and it would be wrong to go
> under these conditions.
>
> While all this is going on in my head, I haven't said
> anything, because it's bad to be accusatory and mean.
> So I put out signals that I'm dissatisfied, and if she
> doesn't pick them up, I have to take action, but I still
> haven't been able to verbalize these bad things that I'm
> feeling inside.
>
> I keep thinking that if I could see more clearly, or if
> I understood her better, or if I found a technique I
> could use, then I wouldn't be so negative. So the ten-
> sion builds until every time she does something wrong
> it's like an electric shock going through my body. If
> she's rude to somebody, Shock. When she behaves un-
> consciously, Shock. When food falls out of her mouth
> at lunch, Shock. When she wears baggy pants, Shock.
> That she even owns those pants, Shock. God forbid
> that she's doing it in public, so that other people see
> how untogether she is—that's a real Shock.

This young husband feels guilty about his own feelings. He
spends a lot of time thinking and not saying much. He has to
be desperate enough to want a divorce before he can verbalize
what he's feeling. From his black-or-white perceptual stance, one

trouble spot blankets the whole relationship. His mind tells him that the marriage stands in the balance over a pair of baggy pants. When the pants are wrong, the whole thing is wrong. The idea that people can be both in love *and* angry seems to be new territory. For him marriage is either being in love *or* being angry. He can't fathom the fact that a certain amount of disillusion is normal or that anger is a way to get things changed and to move on.

He could win twice by observing his bias against anger. If he got angry about the pants, they would probably disappear. He might then begin to ask for other things that he wants, and he might know that he's loved even when he gets angry.

The Signals Ones Send

Positive Signals

Ones challenge you to correct action and effort. You can count on their keeping their promises and accepting responsibility to make things right. The buck stops there. They value right action for its own sake without expectation of benefits. Virtue is its own reward. They can inspire you with, and show you, the joy of a job well done. Perfection of skills, effort, and character can lead to self-reliance and an independent life. They project ethical idealism and push you to embody the ideal. Making the world a better place. In touch with the practical areas of life: health, honesty, right livelihood, good fun.

Negative Signals

The One's criticality and the superior stance make you feel inferior, rejected, defensive, or alienated. Feels like you seldom get it right. Ones always see room for improvement. Criticism is a kind of compliment, a proof of caring. "We should try for perfection." Emotions have to be controlled. Perfectionism sidetracks pleasure and spontaneity.

You can feel the force of One's anger and control, even when it's not explicitly stated. You're punished by unspoken criticism, without knowing what you've done. Ones compare themselves with others' achievements and can feel inferior when other people win. This creates a difficult bind for the One's partner. You're wrong when you don't do your best and wrong if you're better.

Mixed Messages

Ones repress their real needs by focusing on what "should" be done. Therefore when they look most committed, when they launch into a corrective course of action, when they seem most determined to set things straight, they may be focused on should and must rather than on what they really want. It helps if a One's partner questions the difference between what seems superficially right and what is actually good for the One.

Perfectionists can sometimes confuse their own self-serving actions with an objectively correct position. For example, if a One likes to cycle, then suddenly bicycles are the right way to get around town, and other means of transportation are wrong by definition. Cars pollute the atmosphere, cars are dangerous, cars are bad. Cycling is clean, healthful, and good. Once they establish cycling as the one right way, Ones will cycle to work and make it clear to anyone they encounter that the world would be a better place if they changed.

Inner Signals

Ones say it's hard to read their own anger signals. They say that instead of feeling angry, they often come up with a false "solution" that replaces anger with "better" feelings. The thoughts say: "She's really a wonderful woman. I think I'll bring some roses home to show how much I appreciate her." Ones are usually not aware that their own thoughts lead them away from unacceptable feelings. They simply find themselves "doing the right thing."

Ones can also misinterpret their own anger signals. The thoughts say: "I'm feeling energetic today. Getting a lot done. Getting things straight." Others will hear a string of critical comments. The thoughts say: "Good, we're getting things organized. We're moving ahead." The comments sound more like barbed one-liners. "Well, you're finally getting organized—it took a whole day for you to call back." What you may see is an angry, stoic presence, tight-lipped, visibly tensed, and emanating silent judgment, who will truthfully tell you, in a polite, clenched, and rising tone, "*Nothing* is wrong," and "I *never* get angry."

Ones are often shocked when people turn from their anger. Their thoughts say: "I'm clear and precise. I'm on target." The feelings say: "I'm on. I'm right. I don't have to listen." Ones who can observe themselves report that the emotional rush is a warning. There's a feeling of certainty, of being unequivocally right, which may well be the signal of bias. Ones would do well to enlist help. The helper's job is to spot the signs of rising anger.

One at Work

In the Workplace

- Likes specific guidelines and schedules. Loopholes are traumatic.
- Practical. Reshapes abstract approaches into step-by-step procedures.
- Likes schedules and accountability, knowing who's responsible for what.
- Keeps track of detail.
- Energy that could go to product may be diverted to details.
- Looks for evidence of ethical character—discipline, manners, appearance, respect.
- Prefers doing over feeling. Wants to focus on work rather than work relationships.
- Aware of critical points about a program but has a hard time proposing broad solutions. Too much room for error.

- *Secure in a formal role. Wants to respect hierarchy and authority.*
- *Aware of the résumé and the record. "Good people have a good history."*
- *Devoted to work for its own sake. Takes pleasure in a job well done.*
- *Works hard for the right cause, for the good leader, for the competent team.*
- *Compares own effort to others'. "If they work, I work. If they don't, I won't."*
- *Keeps score. Notes what others do right and wrong. Will defend others if they're in "the right." Airs the grudge list if they're in the wrong.*
- *Can mask sense of personal entitlement by working for a good cause. "I deserve respect and special treatment because I do good in the world."*
- *Wants rewards for effort and competence but will not ask. May displace resentment over nonrecognition onto details and petty interactions. Legitimizes hurt feelings by finding fault with others.*
- *Finds it hard to delegate responsibility. Worries about getting the job done right.*
- *Doesn't want to be compromised by the mistakes of others. Will hold a loner's stance until the source of error is assigned.*
- *Afraid to be wrong. Prone to power struggles and arguments about who's right.*
- *Shifts blame. "There was a reason," "It wasn't my fault."*
- *Avoids risk. Risk leads to mistakes. When in doubt, wait. Don't take chances.*
- *Strong advocate for those who work under a disadvantage or who improve as a result of personal effort.*

Leadership Style

The guiding notion is quality control. Quality and control go hand in hand. Supervision is a keynote. Leadership is executed by initiating a perfect plan and designating responsibility for each sector. The plan is then implemented in a stage-by-stage fashion by managers equipped with clear guidelines. Communication is about the plan. The key question is, Who is responsible?

Ones take pleasure in a job well done. They like to work alone, for hours at a stretch, with lists and plans and diagrams, poring over alternatives, assigning responsibility, and deciding what to bring into play if problems should arise. Refining an idea is challenging. The leader takes in new information during the search-and-discovery phase but tends to implement mechanically, in a step-by-step way. Thinking becomes inflexible. A previous solution looks safer than a new direction. The black-or-white bias makes it easy to see information that fits the perfect plan and not to see valuable data that doesn't fit the scheme. Once the first stages of a plan are activated, it's hard to shift Ones' attention or to get them to change their minds.

Decision making can be slowed in the face of uncertainty: "Why go this way rather than that way?" "How do we know for sure?" The classic One style of leadership is highly effective when planning and structure are called for but is ineffective for on-the-spot decisions or dealing with crosscurrents of new information. To influence a One who is rigidly following the program, restate the standing plan and insert a simple accommodation. Do not throw the whole question open. You want a one-step move from the old plan to the new plan without opening options. Ones need good point men in the field. It's a point man's job to question constantly, to bring new data to light, and to suggest changes in strategy. Ones in leadership like to rely on a trusted associate, which eliminates the trauma of decision making.

This leader is likely to have risen through the ranks through honest effort. She or he will notice who puts in overtime, who participates, and who does not. Honesty, family loyalty, a good personal appearance, and respect for authority are bottom-line essentials for every worker.

Ones' projects have a tendency to spread, to take longer, and to cost more than originally estimated. You start with a step-by-step projection. No waste. A perfect plan. When the inevitable, unforeseen glitches arise, they have to be handled correctly. Laying cement for a garden patio, for example, may reveal a badly installed drainpipe. In rerouting the pipe, you could unearth a crack in the house foundation. The crack should be fixed. You delay ordering sand for the patio and shift the crew to the foundation. The crack might indicate structural weakness; you should dig around the entire foundation to be sure. Now a week has gone by, and you have a ditch approaching the size of the Suez Canal that isn't included in your time and cost estimates, but is surely the right way to go, and you're getting angry because you have to renegotiate the costs, you're falling behind schedule, and it's gotten out of hand.

Conflicts

Ones feel secure with guidelines and strict accountability, and that style of management will permeate the organization. The leader may well believe that accountability provides a secure base that encourages creativity to flower, but the subtext of accountability is control. People feel controlled and creatively stifled by meetings and reports. Ones can also limit other people's options and ambitions. They like to make rules that bind people to the system. For example, special benefits may be made conditional on "continuing your good work record from now until retirement."

Peer conflicts typically focus on the One's need to be right. "It wasn't my fault" is a key phrase. One-upmanship also creates conflict. The complaint is that Ones won't pick up anyone else's pieces. "It wasn't my responsibility." These conflicts often originate in a One's belief that support to others disempowers oneself.

Conflict Resolution

See Part III, "The Directory of Relationships," for tips on conflict resolution between Ones and others.

Employee Participation

Ones identify with work that models integrity. They are impressed by an organization's image and long-standing reputation. They want to be evaluated on their skills and merit. They are not self-promoting and will want to be recognized without putting themselves forward. They like to be evaluated on their skills and are uncomfortable with subjective criteria like "a good personality."

It's easier for Ones to critique a set position than to come up with a new approach. They are, however, highly innovative within established guidelines. New ideas or changes of procedure should be accompanied by implementation guidelines. Ones can be flexible if the guidelines tell them how to be flexible. They're not happy with general directives that can be carried out in different ways. Designate the options. Give a clear example of each and state the conditions under which each option should be exercised. If you want a One to be flexible, then state the conditions under which flexibility comes into play.

Ones are oriented to goals rather than process. A One's idea of process is having all the pieces in place before beginning. They do not share the usual tolerance for learning curves, human error, and systems failure. A mistake signals full stop, full review, and a return to the beginning. A weak spot blankets the whole operation until the error is explained. Ones balk if not fully prepared and can blank-out intellectually under pressure. They can fuzz-out in a sudden emergency. It helps to remind Ones of past success, and the success of a similar venture, against which they can compare their current progress.

The process speeds up when someone else is willing to ask questions, to speak up about being confused, to mention problems that might arise. It also helps to model process. Repetition of process statements like "We're working out the steps as we go along," "This is an experiment for all of us," "Here are the problems that I see," is a good learning format. When a step is fully learned, have the One review it by teaching others before you move ahead. It's easier for Ones to ask questions for other students who are confused than to admit their own inexperience. Ones are natural teachers. They get pleasure from the perfection of a task and are in a protected position as the ones who know. They have unusual sensitivity and patience toward people who are trying to improve.

Direct questioning in public may be threatening. Ones need to keep areas of uncertainty hidden, or structure the meeting so this won't arise. Perfectionists feel they should go home and study the manual all night rather than embarrass themselves by asking an obvious question. The framework for learning should model the fact that we're supposed to ask questions, that mistakes are part of the learning process, that we don't have the full answer yet.

Ones assume that there's one right way to proceed. They want to know exactly what's expected; they feel trapped and anxious if directions are vague. They need to know the rules and how to follow the rules to get the job done. "Where's the protocol we're supposed to follow? Where's the technical manual?" Anxiety increases if the rules change without an explanation. They're either in the hands of incompetents or have been positioned in ambiguous territory without a map. For maximum comfort, announce any change of procedure well in advance.

Team Building

The One on a team needs to be right. They find it traumatic to be publicly contradicted. They do, however, thrive on controversy and debate, which can build consensus. The best procedure is to put them in charge of a tight sphere of influence that they can control.

Participation will be affected if there's a strong self-promoter on the team. Comparing themselves with others, Ones will hold back if their work supports someone else's gain. It helps to designate the area of influence or authority of each player's role, to emphasize that the group is working as a team rather than backing a star. Likewise if the team is weak, the One may hold back by matching the other players' efforts. The focus should be on skill development rather than competition.

Ones are alert to the glitches, the flaws in reasoning, the weak spots in a plan; but they prefer not to be the lone critical voice and do not want to go first if there's a chance of being made to look foolish. A One's confidence in the team is improved if someone else will speak. Ones think that people look more astute, more on the ball, if they can troubleshoot. Ones will discount you as a lightweight if you can't foresee the flaws in your own sector of the project.

Ones work well on a team where the others are motivated and well-trained. They love good work and are at their best when they can match their energy and output with people whom they respect.

2

Two ⬡ *The Giver*

PERSONALITY BIAS		ESSENCE QUALITIES
MENTAL	*flattery*	*will (freedom)*
EMOTIONAL	*pride*	*humility*

SUBTYPE FOCUS	
SEDUCTION/AGGRESSION	
AMBITION	social
ME FIRST (PRIVILEGE)	self-survival

The Two Bias

Worldview

People depend on my help. I am needed.

Spiritual Path

Two's involvement with pleasing people points to a search for *will*. From the spiritual perspective, the promptings of higher will were subverted when the child's attention turned to *flattery*, which serves the will of others. *Pride* is an inflated sense of self-worth that masks dependency on approval and the *humility* of knowing our real worth to others. A Two's bias toward strategic giving mimics the action of higher will. It is a child's attempt both to survive by pleasing and to protect the sensitive connection to essence, one's spiritual being.

Concerns

- *Wants to gain approval and avoid rejection.*
- *Feels pride in being needed, being central in people's lives, indispensable.*
- *Acts out pride in three key areas of life:*

  AGGRESSION/SEDUCTION *in sexual or one-to-one relating.*

  AMBITION *in the social arena.*

  PRIVILEGE *concerning personal survival.*

- *Has difficulty recognizing own needs and will. "I have no needs."*
- *Represses feelings in order to be loved.*
- *Manipulates others to get what is needed.*
- *Has boundary issues. "I'm not taking over; I'm responding to a need."*
- *Has a sense of many selves, each attuned to someone's needs.*
- *Confuses the many selves. "Which one is really me?"*
- *Sees the potential in people. Inspired to own best by others.*
- *Finds it easy to support others. Own needs are met through others.*
- *Craves freedom. Feels confined by having to support others.*
- *Self-presentation alters to meet the needs of others. This way of paying attention can lead to:*
  - *Empathic emotional connections or:*
  - *Adaptation to the wishes of others as a way of gaining or retaining their love.*

Personality Bias

We all adopt the Two perspective when we see the potentials in people. We want to be generous when we see their worth. Their struggle inspires us. Their progress becomes our progress. Their needs determine our work. We're not concerned about remuneration when the value of our effort lies in their success. We feel suddenly grateful that our efforts matter. The gift is pure and selfless when the joy of others is felt to be our own.

A Two's window on life looks out on other people—their wants, their potentials, what they need to keep warm. Growing up in a context where survival depended on pleasing, Twos gave to others to get their own needs met. As adults they naturally move toward people. Wanting approval, they form an association in which they become indispensable. People feel chosen and flattered. Relating now depends on what Twos will or will not give. This maneuvering for position can occur without conscious awareness. The other's needs broadcast loudly, and Twos respond by adapting. They mold themselves to please, they are highly supportive, and they're proud to be of help.

Pride is that rush of elation we feel when someone special adores us. Twos get hooked by that kind of attention and adapt to keep it coming. If wanting to please becomes a habit, self-observation stops. You don't know that you have forgotten your own needs and have altered self-presentation. All you know is that rejection feels like annihilation, and you desperately need reassurance. Rejection is so painful that you try to get back into favor. You look for ways to fit in, you position yourself with the right people. You find that spending time with the right people is comforting. You become intrigued with their interests. You stay informed about the critical topics. You become a good source of information and can be counted on for lively discussion. In a very short time, you're so involved that you've lost yourself and become indispensable.

Twos grow by discovering what they want. They grow by being alone. You have a choice when you know your real worth to others and can watch yourself enhance that worth by meeting people's needs. Twos are helped by significants who are not seduced by adaptation, who love them apart from what they give, and who see them through the crisis of having to stand alone.

Subtype Focus:

Pride Affects Sexual, Social, and Survival Attitudes

Seduction/Aggression in Sexual and One-to-One Relationships

Pride enters one-to-one relating through seductive adaptation. We become attractive by adjusting our focus, taking on a partner's interests, and sharing their tastes. Twos have a talent for making people feel good about themselves and can please notoriously difficult people. In fact Twos take a certain pride in being the favorite, the trusted confidant, the one who can handle a difficult case.

The aggressive stance entails pursuit, especially in overcoming obstacles to the relationship. Taking the active role of pursuer and the one who shoulders difficulty effectively spotlights the partner and deflects attention from yourself. Going toward people in helpful ways eliminates anxiety that you might be overlooked without these special tactics.

Accomplished Givers can fine-tune the amount of attention that they get and can pursue/seduce different kinds of attention. Twos feel that they have many selves, and they often have a wide spectrum of friends. There are different qualities of regard to be sought. There are different tactics for parents than for studs and party girls. Seduction/aggression is not gender related. Both seductive males and aggressive females appear in the sexual subtype.

Social Ambition

You maintain pride of place by ambitious social positioning. Who you know and where you're seen. Who came to your party, and were they impressed? Public image is crucial. People know you by reputation and the professional letters after your name. You attract people of stature to your circle and find yourself hosting social events.

You wield influence indirectly, by arranging meetings, facilitating projects, and by putting people in touch who could do each other some good. Social Twos like to back a winner. Sensing the potentials, you are attracted to people on the way up. You serve ambition, often unconsciously, by aligning your own professional interests with those of a mentor, employer, or public figure in the field. You and your friends look out for each other. You get things done by calling your friends. Inner-circle membership is the hallmark of ambition. I pat your back and you pat mine. Being left out makes you feel insecure. You develop an acute awareness of shifts in allegiance and social respect. You protect your people by working the power structure. You want to warn them of danger and alert them to new opportunities. Twos become devotees, dedicated fans, and the hubs of the family.

Privileged Self-Survival

People appear to be needy. They depend on your help. Your need to help does not seem to have come from within you. Feeling like a selfless Giver masks the need for approval and protection. Twos take pride in their own independence, believing that others depend on their help.

Privilege is unveiled when you help people to become successful and find that you're angry when there's no reward. Selfless giving and good support should have protected your privilege. Exerting power indirectly and through other people seems more natural than saying what you want and working openly for your own interests. The indirect approach eases the pressure of public competition and the risk of social humiliation. If they win, you win, and in celebration of their success it's natural to expect some preferential treatment. Box seats for the inaugural. Special attention at the victory ball. Privileged people take their place at the head of the line and survive well.

Focal Issues

Other Referencing

Twos define themselves through the eyes of others. They find their identity in relationships, in the same way that Performers (Threes) find their identity through work. Their habit of attention is to focus on other people's reaction to them, making them unusually sensitive to a loved one's agenda. Whether or not their perceptions are accurate, the fact remains that a Giver's attention is habitually split between other people's feelings and their own. Other referencing can lead to marked qualities of empathy. It can also lead to great confusion. As one socially involved Giver remarked: "Trying to be yourself when you're at a party with all your different friends feels like being in a salad spinner."

Many Selves

Because their sense of themselves alters slightly depending on whom they are with, Givers are not inclined to see relationships as emotionally fixed. They are affectionate and forthcoming with people; they have a good sense of how to make contact in terms of conversation, mood, and body language. They mold themselves appropriately: "Should I be a soft person, an aggressive person, lighthearted, or dead serious?" It's not a matter of faking it or putting on a mask; it feels more like getting along with people so that we all like one another. Givers say they feel torn between their different attractions, especially when they're romantic. Which thread to follow? Which stirring is authentic? Which relationship to pursue when they lead to different ends?

Living in Feeling

Attraction produces immediate energy. Emotional hits are juice. Your mind weaves scenarios of the future. You imagine ways to bump into one another. Could we ever be together? Maybe there's hope. There are many kinds of attraction. The heart opens unexpectedly and at odd moments. When the heart connects, you want to sit on a park bench talking to old people, you want to hold a stranger's baby, you want to telephone your friends.

Relationships develop through currents of feelings that intertwine a conversation. You sense how you're both the same, and how you're different from each other. You test out your emotional blend. It's sometimes difficult for feeling types to describe the line of reasoning that guides them. They make decisions from both feeling and the facts. Qualities of emotion vary from day to day and person to person. "I'll see how I feel when the time comes," "I might feel differently next week."

Chicken Soup

When you're used to people watching, you naturally notice their likes and dislikes. The colors that flatter them, clothing they favor, the sandwiches they like to eat. Twos give naturally and easily, and this can sometimes be actively manipulative: "If I give them something that they want, then I'll get what I want in return." More often their own motives are hidden from themselves. Givers are usually not aware of their own unconscious agendas until they feel resentful because they didn't get what they wanted. It's the chicken soup syndrome. Giving is a way of being, and if you nourish people, they'll be happy and appreciative.

Boundaries

Givers are sensitive to what's needed. Doesn't everybody need help? They are aware, quite correctly, that people often deny what they need most. Soft people need to be hardened, aggressive people need to soften up, extroverts need social playgrounds, introverts need social help. When a Two is heavily fixated, he or she becomes immersed in the loved one's life. Convinced that others couldn't make it without them, and unaware of taking control, Twos can become intrusive. Other people feel railroaded into filling the Two's agenda, while Givers think they're responding to needs. Underappreciated Twos can be invasive. They forget the appropriate boundaries of privacy and take charge of a partner's life. In extreme cases Twos think that everything a partner owns is theirs and that everything that the family ever accomplished was the result of their good care.

Giving to Get

The helping strategy involves being attracted to a potential need, seeing what's needed to fulfill that need, and moving in to render support. The blind spot in this process is that the Two's attention has shifted from personal needs to others' needs. This shift of attention can cause Twos to become so involved in thinking about, and trying to improve, a loved one's life that their own feelings are shut down. Twos think, "I'm doing this for you," when they are actually working for the relationship and have repressed awareness of what they expect in return. Underappreciated Twos can be very angry. If a relationship becomes disappointing, Twos, since they are relationship-bound, will blame the partner. "Look what I've done for you" is the cry. They feel that with such good help, the least their partners can be is productive, attractive, attentive, wise, and well respected. And then the partners would feel much better about themselves besides.

Being Alone

When your identity hinges on the way that you relate to different people, being alone can be difficult. If you're not in a relationship, you feel like nobody's home. Your reactions to others are far more developed than your relationship to yourself. Being alone and doing things by yourself can be terrifying. "It feels like a black hole opens when I look inside. There's nothing there." It takes courage to look inward, to be an inspiration for yourself. Most mature Twos have spent time by themselves. They have had a long period out of relationship or have made a determined effort to be alone and to find the core of themselves that is steady and unchanging.

An Unchanging Self

Givers' sense of themselves is usually anchored in the way that they relate to a partner. It's like athletes relating to their game. When you go into training, your game gets inside you.

Your time, energy, emotions, and thinking are shaped around your game. When you're in training, your sense of yourself shifts slightly. Now you're wrapped around the being-in-training identity, and your other selves recede to the background of your awareness. You're just not as focused on career or school or your love life or being someone's friend.

Like an emotional athlete, Givers can be thinking, being, and feeling their relationship. The sense of self invoked by the other becomes central. As Twos mature, they usually become more impatient with being central to so many. A confusion arises among the many selves. "Which one is me?" Recognizing a constant self is at the heart of the matter, because a self has definite needs.

Having needs feels like a fight. "Who do I serve, you or myself? You like me when I serve your needs. Who are you to hold me back?" The fact may be that a partner is not willfully holding the Two back, but it may seem that way from the Two's perspective. Working directly for their own agenda rather than through others' is new territory.

Cos

"Are Twos codependent?" is a commonly asked question. It would seem that codependency is a major factor in their character, as with Nine (Mediator), the other Enneagram type that habitually merges with significant people. I don't see addictions as type related. Given the opportunity, the social pressures, and ripe inner conditions, anybody can get addicted to anything.

Type differences do, however, affect the motivations leading to addiction and the ways in which an addiction is acted out. It also follows that different types of people have their own best route to healing. A striking example would be the difference between rousing anger as a healing strategy for Mediators (Nines) juxtaposed to anger management for Bosses (Eights). Yes. Twos can be codependent, and so can every other type.

Security and Risk

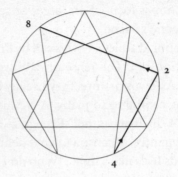

Security

A secure life situation, for example a satisfying job, will relax the focal issues. A secure Two keeps clear boundaries and is not compelled to please. The shift to Four occurs when it's safe to know what you need, and the Two is ready to move deeply into feeling. Attention turns to Four-like interests, which are approached from a Two perspective. The focus is on self rather than others. "What are my personal likes and dislikes? What interests me deeply when I'm alone? What are my authentic feelings, rather than feelings adapted to gain approval?" The development of a constant and unchanging sense of self is conducted from a Two's perspective. You form a relationship with yourself. You befriend your own potentials and learn to honor them with the same enthusiasm that you give to significants'. A secure Two knows what others feel and can separate at will from their emotions.

The opening of real needs is almost always attended by difficulty. Twos commonly get depressed when they see that being for others is easier than being for yourself. They feel used. They have betrayed themselves. They feel that they have sold themselves out for affection and a pat on the back. The downside of the Romantic Four position opens a well of self-pity: "It was easier for every-one else," "Why did I wait so long?" "Poor me." It can be produc-tive for Twos to explore their Four-like grief and envy. Sad about what? Envious of what? These inquiries can lead to the recovery of repressed needs, or, following the Four agenda, to the discovery of what is missing in life—the realm of one's true emotions—that needs to be developed.

Risk

Relationship is in the foreground of attention and is the source of greatest stress. Paradoxically a secure relationship can precipitate anxiety for Twos, because in order to live with some-one, you have to be yourself. Early signs of stress appear when the basic Two defenses tighten. The Two increases the preoccupation with the partner's needs and represses personal needs. A hysteri-cal emotional edge makes its appearance with short bursts of irri-tability and increasingly superficial emotional connection. If the stressor continues, the Two, who classically moves toward peo-ple, adopts an Eight-like stance of moving against. A Giver in Eight can be relentless. It feels like fighting for freedom, and they take the case to court.

To the extent that the Two is fighting against real emotional tyranny, the move to Eight can be liberating. Many Twos report that they found themselves under adversity. They knew exactly what they needed because it was being taken away. They main-tained their clarity, they learned not to fuzz-out, and they fought well. To the extent that Twos shadowbox with their own repres-sion, the move to Eight accomplishes nothing. They simply resent serving the will of others and rebel, but other people's needs are still the focus of attention. Twos can mobilize against the needs of others without discovering their own.

From the Two perspective, the low side of Eight involves punishing people for ingratitude. An aggressive assertion of will against the will of others. The case gets taken to court with heavy claims for damage.

Two in Love

Living with Twos

○ *Wants to be the central figure in your life. "I don't need you, but you depend on me."*

○ *Learn to recognize the Two's manipulation tactics, complaints and guilt, for example. The Two will try to maneuver you into doing what he or she wants.*

○ *Twos exert control while appearing to bend and to be subservient.*

○ *Their heavy emphasis on relationship makes Twos vulnerable to rejection and loss.*

○ *Encourage the Two to be authentic.*

○ *Expect big emotions. Anger and rising hysteria are signals of unmet needs. Twos may not know what they want, but they can get hysterical if they don't get it.*

○ *Be aware that short bursts of superficial feeling scatter concentration. Hysterical laughter, hyperactivity, and flirtations cover insecurity about the Two's own needs.*

○ *Realize that sex or affection seem equal to love.*

○ *Be sensitive to the Two's likely inexperience with real intimacy. Sexual and emotional feelings have been repressed in the interests of altering to attract attention. "I can please you, but what do I really feel for you?"*

○ *Allay the underlying belief that personal will must lead to abandonment. The Two needs to be reassured that you will still love her or him even if the Two doesn't meet your every need.*

○ *Beware: Twos are attracted to relationships with obstacles. Obstacles forestall having to face the confusion that surrounds an available, intimate relationship.*

○ *Twos like to triangulate, to be attracted to some "great man" or inspiring woman ("muse") while being involved in a more available romance. That way they can hedge on commitment, not risk rejection so much.*

○ *Don't be surprised when the Two starts fighting for freedom, feeling sold out by the habit of pleasing others, including or especially you. "I've served your needs, what about mine?" "Go take care of yourself!"*

° *Expect Twos to get angry when emerging real needs differ from their usual pleasing behavior.*

Intimacy

Appreciation is like oxygen. A Giver's best comes forward in response to the best in others. They are usually buoyant, energetic people who bring their enthusiasm and drive to relationships where they feel needed. Because Givers typically strengthen their own capacities while facilitating others, it is important to notice who is selected as a candidate and what help is offered. Their help is selective and specific rather than random or general. They are commonly attracted to physical beauty, to potentially successful people, and to helping those abused by life. In secure relationships their talents are stirred when their own well-being is identified with a significant's success. Appealing people who require help are Two bait.

It's a small shift from helping to manipulating. If you live with a Two, you know what he or she wants when you feel guilty about disliking something that's "for your own benefit." You know you're in trouble when your Two complains of overwork and you feel bad when you see just how much he or she has done for you.

Emotions get big if Twos don't get what they want. Their anger has the flavor of a hysterical, accusatory outburst, usually centered on lack of appreciation or feeling controlled by people's needs. A partner can help by fending off accusations and getting to the buried agenda. What does the Two need? Why the disappointment? What should we give? An angry outburst quickly passes. A hysterically energized moment. No grudge. No remorse. That was yesterday. Anger doesn't stick when the agenda is positive approval. Feelings flare like fireworks and quickly fade away.

Twos move toward people. They are affectionate and outgoing, which can look seductive but is usually just a social style. The prime directive is attention from significant people. To get that recognition, Twos can be oblivious to the fact that they are broadcasting their intentions to the rest of the room. Attention getting inadvertently creates jealousy when other people feel de-valued. The Giver style can be difficult for people who, perhaps out of touch with their own sexuality, see flirtation as foreplay, projecting the idea that pleasantry leads straight to the bedroom.

Going after someone can be a lot of fun. It's a natural posi-tion for Twos, whether by seduction or moving in to help. There's a rush of excitement when someone finds you attractive. You're challenged when there's click. That first recognition is a promise. You want to follow that promise; you want to be emotionally met.

When a relationship deepens, the aspects of self that were neglected during the heat of courtship reappear. Chances are Twos haven't revealed some essential parts of themselves and have slightly altered themselves to win favorable attention. It takes time for those feelings to emerge, and when they do, the well of need feels bottomless. It's terrifying for Givers, who take pride in being needed, to realize the extent of their own dependency. They think nobody can meet those needs. They need to be in-spired, to be wanted. They need to be with people so they won't be left alone. The paramount need is to get their needs met with-out knowing that they're needy.

Having needs equals rejection. In childhood Givers earned their way by accommodation. Being on the receiving end is new territory. This is a time of confusion in the relationship. Part of the difficulty lies in the fact that intimacy is developing. The ini-tial pull of seduction shifts to knowing someone deeply. To live with someone you have to know yourself. When the challenge of first attraction is played out, some Twos get bored. Now what? It's too exhausting watching for approval and too limiting to be molded to a single aspect of yourself.

Successful relationships have survived periods of rebellion, in which the Two fights against the restrictions of meeting a part-ner's needs. The partner may in fact be permissive and uncontrol-ling, but the fact that she or he is so emotionally central is bound to feel restricting. The Two feels taken over. The Two fights for freedom. The Two will no longer do anything to please. It takes time for Givers to see that they can follow their own will in a relationship without being abandoned and that they don't need their partner's permission to live their own lives.

Young Twos have a hard time being alone long enough to define themselves. They take pride in being popular with different social circles—student leaders, rebels, jocks, frats, nerds. The orientation is toward approval and away from rejection. Rejection can be devastating. If you don't get a response from someone you care about, it gets urgent inside. Rejection feels like losing your identity. "Who will I be without you?" "I may never feel this way again." You stand to lose a big piece of yourself when you're rejected, when the way that you know yourself is through the eyes of others.

The Signals Twos Send

Positive Signals

Twos make you feel special, that you're worth it, you're worth the time. Being helped and considered. Romantic meetings. Sensitive care. There's a magical quality in relating. A storybook flavor. Twos represent your interests. They interface with people you need to know. Your prospects are kept alive. Twos send a signal of exuberant aliveness. Energetic and expressive. Willful and willing. Twos will do for others what others normally do for themselves.

Negative Signals

You may experience Twos as dependent. They want a lot of your time. The ongoing demand for emotional excitement can be draining. You're expected to be inspiring. You're expected to confide. Feeling nudged into their agenda. Wondering who calls the shots. Once you were wonderful, now you're less intriguing. You feel that your life has been subtly rearranged.

Mixed Messages

If your interests run counter to Two's, a dual message develops. You may not be told a direct lie, but information is finessed. Twos manipulate with a light touch. Your perceptions feel clouded. Your mind is wrapped in a gauze of ignorance. Support is withdrawn. Meetings happen. Didn't you get the memo? Wrapped in ignorance, you are carefully transferred from the in group to the out group, from which perspective you see the Two busily managing other lives. The message is either come to heel or make it on your own.

Inner Signals

Pride is well hidden because it masquerades as helpfulness. Twos who are new to the Enneagram commonly go blank when it comes to the question of pride. The Giver characteristics that they observe in themselves don't have an obvious common denominator. It doesn't seem prideful to be concerned about what people need. The perception of people as needy doesn't seem at all biased. You don't see pride at work when you take control; you simply find yourself deeply preoccupied. The thoughts say: "I could suggest," "I could arrange," "I see how they could." It seems so obvious. Make sure that everyone gets what they want, and then they'll be happy. It's a Christmas-morning feeling. A generous swelling of goodwill. You go into action wholeheartedly. Magnanimous, not prideful. The feelings say: "They'll feel good about this."

The blind spot in this way of being is that you think of others' needs but rarely of your own. The thoughts seldom say: "I will take," "I will receive," "I'm in this for myself." It helps to notice when your mind has become saturated with someone else's future. It helps to separate your awareness several times a day and focus entirely on yourself. What appears in your mind when you ask, "What's in it for me?"

Pride is unveiled when you can tell the difference between freely given assistance and self-serving involvement. The thoughts say: "I'm blanking-out on this," "You have needs. I don't." It helps to bring your attention back to yourself. To inquire again, "What if I don't give? How will I feel if I do nothing?" If you do not draw attention to yourself, the connection between pride and needs becomes stunningly clear. You feel humbled if they love you anyway; and it's devastating when love that you could have earned goes to someone else.

Two at Work

In the Workplace

° *Takes own identity from authorities who can offer support. The right-hand man. The secretary who knows the secrets. The power behind the throne.*

° *Highly responsive to approval and encouragement. Crushed by disapproval.*

° *Keeps tabs on office interactions. The information pipeline, the party coordinator, the one who knows when invitations get sent.*

° *Associates with "worthwhile" people. Sidesteps those who aren't.*

° *Has complicated office strategies. Backs favorites. Often an unrecognized conflict between an ambition to be first and wanting to please.*

° *Works for the respect of important people in the field, the power elite. "Who do we know that will endorse our project?"*

° *Safety lies in pleasing authority. Fears opposing power alone.*

° *May choose work because it has value to a loved one.*

Leadership Style

Twos are effective leaders, although many position themselves as the power behind the throne. They are attracted to promising new directions and potential talent on the way up the business ladder. They rely on developing key people rather than a meticulous structure. The business vision is of a flourishing, well-knit community that prospers with good care.

There will be an in group and an out group, and, if possible, decisions are weighted toward the favorites. You know that you're being groomed for in-group membership when you get access to the leader. If you're out, you'll be dealing with someone else.

Image is crucial. Twos align with power and success. Twos who are corporate leaders will be ambitious about achieving a prestigious record and will support that image by seductively or aggressively aligning themselves with key figures in the field. Who you know makes what you do successful. A prestige-minded leader is more likely to establish some basis of collegial connection than to stake out a territory and fend off the competition. Twos have an intuitive predisposition to feeling the needs of others, and the line of least resistance is to align with power. Givers can be highly competitive. They need to be recognized and seen. The image of choice projects helpfulness over aggression. They are popular figures who magnetize public approval without looking like they need it. Sensitive to the office climate, they model the enthusiasm and personal charm that they want to see in the workplace. The bottom line is vital, but if you equate success with good human resources, you will be generous about the quality of life.

This leadership style emphasizes identifying and filling client needs. If the needs change, so will the organizational structure. The focus is on client satisfaction. Wooing the client rather than warring with competitors. Presenting a product or service in such a way that customers get what they want. Givers happily minimize the meticulous work of reports and procedures in favor of human interaction. They are more productive in an interactive setting than in isolation. Decision making is often in concert with trusted advisers.

The power-behind-the-throne approach is a typical Two strategy. It's just a whole lot easier to lead indirectly rather than having to deal with face-to-face hostility or rejection. By taking the chamberlain role, Twos are free to observe, advise, and test the waters. Thoroughly identified with the throne's agenda, they will develop a strong in-group network throughout the organization. This is a perfect power position. Their advice determines what needs will be met. They can facilitate the in group and mold policy to conform with their own interests. Under pressure, the in group pulls together.

Conflicts

Givers can be temperamental. They thrive on recognition and will be irritable and rejecting at implied disrespect. Pride makes it difficult to be kept waiting, to move methodically through an obstruction, to feel slowed down by the mundane. Their usual generous and upbeat attitude can shift very quickly to an angry outburst if they feel overlooked. Personal problems may leak into the workplace. A fight at home is brought to work. If the Two is in authority, staff will begin to "handle" the boss. They also learn to disappear on cue when big emotions hit. The types that thrive on consistency may feel emotionally manipulated; but rather than taking an outburst personally, it's far more effective to remember that a Two's anger dissipates quickly. Twos not only forgive, they forget.

Conflict Resolution

See Part III, "The Directory of Relationships," for tips on mediation between Twos and others.

Employee Participation

Happy Twos are a workplace treasure. They represent you well, they offer constructive suggestions, and they have a driving energy to protect your interests. They back you from behind the scenes. They know everyone and can mobilize support. They stay on top of shifting alliances and will keep you informed. They are a fixture in their sector, and an indispensable ally. Nobody is more successful at outreach and promotion than a happy Two.

If the system colludes to keep staff positioned in menial roles, it may be difficult for Givers to participate. They are incredible promoters for those they believe in, but lose interest if there is no positive feedback. It fuels the tendency to exert power indirectly or by manipulating the goodwill of a powerful associate. Twos are molded to the inner dreams of others, and the road to advancement begins with co-teaching or co-facilitating.

There may be some glitches to this system, such as the Two becoming prideful about his or her actual contribution to the project. Attendance at meetings and a few useful comments hardly constitute leadership, but it may seem so to participants who overrate their own influence. This comment, taken from an ambitious young Giver, says it all: "I personally have no interest in appearances, but I spend at least a third of my free time shopping so that I'll represent the firm well."

Two employees must be strongly supported at the beginning of a venture. Standing alone is hard enough, but if the task is compounded by the possibility of public humiliation, it invites the employee to withdraw and scheme. Once in motion, Twos perform well. Their difficulty is at the beginning. They tend to space-out and lose mental focus when they first stand in the spotlight alone.

Team Building

A team of equals presents a bind. The Two will feel split between wanting to be liked by the group and wanting special attention. Being liked means being the same as. Fitting in via a common ground of interests. More often, Twos are competitive with their peers and look for ways to get special attention from someone higher up. A team whose members contribute different skills is better, but the real hook is emotional juice. Does someone of significance to the Two care about the outcome? Participation improves exponentially if the Two feels sympathetic to the needs of the players or is in liaison with a respected mentor. Twos stay interested when they're aligned with others' needs or when they feel for the project. They want more than content. They want emotional connection to the content. Their best work is produced when they are positioned to suggest, prod, cajole, and extend a project that is of great concern to others.

3

Three ⬢ *The Performer*

PERSONALITY BIAS		ESSENCE QUALITIES
MENTAL	*vanity*	*hope*
EMOTIONAL	*deceit*	*veracity (honesty)*

SUBTYPE FOCUS	
MASCULINE/FEMININE IMAGE	sexual
PRESTIGE	social
SECURITY	self-survival

The Three Bias

Worldview

The world values a champion. I must avoid failure.

Spiritual Path

The preoccupation with personal performance points to a search for *hope*. Threes place hope in their own efforts rather than in work aligned with universal principles. *Vanity* elevates personal achievement to a place of great psychological importance. Projecting the image of an achiever mimics *honest* efforts that are carried by universal energies. A high-profile image of productivity is a child's attempt both to gain approval and to protect a connection to the powerful energies of essence. *Deceit* involves maintaining an image of success in the eyes of others. Hope and honest effort are both a psychological growth edge for Performers and a potential access point to higher awareness.

Concerns

- Wants to be loved for performance rather than for self.
- Has to be first. People love a top performer.
- Efficiency, product, goals, results.
- Competes only when winning is assured. Avoids failure. Leaves before the loss.
- Self-presentation alters to enhance effectiveness. Concern about image.
- Self-deception. Takes on the feelings that match the public image.
- Acts out the false persona in three key areas of life:

     A successful MASCULINE/FEMININE IMAGE in one-to-one relationships.

     PRESTIGE in social relating.

     Accumulating SECURITY to ensure survival. Money and possessions.
- Heart is in work. Emotions that serve a role are easy.
- Chameleon. Abandons genuine feelings in favor of a role.
- Confuses real identity and job identity.
- Has trouble accessing deep emotion. Attention turns to tasks.
- Free time brings anxiety. Packs vacations with activity.
- Tends to look to image, status, and material objects for happiness.
- The instant expert. Overvalues own ability.
- Polyphasic thinking. Does many tasks at the same time.
- Has tunnel vision for tasks. Gets angry when tasks are interrupted.
- Effective leaders, good packagers, competent promoters, captains of winning teams.

Personality Bias

Each of the nine types is focused on a special sector of information. Threes are focused on high-profile achievement. Data that promotes that point of view shifts to the foreground, while other data fades away. It's an efficient mind-set for getting the job done, and everyone adopts it in professional life. When a juicy project comes into play, we naturally shift gears and, like Threes, move into performance mode.

Threes were loved for their achievements rather than for what they felt. Doing, rather than feeling, was valued. Image was valued, rather than depth. As a way of flourishing in this environment, Three children learned to perform well and geared up for success. They learned to compete, to handle several jobs at once, and to promote themselves. They learned how to impress people. If the way to love is being a winner, you learn to project a winning facade.

Image can be deceptive. It's tailored to enhance results rather than to express one's needs. Self-presentation will shift in response to different occasions. You become the perfect lover, the effective doer, the leader of the pack. If your own feelings are insubstantial and unfamiliar, you can still feel good about yourself if you stand well in other people's eyes. Without the rudder of a strong emotional life to guide you, it seems natural to take your cue from other people, figure out what you're supposed to look like, and give them what they want.

When projecting an appropriate persona works, you can assume the characteristics of a role. You forget that you're projecting an image. You are only aware that you hate being disliked, that people like you when you look successful, that you can shift your presentation at will, and that everyone seems happier about you when you look good. If this habit becomes automatic, self-observation stops. Threes can then become victims of massive self-deception, unable to distinguish their own feelings from the feelings that come with a role.

Performers grow by seeing themselves as separate from their image. You have a choice when you can hear yourself becoming self-promoting, putting a spin on your accomplishments, or adjusting your manner to enhance the impression that you make.

They are helped by people who reframe the goals of relating from emotional appearance to emotional depth; who are patient with a Three's habit of slipping away from feeling; and who offer loyalty to the person without buying into a convincing facade.

Subtype Focus:

Deceit Underlies Sexual, Social, and Survival Attitudes

Masculine/Feminine Image in Sexual and One-to-One Relationships

Threes can be masters of appearance. In intimate relationships they become a prototype of what a mate finds pleasing. In business the facade alters for maximum appeal. A top producer. A strong contender. An attentive lover. The ideal mate. The emphasis is on form and surface. Having the right look and the best lines. How do strong contenders take charge of a meeting? How should attentive lovers style their hair? You research the perfect spots for romantic dinners. What current books are top performers reading?

The sexual subtype makes a task out of conquest. To be convincing you have to believe in yourself. You connect by projecting self-confidence. You put out hooks and see if they take. You sink the hooks that recruit approval and wear the mask that falls into place.

Seeking identity through a role, Threes become a role model of whatever characteristics a partner finds appealing, and in the process deceive themselves that the appropriate feelings are genuine. The image of choice emphasizes sexual attractiveness; and it's confusing when the current trend doesn't fit your nature. You have to wear bright spandex even when you're not a runner. If your natural look is John Wayne macho, then New Age soft male doesn't quite fit.

Social Prestige

Anonymity makes you anxious. You have to be somebody in the eyes of others or you're nobody within yourself. There's often confusion between being the best and being the best known. Social Threes are concerned with immediate public visibility rather than a private reputation. They place great value on social credentials, titles, public honors, and influential connections. What schools did you attend? How many letters come after your name? Do you know somebody famous?

Deceit involves shifting self-presentation to attract social attention. You may not be aware of slipping into the role of a valued performer. You may not be aware of saying what the group wants to hear or projecting the persona of what they're looking for. All you know is that it hurts to see someone else hold center stage. They may be good, but you could be better. It hurts to be nobody in the crowd, so you lobby and get elected. Along the way, it's natural to take on the mannerisms of a prototype. You lend yourself to the appropriate thoughts and feelings, like an actor beginning to live out a part. It makes you feel secure when heads turn in your direction.

If you're moving between groups, you'll have different sets of clothes. It's important to look the part at the symphony or driving a truck. You shoot for an image that the group values, and you know where you stand by the degree of their regard. If it's not working, you adjust, because you feel like somebody when you're appreciated.

Survival Security

A preoccupation with the security that money can buy. Often rooted in the conviction that money buys safety, survival-minded Threes develop many skills to ensure job security. Even when Threes have a background of wealth, they are terrified of being incapacitated and unable to work. Emotional survival is attached to earnings, and a great deal of attention is paid to accumulating assets and possessions. Your value as a person is associated with material worth. You can deceive yourself and others about the extent of your success by projecting an affluent image. A costly home with a good address, expensive travel, designer clothes.

Losing assets can feel life threatening. You keep working, because you become anxious when you stop. Unbooked professional time produces high anxiety. A job without advancement makes you question your worth. At work the survival concern is focused on single-minded pursuit of the bottom line. Free time takes on the specter of an illness or a layoff. You prefer long hours of work. Happiness is equated with affluence. Material assets will be a centerpiece of your relationship, often with a tendency to confuse financial well-being with emotional pleasure. You'll relax after the next deal, the next promotion, the next raise in pay.

Focal Issues

Chameleon

Threes know what others want them to look like, and they become it. They know what others want to hear and will feed it back to them. They see what will impress others and assume that persona. Skillful in image management, they can change identity in midsentence. They start off in the wrong direction, find that it isn't working, and adjust so smoothly that the end of the sentence affirms an acceptable opinion. They take on the protective coloration of an image that the group respects. By assuming the look, the style, and the status that are valued, like an actor who takes on the characteristics of a part, they can step into the projection and become it.

Polyphasic Activity

In the interests of efficiency, Threes like to do several things at once. If you have to go from the kitchen to the cellar, all the small tasks along that route suddenly come to mind. At work you walk down the hall to another office mentally flipping through the items on the calendar that concern that office. Maybe you could squeeze two jobs into one trip. Efficiency is energizing. The more you do, the better you feel, so you go for quantity.

When there's a main task focus, several tracks are engaged at the same time. You're remembering relevant data, recalling useful contacts, and mentally working tomorrow's list while you're on the phone with today's. Several projects often crest at the same time. To be efficient, you spend as little time as possible on details and move quickly on to the next item and the next and the next. Doing is a form of control. Performers feel secure as long as they can be actively engaged.

Competition

Threes are naturally competitive. They like to stretch their limit, to play full out, to compete with the best. Like most good competitors, they play to win. A good opponent galvanizes the game. Distractions drop away, and you tunnel in on the fastest, most efficient way to get to the goal or the product or to a mate's affection. The strength of a competitive edge is that the job gets done, but the liability is a faulty feedback system. You see the cues that concern the goal, and everything else is irrelevant.

Competitors act on partial information. They can't stop to listen. They're too focused to hear. People and their resources are reduced to what they can do for the project. When project feedback is negative, they work harder. When feedback is positive, they speed up. The message is: "Don't mess with me when I'm working," "I'll call you when I'm done."

Personal Marketability

Competition involves both ability and self-promotion. North American culture is largely Three. We reward youth and vitality. We support a competitive marketing system. We expect to be propagandized by the media. We know that ads enhance the facts. It's not that advertising is a pack of lies, but the product description is tailored to what the public wants.

Other-directed Threes take on roles with public appeal. Their identity depends on positive regard for an attractive persona. It's not that they tell lies about the facts of their life; it's more that they market themselves like a product. The résumé figures heavily into their thinking. You find out what a potential employer wants and put that spin on your résumé. You follow a partner's interests and become a living expert. You look for characteristics that attract them and begin to embody those traits.

Can Do

Threes like a clear course of action with an identified goal. They feel in control when there's something constructive to do; they're furious when tasks are interrupted. Their rage covers deep anxiety about losing control. Needing a win, Threes assume their own ability. "I know the answer. No problem. Can do." Attention shifts to the final result, minimizing the perception of danger. Self-doubt isn't part of the picture. Steps one through nine are blurred when you're already at ten. Moving into fast-forward, Threes outrun their anxiety. "We'll wing it when we get there. Let's go."

Fraudulence

Image is both deceptive and protective. It shields Threes from rejection. If a relationship doesn't work out, you can move on and feel yourself changing into a new life, a new persona, a new set of friends and expectations. Threes look ahead, to the future and to success. They pay very little attention to past regrets. Self-aware Threes know the difference between their image and real feelings. They can tell the difference between a leader and a bluffer. It is a moment of truth when Threes discover that they are living through a persona. They have a sense of being a phony, of betraying themselves. Their own connection to the power of illusion makes Threes somewhat mistrustful. They can spot a phony, because they see the impact of surface appeal. It is a significant moment when Performers become themselves in public. It's so much easier to emanate an appropriate facade.

Efficiency

Security is in doing, so ideas of quantity and efficiency are appealing. Goals and lists are ongoing, often with an impatient feeling that there's not enough time to get it all done. Efficiency is calculated. A choreographed rolling up to the stop sign so you don't have to stop. A certain routine that gets chores done as quickly as possible. Threes have a mental attitude of planning swiftly so as to reduce the time spent on an individual item. The ongoing pressure of tasks makes it difficult to sit and talk. Threes have the feeling that life is passing by. When the energy rev comes on, Threes are the first to jump out of bed, first on the tennis court, hitting the most balls in the shortest amount of time. Even seconds count. Lunch is a sandwich in the car or at the computer or timed for when there's no line in the cafeteria so they won't have to wait.

The Hurry Habit

When a project picks up speed, attention narrows to just those items that will get the job done. Other interests drop away. Distractions disappear. Goals become clear when the pieces are in motion. You set up time sheets, calculate expenses, start making calls. Doubt vanishes, questions disappear. You're on your way.

A project can also dominate your life. It determines priorities. It controls your time, your money, and your mind. It determines who stays in your life and who's left behind. Once committed, you can't let go. A mind split develops. The project stays with you even when you've moved to other goals. You can't dump it. You commit attention to the next step, and halfway through that step you've moved on to what's needed for the next and the next, with no stops between. You experience short bursts of anxiety when results fail to materialize. You quickly adjust to maximize results, sometimes with a desire to adjust the results to conform to the goal. The key word is *stop*. It's very difficult to stop and listen to yourself once the habit takes over.

Security and Risk

DYNAMICS OF CHANGE FOR POINT THREE

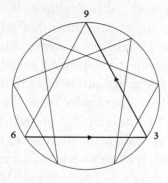

Security

Paradoxically Performers become more tentative and afraid when they enter a secure relationship. Their strength lies in leadership, where the placement of attention favors tasks over feelings. Doing is easy, but the feelings that relationship calls out are new territory. It's far more familiar to rev up than to relax and look within. A secure life situation, for example, a satisfying job or a good marriage, allows Threes to discover an agreeable work pace, but the focal issues may not be called into question. Generally people are reluctant to see self-promotion or a high profile as other than an indicator of valid accomplishment. Threes prefer to work at a level that most of us would see as stressful. They tend to add a relationship to their hours of overtime rather than relaxing the pace. The shift to security occurs either at the behest of the partner who wants greater intimacy, as the result of tragedy that forces feelings to the surface, or when a Performer becomes otherwise convinced that emotional life is worthwhile.

The up side of the security position lies in the discovery of real feelings, which makes empathy and emotional loyalty possible. The down side creates insecurity. Threes doubt their feelings. "Maybe they're not genuine." They feel fraudulent. "Is this what I'm supposed to feel?" Suddenly they are less certain, less confident. Attention turns to Six-ish concerns that are approached from a Three's perspective. They become dependent on a partner to boost their image. They want adoration but are now suspicious of it. A Three in love is afraid to be unmasked. It helps to frame the "unmasking" of image as a useful activity, to emphasize the positive benefits to health and to family life. It also helps to see that doubt can modify a Three's unrelenting self-confidence. In learning to reconsider, to ponder, and to wait, a Three in stress not only learns to love but can also forgo a quick-fix mentality in favor of authentic creative ideas.

Risk

Threes put their hearts in their work, so any professional threat is highly stressful. The obvious stressors are a layoff or illness, but Threes are also at risk when an important relationship declines. The first indications are a tightening of point Three defenses. Attention narrows to the task at hand, which blunts feelings of anxiety. If the anxiety persists, Threes move into hyperdrive. "I'm doing very well. I get home at midnight and leave by seven A.M." The real task is to stay with the impulse that precedes the action, so as to uncover feelings. But in the face of failure, Threes switch to any direction that will keep momentum going. If an exit can't be found, the usual shift to Nine takes place by moving from big projects to small tasks and errands.

Threes inhabiting the low side of their risk point space-out by throwing a lot of energy at trivia. Trashy novels, watching TV, and endless chores. It looks numb from the outside. Anxiety is stated, but there's not much emotion behind it. Questions of self-worth are in the forefront. "Who am I if I can't produce?" "What do you think I should do?" They are most vulnerable in the morning and at night, when they are undistracted by activity. The low side also shows a tendency to blame the fates. "There was nothing I could do," "This is not my doing."

The best use of Nine serves to open trust in relationship. Unable to function at their usual pitch, Threes have to pin their hopes on someone else. This can lead to a reconsideration of the childhood conclusion that only winners are worthy of love. When you expect to be rejected for failure, you are unusually open to acceptance. When you feel you have little to offer, you are grateful to those who reach out. Many Threes report that they became fully committed to their relationship during a business crisis. They felt surrounded by love at a time when they least expected it. The concept of being loved for oneself, for one's being rather than one's doing, can become a lived reality in stress.

See Part III, "The Directory of Relationships," for interactions between Threes and others in intimate life.

Three in Love

Living with Threes

- *Threes feel loved for their achievements, not for who they are.*
- *The Three frames the relationship as an "important task" that can be built.*
- *The Three expects appreciation from a mate for a winning image and style.*
- *Be aware of your Three's tendency to "do" feelings, for activity to replace affect, and to adopt the role of the perfect lover with a script of endearing things to say.*

° *Help your partner slow down activity related to intimacy long enough to be affected by intimate feelings.*

° *Your Three partner will be intolerant of "darker" emotions. Wants to tune out negative feedback. "Let's stay energetic and happy," "Let's do something together," "Let's have fun."*

° *If the Three partner takes responsibility for other people's "negative" feelings ("What should I do to make you happy?"), hold out the possibility that there is no quick solution to pain.*

° *Understand that your Three can readily confuse ideas about emotions with the real thing.*

° *And, as real feelings emerge, your Three can be in a quandary: "Do I have the right one? Am I doing this right? Tell me what I should feel."*

° *So Threes become especially anxious when activity is suspended and feelings begin to come forth.*

° *Three partners need to be assured that they are loved for themselves, not as the prototype of the perfect mate.*

° *A Three's heart is in his or her work. The Three will therefore need a strong push from a partner to take time away from work.*

Intimacy

Threes have a tendency to do feelings. Doing entails seeing how others react and imagining that you're the same way when deep feelings are called for. You see how people's faces change when they're sorrowful or filled with love, and you get used to behaving that way while at the same time watching your mind spin out on lists of things to do. Doing your feelings is a lot less threatening than turning attention inward and finding an empty place where authentic feelings are supposed to bubble up.

Different types of people love in their own way, and Threes promote upbeat, active love in a very convincing manner, without seeing the narrowness of the definition. Believing that their optimistic doing mode is the same as what other types of people call love, they compound the confusion between a feeling role and the real thing by their own self-confidence. Love is doing things together, love is productive and happy. Love is not supposed to be overwhelming or evocative or painful. How could it be otherwise when as children Threes earned love through achievement?

Negative emotion triggers immediate action. "Let's not wallow. We can do something about pain." Activity cuts feelings and reduces anxiety, but because they act in the name of feelings, they seem to be experiencing the real thing. A successful Performer can be shocked to discover that, at first, very little appears when activity stops and attention turns inward. Voluntary suffering is a total mystery. Threes would rather turn to something useful. They're frightened when a partner surrenders to sadness. The Three thinks, "Nothing good can come of this." Even marginal dissatisfaction brings up anxiety. A concerned Three thinks, "I should have done something sooner. Was it something I did or didn't do? What can be done to fix this, and can I do it quickly?" It's stressful to sit down and talk things over. It's stressful to feel and not act.

Because they expect to be loved for performance, Threes are willing to do a great deal for the couple. They want to provide "for the family." They want status "for us." Threes come home late and tired and wonder why they're not appreciated. From the Three side, it's a real dilemma: afraid of rejection if you don't produce, and rejected when you do.

It helps to put intimacy on a schedule; far from being mechanical, this is made to order for Threes. Hanging out with no agenda. Measured doses of being loved without a product to show. Taking a walk without an activity buffer. No running shoes allowed. Just a walk by yourself when the only task is to let your feelings surface. Being is hard. "How do you do being?" "Am I doing it right?"

Intimate life takes on a picture-book quality. A cute couple. An ideal family. Things to learn and do. There are enormous personal rewards in encouraging family interests, in raising healthy children, in making life work. Committed to productivity, Threes can fall into relating as an activity. Love is fused with an appearance of well-being. An activities schedule, things to do for the house, for the kids, for us.

Significants assume that Threes have complete access to their feelings, instead of having to discover them. In this they are abetted by the Three, who, chameleonlike, can role-play emotions, confusing them with the real thing. When real feelings develop, Threes reach a great turning point. It is a testimony to the value of the relationship in which they open. A partner has to call out something in a Three to make change worthwhile. Things get worse before they get better. The shadow comes into play. Stung by the self-betrayal of chameleon living, a Three feels like a phony when attention separates from image and shifts to the heart. "Who am I without my roles?" "Who am I supposed to be?"

Role is deceptive, but it also protects a Three. Having assumed the identity of a lover, for instance, the Three can believe that it's the role that's rejected if there's a breakup. Self-observant Threes know that they're separate from the image they project. A split sometimes develops between the public, performing self and a more private, personal self that emerges when it's safe to move out of a role. The private self feels fraudulent and wonders, "Is what I'm saying true to myself? Is this genuine?"

The Signals Threes Send

Positive Signals

Threes project an optimistic worldview. "We can make it happen." You'll find them enthusiastic and encouraging. There is hope in action. They come across as highly practical, dedicated to the goal, to the team, to the family, to a result. Performers can be dedicated leaders: you can count on them to take responsibility, to stay with it, to be willing to do the most.

Negative Signals

You may Perceive that the Three doesn't care about you, especially about your feelings. Threes can look artificial or superficial because they change to give the crowd what it wants. Things and goals may matter more than people to them. Difficulty in relaxing, in letting go, being on vacation. As a Three cuts corners on relationship time, softening the truth with partial truths, you can feel manipulated by a Three's accomplishment agenda. Threes can let personal friends disappear, while work friends stay.

Mixed Messages

When Threes are most productive, they are often least aware of themselves. Moving effectively from one project to the next, they can achieve robotically, seeing their value as a person in what they produce and do. Happiness is often identified as recognition from others and owning what other people want. Tangible wealth and social awards are priorities. Others can read the subtext of material happiness as missing out on the full range of human emotions. Confusion exists between the pleasure of things and emotional satisfaction. Moving swiftly on to the next project produces incomplete gratification. The Three doesn't stick around long enough to absorb the pleasure of accomplishment. The rush into activity replaces the real task of reflection and accepting pleasure.

It helps if a significant frames the relationship as an important task that has its own goals and results. Threes have to see results for effort. Relationships can blossom if Threes feel confident of their ability to "get good" at being emotional.

Inner Signals

Threes like to charge ahead. They worry about details later. By the time they're halfway into the project, it may be too late to stop and correct course. The thoughts say: "I know what I'm doing. Fill me in as we go along." It's hard to read warnings and negative signs when you're in midstride. There's too little time between idea and action. No time to reflect. A voice raised in disagreement sounds like interference. Threes think: "We can deal with that later" or "That's negative thinking." Criticism can make the Three want to push harder. The feeling is: "These people are jealous," "Gotta get there first."

Energetic conviction and impatience well up. The feelings say: "This is going to work. Let's go for it." When the energy picks up, inner conviction is coupled with imagining how it will feel "when I'm on top of this" or "when I'm elected." Abundant physical energy feels wonderful, and when that energy is tied to an image, it makes the image seem worthwhile, regardless of its actual merit.

Threes need to become aware of when the mind takes off to the finished goal and final results. It helps them to wait. Self-aware Threes can use the energy surge as a reminder. They ask, "Will this goal serve me, or does it serve my image?"

Three at Work

In the Workplace

- Assumes own ability. The instant expert.
- Confuses real self and work role. "I am what I do."
- Takes on the image and feelings of a task. Prototype of the profession.
- The priority is to be efficient and save time, even if this means cutting corners. Takes the shortcut. Does several things at once. "Details later."
- Will stay on an expansionist track until the task is opposed, then parlay options for the biggest possible win.
- Feels rage when tasks and goals are interrupted. Anger is usually task specific.
- Values product over process. "How much did I produce?"
- Being respected for ability as a worker is more important than being liked.

- *Machinelike achiever. Expects others to work in the same way.*
- *Projects a high-profile image—credentials, social standing, "who's who."*
- *Exerts power over people; competes for leadership roles.*
- *Wants a clear path to success. Shoots for defined goals. Wants reward for effort. Intolerant of ambiguous returns.*
- *Pays selective attention to positive feedback. Image has to be maintained. Intolerant of criticism. Places responsibility elsewhere if failure occurs.*
- *Avoids failure. Switches tracks. Finds a presentation that works.*
- *Has difficulty telling the difference between being admired as a leader and being liked for himself or herself.*

Leadership Style

Leadership is the preferred position. When self-esteem is earned by effort, you roll up your sleeves. Boundless energy wells up. "Let's go. I can do it. Why are you tired?" Of course people will follow. Of course they'll join. The typical American Three does business like a football quarterback. You try every trick in the book to keep the ball moving in the right direction. This is a classic leadership style for a business in rapid expansion, and it suits the U.S. ideal; but, like chameleons, Threes adapt to any milieu. A Japanese Three will aggressively espouse the process-oriented facilitations that are typical of the Deming style of management. If a participatory structure is popular, then a good Performer will become that kind of leader. If the people want a fighter, a Three climbs into the ring.

Once in motion, Threes get tunnel vision and tune out the opposition. You can't afford to doubt yourself at high speed. Momentum alone propels you forward. You can't look back. Focused on the goal, Three leaders keep going unless a strong counterforce stops them in their tracks. Then it's a fight. The Three leader is a formidable competitor. The goal is the thing, and any risk that can get you there seems feasible. They will wheel and deal. Beg and borrow. Go to the edge and over. Instead of slowing under pressure, Threes expand and franchise. Any risk is worth it if you get there fast and first.

The unwillingness to tolerate interruption makes it difficult to absorb new or contradictory information. The message to the company is, "Just Do It!" Threes delegate with the assumption that everyone will cut as many corners as possible in the interests of efficiency. Quality control is often sacrificed. Attention goes to quantity over quality, expanding opportunities over the quality of current commitments. If the prime directive is "Do It!" there's not much time for detail.

If a business reflects Three leadership, the vision focuses on expanding goals. Threes can experiment beautifully with known ideas but are not usually original thinkers or innovators. They apply known ideas to new situations and package them very well. Original thinking takes a great deal of time musing over the idea and dealing with questions that arise. Threes don't have the patience for prolonged search. They want to extract known solutions from previously successful projects and apply them immediately to a new goal. They thrive on practical results. Performers get a great deal of validation for their personal style. The world loves a winner, and most of us are quite willing to let someone else step forward and take charge.

Classic Conflicts

Threes are identified with task and role. They expect everyone else to be equally motivated and are infuriated when projects are interrupted. The goal is the thing, without much sense of process along the way. When trouble arises, impatience cuts into a discussion. The fact of interruption is sufficiently threatening to make Threes either want to fire the troublemaker or leave and better themselves elsewhere. If you have to bring bad news to a Three who's focused on final result, you would do well to reaffirm the goal and then encapsulate the problem in as few words as possible. A good format would sound like: "We're on schedule on every front except for one sector, which needs attention." Reassured that the goal is still possible, Threes can get excited about brainstorming a solution.

Predictably there are power struggles between Threes and others. If only one leadership post exists, the Three will go full out to get that position. The best way around this is to model the type of cooperative structure that can get the job done effectively and to stay with the fact that we can all profit from the same goal. The structure of cooperative leadership must be clearly designed from the beginning. A power vacuum in leadership invites warfare.

Conflict Resolution

See Part III, "The Directory of Relationships," for tips on mediation between Threes and others.

Employee Participation

This is the type of person who responds to classic rewards for good work. Threes will produce for a bonus and compete for titles. They are unusually aware of differences in status. They are happiest in a work situation that has stated goals, reward for earned achievement, and promising opportunities for advancement. Nonrecognition incites competition. If they're not singled out, they feel it in the pit of the stomach. "I should be up there doing that lecture," "I should be on stage," "I could do that job." They gravitate to a workplace that has prospects; but when the route to advancement is obstructed, they may well manipulate the system. They will work their way around the incumbents, lobby for their own interests, and set up competitive programs. They look like greyhounds straining on the leash.

Threes' attention goes to their own performance. They want to know that they're doing well and that they look good doing it. They learn best when the material serves a function. They focus on immediate use. "What can I do with this?" If they can use it, the material becomes exciting. They want fast-paced, stimulating activity. They want to get it. They want to be shown a few basic principles and move immediately into hands-on, practical applications.

Threes learn on their feet. They raise their hand to answer a question before they know what to say. They're impatient with long-winded theory. The bias toward action makes it easier to learn by doing. They're not inclined to hang back. They'll jump in and wing it, without being embarrassed if they can't do something immediately. They want to get the pieces in motion, and they'll try before they think.

Driven by immediate goals and results, they may have a tendency to close down options prematurely. A short-term gain seems immensely attractive when you're primed for action. It just seems easier to shift to an immediately promising direction rather than to face a period of questioning or opposition. Threes can succeed at long-term projects by staging them in small chunks that offer rewards and recognition after the successful completion of each stage. An awards dinner. An article in the company newsletter. A public announcement of success.

Team Building

Threes will tend to take over a team when the spheres of influence are not specifically designated. Needing tangible evidence of their value, they will volunteer, set up brainstorming sessions, and expect to work late. This level of commitment is going to have an effect on the team. Some will respond, some will feel pushed, and others will back away. The actuality may be that the activity flurry is more about recognition than about the project. Threes feel helpless when others take charge, so they want to be impressive.

It's important to enroll Threes by demonstrating ways in which the goal furthers their own interests. They can be powerful team players if they are identified with the goal. They are usually specialists rather than generalists. They like to have an area of expertise in which to excel and will be truly interested in skill development and new applications for their area. They are also inordinately aware of status and will surpass themselves when placed in prestigious company. Threes are go-getters. They virtually guarantee that the project will move forward; when they're identified with a team, that momentum serves the project rather than private ends.

Performers are not detail oriented. It helps to pair them with people who are conscientious about procedures and quality control, people who balance the need to demonstrate product. Threes often finesse protocol in the interests of efficiency and can amplify the value of results without noticing a subtle exaggeration. Other star players activate Threes' competitive edge. Those natural sparks can be harnessed to good advantage when team values are properly focused. Threes shoot for the middle of whatever their group values. They become tough team players when that is the valued prototype.

Threes can sell and promote well, which can be a useful skill for the team but may also create concerns about being manipulated. Performers can change hats several times on the same idea. They are motivated by what seems to work for different people, a procedure that can look inconsistent to those who favor a single course of action. Threes will promote and adjust, promote again and adjust again, looking for agreement. It behooves Threes to underscore their own choices so as to dispel loyalty concerns.

To get along, Threes will have to temper an impatience with people who don't work at a consistent pace and who need time to speculate and discuss. They are rarely absent from work because of illness and do not relate to people who can't function when they're upset. They believe that feelings should be set aside until the job gets done. "Let's not be lazy about this," "Let's not wallow around in emotion." Depending on people who worry about details makes Threes anxious. So do people who bring their love life to the office. For Threes on a team, feelings are expressed through team spirit. Fully identified with goals and results, they can rally a flagging enterprise. When trouble hits, they dig in and work harder; and when the team wins, they organize the victory dinner.

4

Four ⬡ *The Romantic*

	PERSONALITY BIAS	ESSENCE QUALITIES
MENTAL	*melancholy*	*original source*
EMOTIONAL	*envy*	*equanimity (balance)*

SUBTYPE FOCUS	
COMPETITION	sexual
SHAME	social
DAUNTLESS (RECKLESS)	self-survival

The Four Bias

Worldview

Something is missing. Others have it. I have been abandoned.

Spiritual Path

Melancholy is a reminder that something is missing; it's a sweet sadness based on the perception of loss. From the spiritual perspective, the child lost the connection with essence, or true being, when attention turned to matters of survival. Unsupported by the *original source,* the child became acutely sensitive to human abandonment and the loss of significant people. The longing for authentic bonds of connection swamps emotional *equanimity* in the pitch and roll of dramatic moods. *Envy* is a reminder that others seem to enjoy the happiness the Four has been denied. A Four's search for authentic moments of connection mimics an ongoing awareness of essence. The search is motivated by the conviction that there is more than ordinary life. We would not be seeking if we were complete.

Concerns

- *Attracted to what's missing: the distant, unavailable, and hard to get.*

- *Envy is the belief that others possess the missing element. "They are happy," "They feel loved," "They are satisfied."*

- *Acts out envy ("Others enjoy while I am deprived") in three key areas of life:*

  > COMPETITION *in sexual or one-to-one relationships.*

  > SHAME *in the social arena.*

  > *A* DAUNTLESS (RECKLESS) *attitude about personal survival.*

- *Melancholy is the sweet sadness of separation. Although based on a perception of loss, melancholy is a sweet and evocative state.*

- *Sense of abandonment by a beloved figure supports low self-esteem. "I would not have been abandoned if I were worthier."*

- *Mood, manners, luxury, and good taste are external life supports to bolster self-esteem. A unique image to cover inner shame.*

- *Feels different from other people, which shifts to feeling unique. "I am emotionally special. My suffering sets me apart." An outsider.*

- *Longs for the missing ingredient for happiness: the absent lover, a distant friend, communion with God.*

- *Impatient with mediocrity and mundane life. Ordinary feelings are flat in comparison with heightened inner intensity. Avoids the ordinary.*

- *Intensifies mood. Amps up through loss, fantasy, artistic connection, and dramatic acts. Drama kings and queens.*

- *Has push-pull relationships. Focuses on the best of what is missing: "When can we have the spark again?" Pulls for the unattainable; pushes away when it's near at hand. This alternating focus reinforces:*

° *Feelings of abandonment and loss, but also lends itself to:*
° *Emotional sensitivity and depth, an ability to give support to people in crisis and pain.*

Personality Bias

Absorbed in an emotional world, Romantics are drawn to relationships. Love and loss are at the foreground of attention. You do feel complete at times when two hearts meet. Far from being negative, the melancholy produced by loss is powerfully attractive. You connect to the universe and each other through feelings that fill and empty and fill again. You connect through pleasure and pain.

Envy is the knife's twist in the heart when others enjoy the happiness that you long for. People seem to be content, they seem happy in their jobs and families. They seem to feel fulfilled, but you have been denied. It's not a matter of jealousy, they're welcome to their pleasure. It's that the sight of happiness reminds you that you're *not* happy. Envy fuels your search for the objects and status that supposedly make people happy—money, a unique lifestyle, recognition, mates. You act out the search by a repeating cycle of desire, acquisition, disappointment, and rejection. Fours pull for the unavailable and push away when it comes within reach. When relationships that were once attractive have passed to the stage of rejection, they begin to seem attractive again, and the cycle repeats itself.

If the push-pull habit of relating becomes automatic, self-observation stops. You don't know that you selectively focus on the positive aspects of distant relationships. All you know is that separation from someone who evokes connection is unbearable, that you want to be the emotional center of her or his life, and that it's hateful to be surrounded by people who have less depth but somehow manage to be happy.

If this habit of attention continues, your immediate relationships seem pale in comparison with the promise of an absent figure. You realize that you've made a mistake, that happiness lies elsewhere. It seems only natural to leave your current situation and try to repair the distant hope.

Fours grow by seeing a half-full glass rather than one that's half-empty. They grow by feeling satisfied, by knowing they have enough. You have a choice when you can stay with a deeply felt connection, when you can watch your mind pulling away by wishing for something different.

They are helped by significants who stay calm during the push-pull phase of relating, who see the good in the here and now, and who can stand fast during intense emotional tides.

Subtype Focus:

Envy Affects Sexual, Social, and Survival Attitudes

Competition in Sexual and One-to-One Relationships

Envy activates the one-to-one relationship through competition. This is an invigorating energy that cuts through depression and ruminating about loss. It's an "I'll show you" rush of energy that can move mountains. Competition is focused in two ways: by competing for approval ("My worth goes up if I get special attention") and through rivalry with people who claim recognition that you want for yourself. Competition against rivals can shift into hate. Reducing their value equals reducing envy. You lie in wait to knock them out of the picture. Competitive Fours are as aggressive as Threes in going after what they want, but the envy motive causes them to focus as heavily on slamming competitors as on the goal itself. Competition is energizing and activating, a guaranteed way to counteract depression.

Competitive Fours want special attention from special people, the unique, exquisite, and especially talented few. Plebs don't matter if you can get the attention of royalty. Low self-esteem is held at bay by courting people of worth. Mentors and noteworthy role models are attractive. These relationships can either produce a satisfying mutual relationship or spiral into seduce-and-reject maneuvers. Who's going to be rejected? Who's in control? By being first to reject, you reduce the other's value and close off the threat of abandonment. The push-pull of abandonment and seduction is a form of control. Not too far away, or you'll miss the other person. Not so close that you can't do without the other. The one-to-one subtype usually does not compete with friends but can be highly adversarial to people in the same field or to a rejecting mate. They are especially vulnerable to envy if a partner leaves to enter a successful new relationship.

Social Shame

In the social arena, feelings of shame can arise when you feel unworthy. You're ashamed when you don't measure up. Feelings of envy arise in comparing yourself to others. You do not seem to possess their merit. When self-esteem is low, shame increases when you see the qualities in others that warrant social respect. You have a sense of not meeting the standards that others are capable of meeting, of an inner defectiveness that will eventually be seen. Feelings of low self-esteem, often based on actual losses in the past, perpetuate the illusion that other people possess and enjoy the things that are missing from your life.

There is a discrepancy between the lack of love in your own life and the finer qualities of feeling in someone else's relationship. Shame Fours can attack themselves by looking for the fatal flaw, that defective quality of being. Surely someone of merit would not feel abandoned.

You have a terror of rejection, of having that fatal flaw detected. You want to hide away from probing eyes, to eliminate social encounters that might bring deficiency to light. You develop an unusual sensitivity to social slights and a parallel desire for recognition. It's terrible to be left out, and worse to hear the names of people who were invited. Image is often heightened as a protective measure: elite memberships, a unique social presentation, looking attractive and somewhat aloof, above the common crowd.

Dauntless (Reckless) About Self-Survival

Life on the edge is attractive when you feel the sadness of your condition. Wedged between hope and despair, why not throw caution to the wind? The dauntless character has a certain suicidal edge, an abandonment to fate. The inner crisis generated by cycles of desire and loss infuses ordinary events with extraordinary vitality. Dancing on the lips of an abyss spares you from the dull mechanics of life. Life on the edge brings meaning and intensity to a life that might otherwise seem mundane.

Survival is marked by a reckless urgency to obtain those things that promise satisfaction. Envy dissolves in luxury, relaxes in meaningful conversation, and vanishes in elegant surroundings. Romantics can ignore basic survival needs in order to follow a dream. The desire for connection becomes so compelling that Dauntless Fours can throw caution to the wind in a high-stakes approach to making that lifestyle materialize. If dissatisfaction sets in when the dream is obtained, they will tend to wreck the basis of security. Fortunes are made and lost and made again. Lovers are seduced, rejected, and reembraced. You wanted it, you got it, you wrecked it, and now it looks interesting again.

Focal Issues

Mood, Manners, and Style

A spectacular image can mask the "little brown mouse" syndrome. Feelings of being small and insignificant inside, drab as a mouse, can be masked by plumage and a sophisticated facade. The sense of being deficient—"I'm not as good as they are"—is contained behind the barricade of self-presentation. Fours are artful in dress, particular about decor, and aesthetically driven concerning their surroundings. External life can become an art form to compensate for life's deficiencies. Life as art is committed to original and distinctive themes. Fours disdain the superficial. They feel affronted by the commonplace and commercial. A graceful manner, original conversation, and candlelight keep the commonplace at bay.

Emotional Intensity

Fours collect around those junctures of the human condition that call out emotional intensity. Life-or-death emergencies, suicide hot lines, creative breakthroughs, and meditation halls. They are attracted to piercing the veil of ordinary existence, finding some deep and final ground of being that surpasses the mundane. Fours resonate to antiquity, ritual, and ceremony. They resonate, they shudder, they take on other people's pain. These exquisite turnings toward eternally evocative themes are an antidote to feelings of separation and loss.

The authenticity of feeling is a primary concern. "Is this a genuine meeting of hearts, or a superficial connection?" "Is this a truly felt moment or merely a passing idea?" Fours are uncomfortable with people who think their feelings and withdraw from emotions, people who swim in emotional shallows rather than going deep. The insistence on intensity makes relating stormy. Fours want to be moved, swept away, taken somewhere higher, and better. They want to plunge in, fighting the tides of conflicting emotion. "We were together once. Can we reach that depth again?" The past, the future, and the distant draw attention. The significant moment is rarely now.

Self-Absorption

The pain of separation creates an illusion that others enjoy a happiness that you have been denied. Fours crave the complete emotional connection that they seem to recall from childhood, "from the time before I was abandoned." You see current relationships in terms of that past attachment. Relationships should be permanently vibrant, consuming, passionate, and alive. You maintain the illusion that love will reawaken complete satisfaction. Self-absorbed and deeply engrossed in their own emotions, Fours do not see other people objectively. They see the aspects of other people that strike an emotional chord from the past.

Fours find it difficult to maintain interest when they finally get what they have longed for. The real thing is not as compelling as the chase. There's juice in longing. Desire is a motivation. You felt complete for a moment and then it flew away. The search is evocative and full of meaning, but the pleasure of the search would have to end if the goal is attained.

Melancholy and Depression

Fours describe depression as a black hole. They feel helpless and inactive. No way out. Life stops while they stare at the ceiling for hours. "If only things were different," "I've made a terrible mistake." Fours feel helpless in the wash of depression. It seems to run its course and lift of its own accord. They want others to listen, to hear their story. They want others to pay attention to how difficult it's been. Their insistence that something will be gained by dropping into the depth of feeling is unnerving to types who avoid negative feelings. Fours are distressed by people who want a quick solution, who try to fix them, brighten their day, and make them smile.

Fours feel unheard and unattended to when their pain is trivialized. They are capable of incredible highs and lows. The full spectrum, not just high-end elation, is interesting. They see people obsessed with ordinary happiness rather than mining the range of human emotion—from pure joy to somber depths of pain. Melancholy, for example, is the mood of preference. A sweet recollection of missing things. A felt connection to absent people and distant places. An understanding of death. Preserved within the preoccupations of their own neurosis, Fours never gave up the realization that we are all connected at the level of essence.

At the personality level Fours can be moody and self-absorbed with refining their private emotions. Depression often lifts with activity. Just getting into action shifts the focus from self to the environment. Some Fours kick incipient depression with hyperactivity. They look like Threes; they stay in motion and accomplish a great deal, all the while knowing that deep emotion, rather than recognition for task, is the agenda. There are three kinds of Fours—chronically down, hyperactive, and swingers. Swingers oscillate between emotional highs and lows. In Enneagram terms, they would be seen as "leaning on the wings": affected by Five if retracted, affected by Three when very active, and affected by both wings if they oscillate.

Elegant Elitism

While Ones have perfectionistic standards, Fours have elite standards. Romantics are unique and special, not easily pleased. A disdain for pedestrian life can develop. They feel trapped in the mundane and surrounded by mediocrity. Fours feel immersed in dreck in shopping malls filled with plastic people. Ordinary relationships are eschewed. They want a miracle. Momentous meetings and gracious strangers. Out of millions, they have to find the one who will understand.

Feeling different and misunderstood, Fours easily identify with those who suffer. They understand disappointment and are attracted to people in difficulty. Their nature is aligned with the disadvantaged. Outcasts and eccentrics, the abandoned and bereaved. The sense of being misunderstood easily shifts to being unusual. A precious jewel refined by suffering. Someone whose sensibilities became exquisite through pain. The secondary gain of feeling elite and deeper than ordinary people can make simple happiness elusive.

Security and Risk

DYNAMICS OF CHANGE FOR POINT FOUR

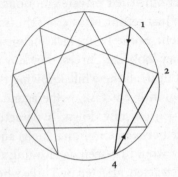

Security

The first security signals look like a relaxation of the focal issues. Sadness lifts and feelings of oppression lessen. Projects seem both interesting and possible. Relationships settle into a realistic perspective in which both positive and negative elements are apparent at the same time. Any situation that renders satisfaction breaks the Four's habit of focusing on things that are missing in life. It's the shift to seeing a half-full, rather than half-empty, glass.

Security for Fours means feeling that they have enough. When you're satisfied with what you've got, it doesn't matter what other people do or do not possess. The merits of a relationship or a project are satisfying enough to warrant commitment and participation. Attention shifts from a preoccupation with self and moves outward to others and to the environment. Freed from self-absorption, you cooperate more fully.

The hallmark of the type is unique style and self-expression. This does not mean that Fours are universally talented, and it certainly doesn't mean that they are inherently more gifted than the eight other types. It is quite true, however, that their preoccupation with being different, and with making a personal statement about that difference, brings an original flavor to their undertakings. That twist of originality comes into being when Fours are productive and happy at their own point on the Enneagram.

The shift to One often occurs when goals are brought to fruition. The One energy makes for well-wrought originality or exquisite perfection. In a practical sense that means shaping a project or a relationship so that it works well. Things get done when Fours are meticulous about follow-through. Creative ideas materialize. Products are refined. Romantics say that they like the precision and clarity of mind that occurs when they can work like a One.

The low side of the security point is very apparent in Fours. The story of the princess and the pea applies. Small, pealike difficulties feel like major irritants. The partner can't do anything right. Boredom sets in, and the petulant princess, or prince, is just too sensitive to live an ordinary life. The push-away half of push-pull relating is amplified. Disappointed Romantics are highly sarcastic. Vindictive backbiting repays associates for having "caused" the Four's low self-esteem. Paradoxically Fours often tense up when things become secure and predictable. Intimacy can generate tension for those with a history of abandonment, and that tension can produce a cut-and-run escape. Fours in the security of One can sabotage a good relationship. A crisis. A bailout. "I feel hurt and it's somebody else's fault." Better cut and run before being abandoned again.

Risk

Fours' usual image has to do with being special. They are one in a billion, not the ordinary kind. Their usual manner of seduction does not involve adapting to suit the tastes of others. They want you to know that you are dealing with an alluring alien, a treasure, an unexpected find.

When loss occurs, the first signs of pressure intensify the defenses at Four. Feelings of grief and abandonment deepen. If the defenses of Four itself are ineffective, there is a shift to Two, a Giver-like perspective. Fours move toward others as a way to counteract loss. The high side of a Four taking on a Two's perspective is a real breakthrough. Attention shifts from self to other, which can break a depression. Focusing on someone else's needs reduces a self-absorbed preoccupation with your own. Giving to others gets you out of yourself and your own sense of loss. The task is to give freely instead of giving to get.

Fours can alter self-presentation when they feel threatened. They move toward people in an effort to please. The pulling phase of push-pull relating is accented. They see the best in things that are missing and pull for relationship when it seems to go away. The pulling, or seductive, phase of relating is stressful to the unique-minded Four. "Why should I have to chase you?" "Would you come to me if I were worthier?"

Four in Love

Living with Fours

° *Remember that Fours feel that something is missing. Others have what's missing. Focused on the quality of feeling in other people's relationships, the Four worries: "They have it. I don't."*

° *You can easily be dismayed by your Four's attraction to the distant and the unavailable, positive attention to whoever is missing: the ghostly lover, the distant friend, the unfulfilled dream.*

° *Count on complex relating. Nothing is simple. Depth is the goal rather than fun.*

° *Expect impatience with the "flatness" of ordinary feeling. "Surely there is more than this." Relating is intensified by sabotage, suffering, and dramatic acts.*

° *For Fours the present seems unreal. All relating is building toward the emergence of the "real" self through the agency of love. The ultimate disclosure, the transcendent moment, the reawakening of the soul.*

- *It's always showtime: mood, manners, luxury, and good taste as a setting for relationship. Unique self-presentation compensates for inner feelings of deprivation. The art form of keeping feelings contained. Conversational innuendo, aesthetic distance, the implication of a special glance. Relating through romantic idealization.*

- *For Fours, it's the pursuit not the happiness that matters: a refined and bittersweet emotional sensibility. A mood of melancholy. Love is many layered and goes through many phases. The stages of letting go are unusually slow.*

- *Fours sweetly reminisce about people from the past and focus on lovers, experiences yet to come. Attention on present opportunities are weak and intermittent.*

- *Push-pull habit of attention. The Four's focus turns to your negative aspects when you are present and to positive aspects with the safety of distance.*

- *This way of paying attention reinforces the Four's feelings of abandonment and loss, but also lends itself to:*
  - *Sensitivity to your emotional states and the ability to support you when you suffer pain.*

Intimacy

The centerpiece of life for Fours is emotional contact. When feeling is triggered, everything else seems pale. It can happen at unusual moments—a shift in the weather, a striking profile, a flurry of talk, the cry of a child. When the heart is touched, Fours have an impulse to follow those feelings, to abandon caution, to be emotionally met. This profound requirement makes ordinary relating difficult. Because connection is the focus of their existence, Fours want absolute emotional presence from a partner. They want unwavering devotion, and they get extremely tense about abandonment.

Fours are like children pressed close to a window, longing to see a familiar shape. You feel a rush of recognition when someone turns the corner; hopes run high when you expect a certain face.

Hope turns to fury when strangers pass the window. The wrong laugh, the wrong eyes, an unfamiliar gait. Fours became devoted to love that was just around the corner. "Why didn't you take me? Why wasn't I worth it? Are you coming back?"

The search for love develops early. Significant moments, possibilities of connection, flutters that easily fade. It would be terrible to lose again. To suffer. The tension grows until you have to pull away. Fearing the discovery of that inner flaw that led to abandonment in childhood, you distance yourself from intimacy. You withdraw from the present and focus on something difficult to obtain. Loss is the familiar index of attachment. "I wasn't sure that I loved you until we parted, and then I missed you again."

Fours' hallmark of relating is the push-pull pattern of their desire. They adore people when they want them and are spiteful when they don't. Tests of abandonment are vindictive. "I've been hurt before, and now you're doing it to me," "Will you leave now that I've said the worst?" Relationships have to survive the push-pull pattern that eventually builds trust. Fours distance themselves when others want them and crave affection when others want to go away.

Fours protect themselves by presence and distance. They seduce and reject. They must have you if you abandon them, but things are less certain when you want to commit. The push-pull tendency spotlights a concern with authenticity of feeling. "Is this a genuine connection, or something superficial?" "Is our love enduring, or simply a passing idea?" Fours live in a changing emotional climate. They need an anchor, a bastion, a pillar. "Is this casual or real?" Connections of the heart are fragile. Moods shift easily. "Will this be enough to hold me?" "Can this partnership bring out my best?" Significants will need to be that anchor, to weather the stormy atmosphere of abandonment. Most of all, significants need to hold ground during the push-pull phases of relating.

The Signals Fours Send

Positive Signals

Fours conduct their lives as works of art and create art to express their lives. Dedicated to passion, they draw you into a cycle of love and hate, creativity and pain. They want your feelings. They plunge you into emotional depths. They can immerse you in every dimension of feeling.

Negative Signals

Fours can make you feel that you aren't enough, that you're not quite worthy of their attentions. Something you've done has failed the Four. If you were different, they would be happy. It's your fault. You get resistance when you try to help and feel guilty that you haven't done more. You feel hurt and alienated by Four's sarcastic rejection in the push-away phase of intimacy. You have to pick up the pieces of recurrent crisis cycles. Their feelings take priority over yours.

Mixed Messages

Love and hate can come together. Fours can be difficult when that happens. Idealizing a relationship and fearing abandonment, they love the parts that fit the picture and simultaneously reject the rest. The message is, "I love you even though it makes me unhappy." The juice for Fours is to be in between, not far enough away to lose you, not close enough to risk being seen.

The push-pull habit of relating sends a mixed signal to significants. As a significant, you see that you're cherished when you're distant, but you feel diminished when you get too near. Fearing abandonment, Fours reject before they are rejected. They bail out and sabotage trust in the relationship. After the crisis they may want you back again.

Inner Signals

Envy is masked as yearning for things that are missing. The thoughts say: "If only I had her hair, her clothing, her status. If only I had his wealth, his family, his fame." It seems justifiably sad that some have plenty while others have to suffer. It seems unfair. The thoughts say: "I'd be happy if only my life could be different, if my husband acted differently, if my body looked better, if my wife were willing to change." It doesn't seem envious to improve your condition. It seems so obvious that you've made a mistake. The feelings say: "This isn't working. My love is dying. My creativity is at stake." The blind spot in this way of being is that Fours notice the things that others enjoy but rarely enjoy their own. The thoughts seldom say: "I have the love that I need to be creative, but my self-hatred holds me back."

It helps to shift from what you are missing and focus on what you have. It helps to review your blessings and to treasure the fact that they exist. Envy is defused when you can participate in the present without turning attention to what other people possess. The thoughts might say: "I can see the counterpart of other people's blessings in my own life." The feelings might say: "I am satisfied now. I have enough."

Four at Work

In the Workplace
- *Wants distinctive work. A job that calls for creativity, even genius, an eccentric edge in presentation, a unique approach to business life.*
- *Must feel respected in the workplace for personal vision and ideas.*
- *Efficiency is tied to mood. Attention gets displaced from tasks when emotional life takes over. Can sabotage business life over a love affair.*
- *Wants to be connected to special authority, to those in the field who stand for quality rather then popularity.*

- ° *Feels demeaned by plebeian work, the definition of which is different for every Four. Gardening can be work for plebs. So can being a CEO.*
- ° *Feels called to emotionally intense lines of work: grief counselor, animal rights activist, the suicide hot line late at night.*
- ° *Aggressive and cutting toward competitors or peers in the same field. Attracted to successful people outside his or her own sphere of interest.*
- ° *Does not flourish in a work environment that requires close cooperation with others who are more skilled, more valued, or better paid.*

Leadership Style

Romantics in competitive settings look and act like Threes. The Performer prototype is the valued business persona that we all tend to adopt in the workplace. We're all supposed to look, and presumably feel, like Threes in order to compete successfully. Fours, particularly the competitive subtype, are highly motivated by material rewards and recognition. They are visible, viable, and usually too preoccupied with worldly affairs to become depressed. But Fours are also acutely aware of the discrepancy between the business mask and the feeling self. Threes work for goals and results. Their motive is to be a champion over others. Fours achieve goals and results so as to be distinctive from others.

Romantics lead with vigor and a highly competitive edge on the upswing when there's something to prove. A Four leader can go for broke. "Why not go down in flames of glory when there's a lot at stake?" They are often more effective at the point of risk than in maintaining an operation. This leader will feel oppressed by particulars. There is nothing to prove in routine. If boredom sets in, Romantics can sabotage their own prior efforts. Disaster reawakens interest. Success seems unavailable and alluring again.

The push-pull pattern of relating also applies to business. Fours are active in pursuing an elusive goal, but the realities of achievement are problematic. It's just not that interesting when there's no drama. The Four leader wants to stay emotionally engaged.

Fours excel in a business approach where unique presentation counts. An original contribution, a presence to be reckoned with, making a distinctive mark on the field. When their self-worth is connected to success, they are fully identified with their work, but attention wanders when it's just a job to be done. If interest dies, Fours will vanish, drawn to a new interest that feels emotionally fresh. They often sell themselves at a high-paying job to support a secondary career that matters. Fours regularly distinguish between "what I do for a living" and "who I really am." Day jobs can be radically different from avocational pursuits. Banker/poet, scientist/dancer, competitor by day/a friend by night.

They often find work that supports a worthy cause. They lead when their hearts are in it and lose interest when the challenge has been met. They are sensitive about putting people together who are compatible and reducing competition by making them feel emotionally secure. They have a gift for challenging others to their best efforts, especially in the dramatic atmosphere of business expansion: "We can pull this off."

Classic Conflicts

People often feel deficient around Fours. You felt attractive and suddenly you've been dumped. You got used to feeling special, now what you say is beside the point. It's that sense of overstaying your welcome. The conversation went stale. So you back off to reevaluate, and suddenly the Romantic reappears. Classic conflicts involve the seduce-and-reject style of relating. A business example of the push-pull dilemma would be Fours not wanting to repeat the known, wanting to follow a new and more exciting route. If the business is in a consolidation phase, Fours are likely to feel limited and to take it out on whoever is around.

They are attracted to excellence in different fields of endeavor but can be biting toward immediate competitors. Four inventors may admire other inventors, as long as they innovate in a different professional sphere. Needing approval to bolster their own self-worth, Fours often insist that their friends choose sides. "Do you like my work or my competitor's work?" "Whose side are you on?"

Conflict Resolution

See Part III, "The Directory of Relationships," for tips on mediation between Fours and others.

Employee Participation

A Four employee has to feel special. They flourish when they are recognized by important people in the field. Perks and special treatment make a big difference. They do no like to be "the same as." They won't be happy as part of the crowd. Above all avoid criticism in the form of comparisons. "Why didn't you do as well as John? You could do better than Susie or Jane!" Fours already compare themselves to other people, and will focus on John, Susie, or Jane rather than the pleasure of a job well done.

Fours need to be heard and have their opinions solicited. They can make an ordinary job interesting as long as they see the worth of the work. Modeling a unique approach to ordinary matters, they inspire others to see routine affairs in a different light. They elevate the ordinary. They make the mundane significant. They can chop wood and carry water when the task has depth. The trick is to present Fours with a challenge; to keep them interested they need to be inspired. They are famous for their commitment to a worthwhile cause. If the business can be that worthy cause, they find their own worth in service.

Team Building

Fours' illusion of specialness takes precedence over seeing themselves as one of a team. Fours have to star in their own dramas and do not want to be upstaged by talented support players. Domains of activity should be divided; if possible the Four should be looked to for a special area of expertise. Avoid counterparts. Avoid comparisons between team members. Play up the team and downplay the star. Romantics come to the fore for a worthwhile project that depends on their efforts. Fours are quite as capable as Threes for a job that they believe in, but unlike Threes, their emotional needs must be met. Group planning is a bad idea. Fours hate to be overridden in public and may confuse their feelings about the other players with the players' ability to produce. They can fall prey to interpersonal drama. "If I'm more talented than John is, my ideas should be accepted over his." Fours can feel personally attacked when their ideas are questioned. They can be highly defensive and retaliatory if they feel unseen.

Their best efforts come forward when they have their own area of expertise highly validated by authority figures who stand above and beyond the limits of the current project. Special recognition can be as important as a raise in salary. If Fours challenge authority or become unproductive, they may simply be asking for recognition. Fours want to be understood. They don't always have to get their way, but they have to know that their feelings have been heard.

Five ⬡ The Observer

	PERSONALITY BIAS	ESSENCE QUALITIES
MENTAL	*stinginess*	*omniscience*
EMOTIONAL	*avarice (greed)*	*nonattachment*

SUBTYPE FOCUS	
CONFIDENCE	sexual
TOTEMS	social
CASTLE (HOME)	self-survival

The Five Bias

Worldview

The world is invasive. I need privacy to think and to refuel my energies.

Spiritual Path

All of the potentials of essence are "paranormal" in the sense that their intelligence lies beyond the boundaries of thought. *Omniscience* clearly refers to a dimension of awareness that is not mediated by intellect or analysis. It is an accurate knowing that appears before any data is analyzed, and it opens a broad range of nonlinear and predictive information that cannot be grasped by logical thought. Following the idea that aspects of essence are mimicked by the central preoccupations of type, the potential for omniscience or pure knowing is mimicked by a Five's lifelong attachment to information and private study.

Stinginess toward oneself and others can guarantee some degree of that treasured independence, because when one has fewer needs, one feels less pressure to reach out. Greed, or *avarice,* can develop for the resources that support private survival. Protecting knowledge, money, energy, and time becomes psychologically important. The desire to grasp reality through force of intellect can be seen as a child's attempt both to detach from painful emotions and to preserve a fragile connection to the *nonattachment* of mind that leads back to essence awareness.

Concerns

- ○ *Craves privacy, a place to be alone and recharge after being with people.*
- ○ *Likes boundaries and limits. Likes precise agreement. Wants time, agenda, and responsibilities carefully defined.*
- ○ *Believes that knowledge is power. Special information is the key to power.*
- ○ *Minimalist. Able to survive on very little and make do with less.*
- ○ *Greedy for the few things necessary for mental survival. Private space, knowledge, and the bare necessities.*
- ○ *Avarice for the necessities of mental life is acted out in three key areas:*

    CONFIDENCE *in the special bonds of sexual and one-to-one relationships.*

    TOTEMS—*an attraction to the ideas and people who influence the social culture.*

    CASTLE *or a private living space that is safe from intrusion.*

- ○ *Tightens the belt to maintain independence. Doesn't reach out.*
- ○ *Compartmentalizes. Different areas of life are separated from one another. Friends from one area of interest may not be introduced to others.*
- ○ *Feels drained by open-ended events. Likes to leave after a meeting.*

- Likes noninvolvement, which can be troublesome, since both love and hate require involvement.
- Unhooks from emotion, which can be confused with spiritual nonattachment.
- Feels drained by people's expectations and emotions.
- Values emotional control. Emotions can best be felt in privacy.
- Enjoys the mind: knowledge, information, analytic systems.
- Watches life from the point of view of an outside observer. This way of paying attention can lead to:
  - Feeling isolated from the events of one's own life, or
  - Taking a detached point of view that is unaffected by fear or desire.

Personality Bias

We all adopt the Five worldview during times of scarcity. When we don't have the energy to meet our needs, we shrink our expectations. In an economy of scarcity, we learn to do with less—less involvement, fewer goods, and less emotional contact. Less produces more—more time, more energy, and more autonomy from people. Less simplifies everything. Fewer desires, fewer needs, fewer rules and obligations. Freed from some of our emotional burden and alone with our own thoughts, Five-like, we may be nourished by the silent abundance of mind.

An Observer's home is like a castle. Low visibility, controlled contact, and uninterrupted private time. The mind becomes a good companion, an endlessly entertaining friend. The mind is also a refuge that is totally safe from invasion. Fives do not have to share the contents of their thoughts. Living in the mind can be remarkably self-sustaining. Observers do not feel deprived unless desire creeps in.

There are certain physical and emotional necessities that sustain a reclusive life, and if one of these is in short supply, Fives will develop a tenacious desire to acquire that commodity. Because they value autonomy, Fives dislike having needs, and that fury feeds their desire. It becomes imperative to possess that person or those books or that small treasure that has penetrated their solitude. Avarice is an angry desire to possess, a greed that overrides detachment. You get so hungry that you have to reach out.

If this habit becomes automatic, self-observation stops. You dislike being forced to have feelings. You don't want needs in your life. You try to let go but you can't. You don't have it, you must get it, and to own it you have to reach out. Caught between emotional emptiness and the fear of being engulfed by people, you begin to enter your feelings.

Fives grow by joining mind with emotion. They grow by finding passion in life. You have a choice when you feel a spontaneous flush of emotion and can watch yourself pull back until you're empty again.

Significants can help Fives through the anxieties that attend an emotional opening by relating without inserting their own emotional agenda, by respecting the Five's need for time, privacy, and space, by pointing out overintellectualization, and by making self-disclosure safe.

Subtype Focus:

Avarice Affects Sexual, Social, and Survival Attitudes

Confidence in Sexual and One-to-One Relationships

Confidential understandings are private bonds of connection. They are not to be shared. Fives often maintain their privacy by keeping their emotional connections separated from each other. That habit lends itself to a kind of lust for intense, brief, highly meaningful encounters. Avarice in one-to-one relationships refers to a preoccupation with key disclosures and emotional ties that can endure periods of separation. Confidants are the few with whom they share an "understanding." The private adviser, the personal moment, the secret love affair.

Bonds of special connection are mental treasures. They can be privately reviewed and imaginatively re-created, over and over again. They are meaningful not only because they are few and far between but because they are deeply embedded in the mind. Confidence Fives say that they're drawn to sexual expression as the antithesis of intellectualism. They also say that a remembered friendship can enjoy a perpetual life in their imagination, that any meaningful encounter can be re-created at will. Because Observers allow emotions to emerge in private, a love enshrined in memory does not fade away.

Loneliness is a by-product of isolation. No matter how interesting you are, you tire of your own mind. You can read and think and imagine just so long, and then you crave experience. You will have to reach out. Confidential exchange can be highly charged because of the secrecy element. "Only we two share this understanding. We two out of millions know about this." Fives carefully censor private material. It's devastating when private disclosure goes public, when confidence has been betrayed.

Social Totems

The totems of a tribe are links between the gigantic forces of nature and the limited human mind. They are symbols that encode a message about ancestral knowledge, and they are the focal point through which the world at large is joined with private consciousness.

The Five preoccupation with mind as a source of power can develop into a passionate search for "power information." Social avarice underscores an interest in ideas and people who influence the culture. Fives are attracted to systems that explain human behavior, to the search for the pivotal formula that governs a field of study, and to those seminal thinkers who can shape the history of ideas.

Social Fives gather in places dedicated to serious study. They like chess clubs, math departments, Yoga centers, and musical events. Fives will not jockey for social place. They want to be called to the inner circle. They like to refine their thinking with "people who know" in a setting that is blessedly free of having to shmooze and make small talk.

Intellectual mastery is very appealing to people who live in the mind. The right model properly understood allows you to grasp the true significance of events. Totem Fives are attracted to systems of study that yield big-picture accounts of social forces: political prediction, stock market analysis, psychoanalysis, and the Enneagram model of consciousness. It's a way of predicting outer events through the command of mind. Knowledge is power and forewarned is forearmed. Insider information is protective.

Castle (Home) as the Focus of Survival

Caught between an intrusive world and the pleasures of private life, Fives tend to reduce their contacts and possessions. Small luxuries can seem extravagant. These are the minimalists of the Enneagram. Dessert may lead to gluttony. Just one sip of piping hot coffee. A tiny sliver of something sweet. They take pride in doing with very little, so what they own and carry with them is going to be important. Their independence depends on a private place in which to retire and think, surrounded by familiar belongings. The home offers sanctuary from prying eyes, draining encounters, and taxing responsibilities. You can examine your thoughts in a haven peopled by memories and significant tokens.

Feelings of scarcity underlie the avarice for independent privacy. Survival Fives hoard whatever they need to guarantee their freedom. Private time and personal space can feel as vital as oxygen. Most Observers store critical information rather than money or possessions. It seems natural to be sparing in the use of precious things. Economy equals independence. You won't have to go without in the future if you remember to save now. You won't be dependent on other people if you have enough for yourself. Fives can be stingy with themselves, even in times of plenty.

They take pleasure in abstinence, and in doing with less, because it frees them from the personal entanglements that getting more would require.

Focal Issues

Commitment

Quitting is easy. It's a lot harder to stay in a relationship than to let it go. When Fives live in the same space with someone else, it involves considerably more commitment than it might for people who like a lot of attention. Fives often measure the increasing depth of their commitments by saying: "I can still do without this" or "I would still be happy on my own." The hardest decision is deciding to stay. Staying means opening yourself to pain. You can't feel deprived when you don't feel much of anything, but your inner emptiness becomes apparent when you feel loss.

When Fives commit themselves to love, they commit themselves to struggle. They choose struggle over the security of being alone and untroubled. They choose the certainty of loss. It's a decision carefully weighed and chosen. This relationship is worth facing that dreadful gap between ideas and practical reality. For Fives, love has less to do with romance than with deciding that a certain person is worth the price of pain.

Renunciation

Mental life is amazingly self-sustaining. Needs can appear as ideas rather than as feelings. Passions are conceptual rather than felt. A possession that would normally arouse desire can be reduced to a thought. The thought of that desirable possession, carefully installed within the mind, can be re-created and treasured at will. An unsettling interaction can be thought through and discarded without being acted out.

Living in the mind can produce an illusion of nonattachment. True, you may not feel deep emotional yearning, or actually

own an object of desire, but you can entrench ideas about significant people and desires so deeply within yourself that they take on
a reality of their own. Fives can look spiritually nonattached, because they own very little and may have few emotional needs; but
true renunciation implies giving up a tangible investment.

Secret Lives

Observers are usually happy to conform to the roles and expectations that people have for them. A job, a family, a certain
standing in the community. An appearance of conformity may be
the simplest way to get along, but Fives can also cherish the idea of
going off and doing things that no one in their wildest imagination would consider. Observers sometimes compartmentalize
their lives into several different sectors that don't overlap. They
may have unlikely combinations of interests and different sets of
friends who haven't been introduced to one another. Compart-
mentalization is one way to maintain privacy: you have a piece of
yourself invested in every sector, but nobody gets it all.

Fives have elaborate ways to preserve their privacy. They can
withhold their feelings, censor information, separate thinking
from emotion, develop confidential bonding in relationships, and
lead secret lives. There is hardly ever anything illicit about the secret, but it can produce profound feelings of freedom. Secrecy is a
treasure because it ensures personal autonomy. You can go off by
yourself at unpredictable times. A perfect escape into privacy.

Loneliness

Fives do not suffer from loneliness when their retreat into
solitude is voluntary. Moving away from people is a strategy for
survival, and privacy feels good and safe as long as there's someone on the other side of the door. Noninvolvement is an active
choice when there is some reason to guard yourself; but when nobody knocks on the door, privacy can feel like a prison.

The noninvolvement strategy is effective in the face of invasion; but it can feel life-threatening when you're cut off from life.

Privacy turns to isolation when it's not of your own choosing, when you're so retracted that it seems impossible to reach out. To reengage, you have to initiate, to disclose, and to make yourself available, all of which is painful when you don't want to be seen.

An Economy of Scarcity

From the detached point of view, a great many activities seem pointless. Why do people run around in circles wasting themselves on trivia? Afraid of being sucked into other people's agendas, Fives deliberate carefully about where to place their own time and efforts. They conserve energy rather than spread themselves too thin.

It seems futile to throw yourself away on multiple plans and options when there's no telling how much time and labor it will take to effect something tangible. Detached from many of the desires and pleasures that feed the flurry of human activity, you watch and wait for something of significance.

Detachment

Fives can go public and still be distant. When thought is unhooked from feeling, you can watch emotional events. You don't need closed doors or elaborate ways to avoid entanglement when you can detach from your feelings. You can talk and respond to people without really being there. You can be far away even when you're in front a crowd with everyone looking.

Detachment can be like watching yourself go through a rehearsed scene. You're not aware of your body while you perform the role. You can even be engaging and funny. It doesn't matter if hundreds of people are watching. There's no anxiety as long as you're not affected.

It's an internal thing, a split in awareness rather than a separate it or he or she located in physical space. Fives have interesting ways of describing detached perception: "It's like seeing myself in a three-way mirror," "I look at myself and have looked at myself looking at myself," "A part of myself isn't attached to me."

Detachment can be elevated to a psychological virtue. Mental types have a certain arrogance about having risen above the more primitive emotional expressions. Lust is for lesser beings. Angry people can't control themselves. The prescription for hurt feelings is to drop them. If they still hurt, think about something else. Desires are going to mislead you and are bound to get out of control. Detach before you get hooked.

Privacy

For Fives privacy means far more than having their own rooms and closing the door. Often detached in public, Observers wait until they're alone to match their feelings to the events of the day. They need time to review their thoughts, to let feelings surface, and to preview tomorrow's events. The reviewing process gives them an emotional platform, and previewing is intended to eliminate emotional jolts and potential embarrassment. All of this inner work happens behind closed doors. It's draining when you have to preview and review an event, as well as witness it while it happens; you are really doing the work of three people.

Partners commonly believe that detachment prevents a Five's "real" feelings from surfacing. Feelings should be immediate and fully expressed on the spot rather than thought through when you're by yourself. The standard Five counterresponse is to point to the damage wrought by lack of emotional control; and of course there is truth on both sides of the discussion.

Avarice

Avarice is one of history's seven capital passions that warrants some comment. How could the Enneagram's detached type be underscored by greed? On Enneagram panels speakers who relate to all of the Observer issues often look blank when it comes to the avarice passion. "Me? Not me! I can do with very little."

One way to identify the passion is to examine the security point for Five. Eights and Fives are run by the same need to resist domination. The apparently aggressive stance of Eights is in fact an attempt to make sure that nobody dominates them. Eights resist intrusion by going against people, and Fives resist, quite as forcefully, by holding out. The preoccupation with domination is exactly the same, but the manner of defense is different. Eights control through force of presence and Fives control by hoarding time and space.

Security and Risk

DYNAMICS OF CHANGE FOR POINT FIVE

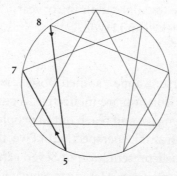

Security

Because Observers' security is the castle, they are likely to be territorial and to exercise somewhat demanding control over domestic affairs. Fives can act like Eights when they're at home. When they feel secure at the office, they are going to want to control the routine. It's not that Fives "turn into" Eights, it's more that a secure life situation relaxes the basic defenses at Five, which allows a Boss-like perspective to emerge.

Sex can be an important area of security for Fives. It's high-level nonverbal communication that lasts for an hour or so and then is done. Although they are primarily mental beings, secure

Fives can be quite at home in their bodies. They like physical sensation, athletics, and sexuality, and may even enjoy an occasional fight.

The high side of the security point develops a full-bodied life. Secure Fives participate physically and emotionally. They can be outgoing, get angry, and hold their ground in a fight. This is often described as tapping into a healthy rush of power, a feeling of waking up, and being fully alive. Secure Fives are every bit as immediate and forthcoming as Eights. They move into action rather than retreat.

The low side of Eight produces a petty tyrant. This tongue-in-cheek one-liner was delivered by a devoted Nine who had been married to her Five for more than thirty years: "You should see him at home—it's Jekyll and Hyde."

Risk

The Seven persona appears when Observers' major defenses of withdrawal and isolation are ineffective. A socially acceptable facade emerges to engage and reach out to people, but it may not be enjoyable. Seen from the perspective of Five, the outgoing and apparently happy self-presentation of Seven can mask unaccustomed levels of inner tension. Having to wing it is terrifying. Fives often feel harried in open-ended, multioptional Seven territory. The primary defense of knowing in order to be prepared dissolves when there are too many choices and there is too much to do. If only there were time to think.

The fact that they are welcomed as open and friendly in Seven adds to habitual feelings of alienation. "Right. People can't see past the surface." "Look how shallow they are." The low side of Seven feels like a nervous inner buzz. A flood of information. An inability to think clearly, to relax. All this activity adds to the fear of being sucked into other people's agendas. The Five feels spread too thin. At the low side of the risk point, attention scatters in a frantic search for any quick-fix solution to buy time and save resources.

From the perspective of Five, the high side of Seven can produce a genuine ability to enjoy the flow of events rather than to contract against surprise. This is a situation where risk can erode social anxiety. In Seven you have to act so quickly that it's possible to jump in and wing it without being prepared.

Five in Love

Living with Fives

° *Because Fives have delayed reactions, their feelings can surface when they're alone. They find intimacy in private reverie. Great tenderness can develop without the need for words or prolonged personal contact.*

° *Fives' cycle of withdrawal can lead to feelings of isolation and the desire to have others draw them out. They are caught between wanting contact and wanting to go.*

° *Intimacy can stimulate detachment. Significants may get the message "I can still do without you," or "I'm committed, but I won't live with you."*

° *You may be compartmentalized, separated from other aspects of the Five's life.*

° *Expect a Five to express intimacy in nonverbal ways. Fives sense that feelings can surface more easily if they need not be spoken.*

° *An emotionally attached Five may become fiercely possessive of you. You may feel like his or her emotional lifeline.*

° *Partners will get lots of support when the Five is free of personal obligations and doesn't feel forced to respond.*

° *Noninvolvement is the Five's habitual emotional stance. Partners should therefore read "negative" feelings such as anger, jealously, and competition, as well as "positive" feelings like sexuality and tenderness, as possible signs of increasing connection.*

Intimacy

When your major defense is detachment, it can seem dangerous to fall in love and join in someone else's life. Disengaging thought from feeling is a powerful defense. Don't feel. Don't fight. Don't let them control you. Eights control by force of presence and Fives by lack of presence. Fives unhook, and by separating from themselves they stop giving energy or emotion.

When you're detached, life can flow over you and slide by, as if it never happened. It takes emotion to imprint an event and to make it significant. An entire episode can drop out of awareness if it isn't felt profoundly enough to make it memorable. Detachment has protective value. It softens unexpected jolts of emotion and cushions unpleasant events. Life is quiet and pleasant when you're unemotional. Why entertain strong feelings when they are the source of pain? Separating from emotion does neutralize negativity. But, over time, cutting off your own reactions can seem like an amputation. By denying yourself the wellsprings of emotion, you deprive yourself of experience.

Making commitments that are going to last for years upsets private independence. It's a lot easier to do without someone than to feel how much they matter. Fives sometimes feel "had" when people become emotionally important to them. Their privacy has been exposed. Suddenly they can be touched and seen and loved and affected.

Fives say that unwanted emotions can seem like being possessed. Unfamiliar pangs of desire, fueled by an Eight's rage. They have wants and they hate to want. They feel used. "How dare life make me feel this way?" Strong emotion feels like indulging a weakness. "Why be run by a weakness?" "I don't need this." Most of a Five's defenses emerge in the initial stages of relationship, when a closed door and unreturned messages still work. They open the door only a crack, because once feelings invade their privacy, detachment becomes impossible.

You become the active party in relating to Fives. You will probably initiate calls and activities, find yourself dropping hints when you need information; and after a great evening together, you may face a protracted period of silence. Fives can employ these distancing measures without conscious intention. Your emotions are demanding. Your needs could lead to entanglement. Sensitive to being dominated, they need to withdraw and think.

The interesting thing is that Observers can be exquisitely emotional when they're not being told that they should be. "Shoulds" feel coercive and make a Five retreat. Shoulds feel draining, so the Five gives less. Shoulds feel invasive, "Now what do you want?" and "When will you want it?" Shoulds are a red flag. Shoulds make Fives bolt. They may love to look at you, but if you say, "Look at me, look at me," they won't.

The rule of thumb is to state your intentions, then give Fives time to consider. Let them come if they want to, and carry on by yourself if they don't. Observers have delicate perceptions about the human condition. They can be sympathetic listeners and can offer solid support as long as you don't insist that they share your feelings.

Fascinated with gathering information, Fives do not like to be seen or to have their brains picked for information. Not being seen in an intimate relationship involves respecting the key boundaries of independence, unpredictability, autonomy, and privacy. Independence has to do with being able to take off without anyone knowing where they're going. Fives can disappear for hours at a time, and you don't know where they are. Then they reappear without explanation. This is disconcerting if you expect a constant presence. "So where did you go?" "I went out." Independence also involves monitoring information. Fives habitually answer questions in a narrow, noncommittal manner, and may not volunteer more than what's required. It's as if the unsaid doesn't exist. When you want to know why you've been left out of a decision, the reply may be "You never asked me about it."

Sensitive to the burden of other people's needs, Fives want emotional autonomy. You can be dependent and emotional, but Fives will not want to be drawn into those feelings. They can pay just enough attention to find out what you want, think of an efficient way to respond, give you what you asked for, and then think, "All right. I've done it. I've delivered. Now you can go away." By giving, Fives can buy time for themselves. "You got it, now go away and enjoy it. Leave me alone."

Observers are highly protective of their inner world, or "the real me." Partners who feel privileged to share that world report an intelligent, offbeat, and strikingly whimsical perspective on reality. A Five's mind is often attuned, sometimes poignantly, to profound questions of deeper meaning.

The Signals Fives Send

Positive Signals

Appreciative of an unencumbered lifestyle, Fives bring a delicacy of perception to relationships. Scholarly, knowing, and thoughtful, a voyager in the realms of mind. Fives are sensitive in their tastes. Ascetic and aesthetic. A single cushion in an empty room. A delicate sliver of something to eat. Dispassionate and calm in crisis. The one in whom others can safely confide.

Negative Signals

Partners may feel frozen out by Fives. You feel unconnected, neglected. The Five's ongoing privacy needs feel like signals of rejection. The burdens of initiation and confrontation fall on you. The Five's self-control reads as hoarding time, space, energy, and access to themselves. You get signals of superiority and secrecy—intellectual arrogance, an appearance of being above emotional expression and beyond the need to explain themselves.

Mixed Messages

Fives are very difficult to engage when they turn inward. There's a clear "stay back" message, like a Do Not Disturb sign etched on their faces. When they're acting out an appropriate social role or reacting to stress (point Seven), you can have difficulty discerning whether or not they're available. Energetic and apparently interested Fives can in fact be hiding in a social pose or watching themselves engage you from a third-party position. If they are doing a convincing job, you may mistakenly perceive a genuine request for contact. It can get to be a guessing game. Is the Five approachable or not? Who knows? The signal looks inviting, but it may be a social cover.

Inner Signals

When Fives are feeling uncooperative, the energy will simply drain out of a situation. The retraction of their personal presence can be so pronounced that you feel as if you're straining to speak with someone who's standing at a great distance rather than face-to-face. If you try to pump vitality back into the interaction, it just gets sucked into empty space until you feel physically drained.

From the Five's standpoint, your energy and interest feel like a demand for attention. Isolated from their own immediate feelings, Fives have difficulty with spontaneity. The thoughts say: "I'm unprepared. I don't know what to do. I need time to think." Open-ended requests can be terrifying. There's no way to prepare. It feels like opening the way to humiliation. The thoughts say: "Don't react. Don't invest. If you get involved, these people are going to want more." The feelings say: "I'll never get through this. It's not worth the time. I don't have enough time. I've got to save time." Inexperienced with erupting emotions, Fives can go blank mentally when they're not prepared. It's hard to think when feelings surface, which undercuts stability. They feel an urgent need to be alone, to find some quiet place in which to calm down.

If the pressure continues, the Five's thinking can become discontinuous. Fives say: "It's like flypaper mind. You remember bits of things that aren't connected to each other." The moment freezes in time. It seems like this morning never happened, that you've always been stranded in public without a place to hide. The thoughts say: "I'll never get out. I don't have a place. I've got to get back to my own place." The feelings confirm the need for flight. It doesn't feel like avarice to terminate the conversation abruptly and search for an exit. It feels like saving the small piece of yourself that still has a chance to get out.

The blind spot in the avarice passion is that attention focuses narrowly on vital things that could be taken away rather than on the more neutral aspects of a relationship. It helps to reduce the surprise factor. Fives contract if they are unexpectedly questioned, touched, or visited. They relax when they know exactly what to expect.

Five at Work

In the Workplace

- *Has a sense of limited energy reserves. Does not want time and energy to be used for other people's agendas.*
- *Works hard for the rewards of privacy and the freedom to pursue personal interests. Works to buy autonomy.*
- *Needs predictability. Wants to foresee in order to be prepared. Expects to have minutes from the last meeting and names of those who will attend the next one.*
- *Attention gravitates to others in the environment. Feels their intrusion. Often finds it hard to concentrate in the presence of others.*
- *Freezes when unexpectedly questioned or when a spontaneous reaction is called for. Needs to withdraw in order to figure things out.*
- *Strictly avoids conflict. Puts up a wall of memos and secretaries as protection against emotional scenes.*
- *Values unemotional decision making. The use of feelings as a rudder for decisions appears to be a loss of control. Can usually see through flattery and charismatic leadership.*

° *Extremely productive when in a decision-making role that is protected from frontline interactions.*

Leadership Style

Fives lead from behind closed doors and a bank of telephones. They are usually found in a cooperative effort with a more aggressive type, particularly Threes. Fives are usually positioned as the thinker/analyst, with the assertive type in the trenches. When public presentations have to be made, Observers may inhabit an appropriate pose; the right look and a memorized speech. Fives can lead in an outgoing, even engaging, style when conditions demand it. I once interviewed an Observer who ran a shipyard. He was very direct, very macho, and could easily have passed as an Eight. He described himself as "walking the walk" in the shipyard. He said that for eighteen years, on a daily basis, he'd get up from his chair in his private office, curse the fact that he had to go out, and, by the time he hit the door, "watch himself" shout orders. "You have to look right," he said. Fives slide into a public persona as if it were a role. These leaders can look extroverted when they know what to expect. They can take charge, delegate, and handle emergencies, but they may have practically no investment once the job is finished.

Observers focus on ideas and on a self-presentation that will get those ideas across rather than interpersonal communication. They deliver the message without embellishment. They state the problem without softening the edges and wait for others to volunteer input. It's a setup. The Five leader wants facts, and to get them, she or he dumps a bloody carcass on the table and waits for input. Everyone in the room will want to know where the leader stands before they deal with the body, but the leader won't go first. Observers do well with an adviser who is sensitive to human issues and who can tell the difference between a blunt, factual statement and one that will engender cooperation and support.

Once a project is positioned, Fives are quick to delegate. To protect privacy they will initiate specific windows of contact for "confidential" meetings with managers, rather than having to deal with them all at the same time. Each sector will be heard, but in a way that discourages information sharing and support among the different sectors of an operation. Following leadership's example, managers may begin to hide or trade their private information in the hope of improving their own position. A worst-case scenario is factionalism and secret rivalries among the various sectors, with a focus of attention toward influencing the leader in private.

Capable of high-level abstract thinking, Fives can reduce a great deal of information to a core proposition. The idea is to form a workable inner image and to replicate that image faithfully in the outer world. Five leaders can wait. They don't panic in the short term as long as basic necessities are accounted for. Still following the initial mental idea, they can ride through times of enormous difficulty while relating new information to their original plan. Safely installed in the mind, the core ideas are relatively immune to the disturbances of a business cycle.

Classic Conflicts

Lack of accessibility is a classic complaint about Fives. Fives just aren't there. They may be sitting in a chair and answering questions, but they give off no emanation or flare. The style is particularly devastating to types who need personal contact and who want to feel connected to the people with whom they work. Unless you're part of the private circle, you may feel that you work *for* an Observer rather than *with* one.

It's easy to project your own agenda onto the blank screen of Five's self-presentation. Low affect can easily be mistaken for agreement, and lack of opposition confused with support. With so little emanation, it's easy to think that Fives seem to be in agreement, as far as you can tell. You could just as easily project that they're not interested. Unfortunately this dynamic adds to Fives' feelings of alienation. If people are going to misread their intentions, why give out more information? It helps to allow time for formal summation at the end of a meeting, so that we're sure where everyone stands. There can of course be an "undecided" category, but it is important that Observers be positioned in a way that accurately reveals their thinking.

Lack of information about Fives' decision-making processes is a classic difficulty. The blank screen suddenly announces a final decision that was apparently made without input from the people affected. Unable to handle conflict and having few defenses against public confrontation, Observers withdraw, think, and decide in private. A decision that may affect many may then appear as a simple announcement. There. It's done. No further explanation. Those on the receiving end are bound to see high-handed, callous intent.

Conflict Resolution

See Part III, "The Directory of Relationships," for tips on mediation between Fives and others.

Employee Participation

Hell for Fives is an office floor with lots of desks, no partitions, and co-workers who go out to lunch and talk about their relationships. Fives want boundaries. They like to be alone with their own projects and will see private space and their own telephone as real incentives. Easily overwhelmed, they want to know exactly how much time and energy to expend. "What do I do? How much is there to do? And how long will it take?" Sensitive to intrusion, they become inefficient in an environment with too much input.

Fives are discontinuous thinkers, which means that they focus on a single piece of information, discard it, and then think about something else. The pieces need not be related to one another. Each bit can be examined independently and then, like a pin on a board, placed in a big-picture context. Big-picture think- ing for Fives could be illustrated as a large board with clearly de- marcated edges that define the theoretical question. The board is filled with independent bits of information that should reveal the central patterns of the theory once they're all positioned cor- rectly. The search for new information is continuous, and each good bit goes into the big picture, but as an independent piece.

Discontinuous thinking makes it difficult to shift attention quickly. The learning curve dips dramatically when there are interruptions or shifts of task. If someone suddenly enters the room, attention goes to the intrusion, and it's hard for Fives to re- focus their thoughts. Fives think of one thing at a time, or one concept at a time, and then move on to the next consideration. They become confused when the grounds of discussion switch too suddenly. "I don't understand the question" is the usual re- sponse from Fives when the piece that they were considering sud- denly doesn't fit into a new conceptual framework. Fives can freeze mentally if they have to switch focus too quickly; and be- cause they rely on their minds, a sudden switch of context can feel slightly threatening.

The same habit of attention underlies compartmentalizing, which means keeping the different sectors of life separated from one another. Fives are highly involved with the sector that en- gages them at the moment. Ten to noon might have been a very interesting bit, but by evening it may be only a vague memory. Fives concentrate deeply, but when their attention shifts, it's out of sight, out of mind.

These employees work to buy their independence. Accu- mulating wealth to support a luxurious lifestyle is not of interest. They commonly see worker incentives such as titles and benefits as a form of entrapment by management that binds people to the system. Fives often feel manipulated by other people's agendas. They hate having their energy used for an employer's benefit.

Their success is measured in terms of autonomy from a system of rewards, titles, and seemingly endless hierarchical involvement. Five heaven is being paid a decent wage to pursue their own intellectual interests in a private office with co-workers who eagerly supply data.

Team Building

Meetings will be a burden unless they are specific and to the point. Open-ended discussion is to be avoided. The Five mindset is not suited to fast-paced brainstorming sessions, where the grounds of discussion suddenly shift from one conceptual framework to another. Fives will get bored and tune out if the discussion gets muddled. It helps to announce the agenda beforehand, so that participants have time to prepare. Brainstorming should be bracketed in a specific time slot on the agenda.

Observers like to be responsible for a small, clearly demarcated area of expertise. They love specific questions involving their own interests but are unwilling to extend themselves into ambiguous territory that hasn't been thought through. Picking a Five's brain is almost impossible. You'll get only what they're willing to give, and you'll get it in the context of their choosing. Fives appreciate specific questions. Do not expect them to amplify your questions, to draw you out, or even to ask for information that they may need for their own purposes. It's simply not their habit to reach out. "I didn't tell you because you didn't ask me" or "I gave you exactly what you asked for" can be sources of complaint among team members. Fives censor their information and often withhold without realizing it. To elicit exactly the information you need from a Five, you'll have to tailor your questions.

Once committed, Fives are unstoppable workers. They're in their element with a difficult, worthwhile project. The problem itself, rather than rewards and benefits, spurs them on. They can remain committed for years to a small area of independent study without the support of public recognition. This commitment sometimes gets in the way of good communication. Fives may get interested and isolate themselves. They may then call team members only when it's a matter of business, ask for whatever they need, then hang up. Protecting privacy, incommunicado Fives look like takers rather than givers, because the sequence of contact is invariably call, ask, take, leave, without explanation.

It helps to draw out Fives on a team so that they demonstrate their real intentions. If they're timid about going first, then let them deliver the summary at the end of the meeting. Do not suppose that Fives are aware of their own isolation or that they necessarily feel deprived by lack of contact. Meet Fives on their own turf, which will be project-related information.

Six ✦ *The Trooper*

	PERSONALITY BIAS	ESSENCE QUALITIES
MENTAL	*cowardice/doubt*	*faith*
EMOTIONAL	*fear*	*courage*

	SUBTYPE FOCUS	
	STRENGTH/BEAUTY	sexual
	DUTY	social
	AFFECTION (WARMTH)	self-survival

The Six Bias

Worldview

The world is a threatening place. I question authority.

Spiritual Path

Doubt involves a loss of *faith*. The child reacted with *fear* to losing the permanent security of essence, initiating a lifelong preoccupation with *courage*. Fear creates dependency on rules and protective authority, which mimics the certainty of faith. The Enneagram's Fear type has a parallel in the Doubting Mind category of Buddhist practice, in which attention shifts from belief to intense internal questioning. Success and goodwill seem particularly doubtful. This *cowardice* and *doubt* of mind are a natural starting place from which to develop faith. The path of faith begins with the firmly held beliefs seen in psychologically mature people, but, like all of the qualities that originate in essence, faith can transform consciousness.

Concerns

- *Thinking replaces doing. Procrastination. Image of the frozen rabbit.*

- *Inaction increases anxiety. Imagining the worst. Fight or flight. The counterphobic Six—confrontational, daring—charges; the phobic Six—furtive, frightened—flees.*

- *Manifests fear in three key areas of life:*

    STRENGTH/BEAUTY *in sexual or one-to-one relationships.*

    DUTY *and law-abiding social behavior.*

    AFFECTION (WARMTH) *that guarantees personal survival.*

- *Has high goals, often with a history of incompletion.*

- *Anxiety peaks with success. Success equals exposure to hostile forces.*

- *Has amnesia about success and pleasure. Often successful in an underdog cause. The loyal companion in adversity. The business turnaround.*

- *Ambivalent about authority. Either seeks to be protected from authority or rebels against authority.*

- *Questions other people's motives, especially authorities'.*

- *Identifies with underdog causes. Leads the opposition party.*

- *Afraid to recognize own anger. Afraid of other people's anger.*

- *Asks the hard questions. Wants to eliminate doubt. Wants an explanation.*

- *Skepticism. The Buddhist category of Doubting Mind. A mental "Yes, but . . ." or "This may not work." Sees the loopholes. Excellent troubleshooter.*

- *Scans the environment for signs of safety and threat. Activates personal radar. This way of paying attention will confirm that:*

    - *The world is a threatening place, but also leads to:*
    - *Recognizing the motives, needs, and inner worlds of others.*

Personality Bias

We all adopt the Six perspective when we feel endangered. The war zone, dark streets, a cliff on the mountain road. We muster up. Adrenaline forces fight or flight. Either brace for defense or run for cover and hide. The Enneagram accounts for both reactions. Phobic Sixes hide, and submit when they feel cornered. Counterphobics, equally afraid, challenge their fears in an aggressive way.

Six children know adrenaline. They learned to be wary, to question authority, to "look for what you really mean." Skeptical and cautious, they search out hidden intentions as intently as Threes seek image and success. Sixes doubt authority, while Threes take on leadership roles.

Paradoxically success can be frightening. Visibility equals attack. A Six looks for clues. "Can you be trusted?" The mind takes over: "What if . . . ?" If this habit becomes automatic, self-observation stops. The Six is primed for opposition and doubtful of support. Flooded by apprehension, thinking replaces doing. When worst-case thinking takes over, it's impossible to act.

Sixes grow by regaining faith in people. They grow by learning to trust. They have a choice when they can separate mental fears from real danger, when they can watch hope rise and then turn to doubt. They are helped by significants who offer reassurance, who remain steadfast when the future looks doubtful, and who are faithful to their word.

Subtype Focus:

Fear Affects Sexual, Social, and Survival Attitudes

Strength and Beauty in Sexual and One-to-One Relationships

When you're afraid of people, caring can make you feel helpless. You feel manipulated by your own feelings. You're in someone's power. "What if they don't love me?" "What if they change their mind?" You crave reassurance, which feels humiliating. You fear abandonment, which makes you feel weak. You contract and, without realizing it, begin to doubt people's sincerity. "They only said that to be polite," "They were being kind." It would be terrible to trust and to be betrayed again. Doubting seems more realistic.

Strength and beauty are a show of power, a mask that covers inner doubt. The motive is to attract and command allegiance. The power of beauty. The mastery of strength. Sixes respect power of all kinds: ideas that command allegiance, aesthetics able to capture people's minds. The reason for this preoccupation is that a beautiful and wise environment offers reassuring feedback. When the environment is lovely and people are humane, you can relax.

The compulsive aspects of the subtype are typically acted out by wanting to see that you can affect an associate or mate. A formidable intellect. A fierce opponent. A handsome woman. A striking man. The power stance is typically acted out by cultivating physical strength/beauty, maintaining a string of lovers, or a dominating intellectualism. Even a frightened person can feel powerful if people think she or he is strong, beautiful, sexy, and smart.

A preoccupation with strength or beauty may well be common to other personality types, but for Six the motive for being strong or beautiful is anxiety management. Fear evaporates when significants look up to us, when we command the respect of associates or a mate. The preoccupation with power is often intertwined with risk-taking counterphobic behavior, which is also a cover for inner uncertainty; but the sexual subtype's focus of attention is affecting an associate or mate. The preoccupation with strength/beauty in one-to-one relating is more obvious in phobic Sixes, because it stands out against a timid behavioral style.

Social Duty

This is a way to contain fear through mutual obligation and commitment. The needs of the group govern behavior so we know what to expect. Self-doubt lessens when opinions are confirmed and backed by the power of collective authority. We can't be isolated, and we won't be attacked.

Sixes can be devoted to their family, to underdog causes, and to those islands of sanity where people are socially concerned. Communes, political leagues, self-help groups, and the church are examples. They often have deep bonds to a social group or cause. The compulsive variation of the social commitment is played out through ritual obligatory duties, which are spurred by guilt and fears of abandonment. Following the rules ensures your place in the group.

Duty Sixes are capable of enormous self-sacrifice for the cause, for the family, and for ideals. Like all Sixes, they are often most effective before a situation becomes fully successful, where strength can be mobilized as "us against them." They are particularly effective when duty calls. They can be encouraging to others in adversity and heroic in a turnaround. The call of duty mobilizes action. It's easy to act for the cause, but a personal success can be alarming.

Self-Survival Through Affection (Warmth)

Fear disappears in the company of friends. You can relax with people who know and accept you. You have history together, you know what to expect, so you let your guard down. Sixes feel safe with people who like them and feel endangered when they don't. There is an ongoing request for reassurance. "Do you still love me?" Distance and silence encourage doubt: "Has anything changed between us?" "What are you thinking now?" Without a reality check, they fall prey to their own imagination and start to wonder, "Why didn't I get a call?" "Maybe it's off." There may even be a sense of relief when no call comes. No need to worry now, because it wouldn't have worked out anyway.

Without realizing it, attention shifts from doubt to imagination and from imagination to fact until you're convinced that it's over. Sixes don't realize that they're scaring themselves, that they've lost faith. They're shocked when the call finally comes, and there's a cheery voice on the other side who doesn't realize that everything's changed. It's embarrassing to see how easy it is to lose faith in people.

Given encouragement, warm Sixes are devoted to friendship. When your safety is tied to other people, you want to understand them. You get close to people by disarming their anger and allying in friendship, by sticking up for them, by taking their side. Bonded by warmth, actions are motivated by friendship. "We're in it together," "I'm in it for you," "We are not alone." Fears vanish when you see that someone likes you. People protect the ones they like.

Because safety is tied to friendship, a change in affection is very threatening. It's like being thrown back into a hostile world again. Six's survival strategy is similar to point Two. Both warm Six and Two want to please and move toward people. Both types align with others in order to feel safe. The difference is that Twos gain identity by pleasing. Sixes don't alter their identity from person to person. Warm Six pleases to feel safe.

Focal Issues

Projection

Sixes are vigilant. Their attention is highly focused, and when they're alarmed, they look outside for clues to explain their inner uncertainty. The environment becomes suddenly meaningful. Faces and gestures seem to emanate a response to the unarticulated questions "Do you like me? Am I safe?" It seems like undisclosed emotion is being demonstrated: "I saw you waver. I saw you freeze." The unstated resounds loudly: "Your voice softened. I felt you relax."

All nine types project to some extent, in that aspects of themselves that are hidden by defenses are attributed to other people; but projection is almost synonymous with the fearful tendency. Danger seems so clearly "out there" until you start getting feedback, like this Six engineer who went to a party one night.

> My wife and I are driving home late after a party. Our teenager, Amy, is at the wheel. She's just gotten her license. Amy takes a back road and enjoys going fast, and I'm starting to freeze. I hate being the crank parent, and I'm thinking that my wife, the One, has to know what's happening. Don't Ones always know when someone's out of line? So why doesn't she say something? Why is it always me? My arm is braced against the dash, and I'm thinking, "Ones wait for you to go first, and then they criticize." By now I feel her silently judging me. "She's waiting for me to stop Amy, and then she'll say I'm uptight." By the time we get home I'm steaming. I hate it when she's on my case, and it's been happening a lot lately. She's a One, right? They always know when stuff goes wrong, so I know it's deliberate. I get out and yank open the back door. In the same second that I see my wife wake up I say, "Why do you always have to be critical?" She answers, "But Henry, I've been sleeping since we left the party."

Certainty

Doubts can be softened if someone else will go first. Sixes are susceptible to people who initiate and who find them attractive. Being on the receiving end is safer than having to go first. Consistency is important. Tell the truth and make it as consistent as possible from one day to the next. Untruth triggers suspicion and is very hard to forgive.

A Six wants to know what you want and what you're thinking, because it eliminates doubt. They can move toward a steady, friendly presence but become increasingly suspicious of moodiness and mixed intentions. Another's change of feeling will be taken personally, because it makes them afraid. They were comfortable with that person yesterday. Now they aren't. Worst-case thinking takes over. The whole relationship is in doubt. "Why are you mad at me?" "What have I done?" The Six will push for reassurance, unfortunately at exactly the moment when a stressed or moody partner is least inclined to give it.

Troopers need certainty. If the news is good, they can be pleasantly surprised. If the news is bad, at least they know where they stand. Bad news is familiar to types that imagine worst-case happenings. They can mobilize to deal with difficulty, but the unknown is paralyzing. Anything could happen. You can't prepare. Sixes get pinned by their own imagination when the news is uncertain. A good way to offer reassurance is to get the basics in order. Get the Six to voice fears and cover each in turn. "If this turns out to be serious, then I'll need money, a car, and a place to stay." Then determine that the basics are available. Locate money, a car, and potential living space. Last of all get the Six to imagine the best-case outcomes and to voice those out loud as well.

Doubt

Six doubt takes the form of inner questioning. Appearances are examined. Face value is less interesting than what lies under the face. Motivations that telegraph from the unconscious are more compelling than a pleasant smile. The objective world is searched for deeper meaning. The eye goes beneath the surface. A lovely face, striking clothes, a polished manner—and what? Questioning appearance doesn't seem doubtful. "What's hidden?" "What are they thinking?" "What's the motive?" "What can we trust?"

These pervasively interesting questions are easy to stereotype as negative thinking, particularly when an obvious answer is overlooked in the search for deeper meaning. Sixes are famous for bumping into telephone poles because they're preoccupied. They overlook the obvious. "An earthquake? Where? I missed it. But look at that interesting face!" Disregarding appearance does not seem at all suspicious. Dismantling obvious remarks does not seem negative. Assuming hidden intentions seems realistic. Doubting does not seem cynical.

It helps to get a reality check. Doubts vanish with honest inquiry. It helps to voice both positive and negative thinking and to get direct feedback. Are these perceptions false ideas, intuitions, projections, or doubts?

The Devil's Advocate

Doubt can produce unusual powers of discernment. The Six mind is organized to question, to discard the obvious, and to cut through overlays of obscure meaning. The joke about paranoid attention is that a query such as "Hello. How are you?" is examined for secret meaning. "Hello? How am I? Why do you want to know?" Safety depends on knowing people's intentions. "Could I be put at a disadvantage?" "Why do you want to know?" Doubt is usually an inquiry about intentions. What is the intention behind the facts?

An unusual mental precision develops from negative questioning. The Six mind doubts, repositions the refined proposition, and doubts again until there is no doubt. It's the appropriate state of mind for sleuthing. Sixes are impressive troubleshooters; doubts are confirmed when the obvious turns out to be devious or mistaken. They see the holes in an argument and inconsistencies in reasoning. They see the context that influences the discussion. Most of all they see intention. What are the motives here? Are they oppressive or kind?

Action

Doubt can create depression. You lose confidence. You're convinced it can't be done. It wouldn't work anyway, so why try?

Unlike biological depression, a doubt-induced depression lifts with a call to action. The challenge is to get Sixes mobilized without looking like you are an oppressive authority, to get them to act without your having to be a cop. The best medicine is a good example. Carry out your part and leave the Sixes' part undone. Filling in their piece is going to be easier because your part works. Sixes are rarely proactive. Going first, especially into success, feels like walking into a trap. Because it's frightening to be alone and exposed and successful, encouragement can feel like a setup. Sixes may read compliments to mean they're being set up to be an authority. Honest support can feel like being thrown to a hostile world again.

It helps to remove as many areas of uncertainty as possible. Reaction is much easier than proaction, because you know what you have to face.

Authority

Troopers remember negative authority figures. As a consequence they overestimate other people's power and tend to doubt their own. Sixes need to account to authority, to explain, to ask permission, to be sure there's power on your side. You prefer the protected place. Many Sixes gravitate to protective marriages and to secure institutions, like the army or the church. But like all "solutions" that involve a loss of identity, submission leads to rebellion. Both the submissive (phobic) and the rebellious (counterphobic) style overvalue the extent of other people's power.

Sixes need to stand on their own, to be guided by their own authority, rather than looking outward. They would do well to deal with their fear of aggression. From the Six perspective, standing on one's own equals conflict with authority, and that conflict could escalate. Dire consequences are replayed in the imagination. Powerful people will be angered, and then what?

Security and Risk

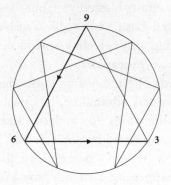

Security

A secure Six can relax. The mind lets go, thought gets quiet, and body awareness comes back. It's like returning to your senses. There's a strange advantage for an alienated type like Six in self-development work. Fear isn't nearly as attractive as some of the other passions. There's no exciting ego inflation. No payoff. Not much of an image, no puffs of pride. When people discover the constraints of their passion, they're motivated to change; but for Six the advantage is immediate relief. You know how much you've been hurting when the pain goes away. Troopers may not catch themselves in the act of imagining the worst, but it feels good when its gone.

A relaxed Six may worry about losing his or her edge. I once interviewed a radiologist who was convinced that his skill improved when he was slightly paranoid. We had a good laugh about the paranoid physician scanning his X rays for clues to hidden intentions, but the truth of the matter was that he thought his vigilance lessened when he was relaxed and happy. Point Six has a sharpness of attention that may indeed be a by-product of unconsciously scanning the environment for danger. When that mental tendency relaxes, awareness shifts to your body. Sensory awareness improves, sometimes blessedly so, but the natural seat of attention is interrupted. Losing your edge translates in Six-speak to feeling afloat, feeling spacy, feeling spread out over the room rather than focused in your mind.

At the low side of Nine, losing your edge feels like losing initiative. You have less adrenaline, less push, and sometimes less interest. Your life winds down. Seems like there's plenty of time when you're unhurried by anxiety. You just don't care as much. No problem. It looks peaceful on the outside. Inside there's not much happening. You may have a real concern about accommodating to the peacefulness of Nine, thereby losing motivation.

At the high side of Nine, a Six opens to people and the environment. Without the screen of vigilance, sexuality, pleasure, and companionship are far more available. A Six at Nine feels the goodness of people, not as an idea but as a tangible reality. It can be disconcerting for a mental type to stay in sensation and feelings. You feel a small panic, a need to retreat into your thoughts, to figure out what's happening. Troopers need a safe way to relax. Sports are a good way to tell the difference between being in your body and being in your mind.

Risk

The first indications of stress show as a tightening of defenses at Six. You get a feeling of dread. Some dire consequence is about to happen, but there's no basis in fact. Phobic Sixes can stay in this state of mind for a long time. It looks like someone with her head down, walking in small circles, who won't strike out on her own. It helps to relax, but the tendency is to tighten. You want to be rescued. You want someone else to do it for you. You want out. When the tension hits a critical point, it triggers fight or flight.

The counterphobic can't stand waiting and moves into action fast. You feel better once you're in motion. It feels like progress, even if you're on the run. The move into Three can either be energizing or terrifying. You have energy, but you're running scared. If attention shifts to the task, the energy release can be constructive. Sixes can act because they're not tied up in their mind. It feels like acting in the face of danger. There's a test to take, a child to be born, a challenge to be met. Things go badly when the adrenaline charges a worst-case scenario. It's like living through a scary movie where you're fighting yourself. The low side of risk behavior shows Sixes in a stuttering start-stop pattern that alternates between mustering up and caving in, with a final crash when the adrenaline runs out. The high side of risk depends on keeping your concentration on the task and relaxing into the energy instead of tensing up.

Six in Love

Living with Sixes

° *Sixes question your intentions: suspecting your positive regard, wondering what you really think, undervaluing romance.*

° *A Six can be a loyal ally, strong in an "us against the world" relationship, a devoted supporter.*

° *Sixes want reassurance to overcome doubt. "Will you always love me?" There's no right answer for this one. A positive response leads to doubt of your sincerity, further assurances are required, and so on.*

° *Sixes tend to project personal dissatisfaction, for instance, denying their own wandering eye by "seeing" that you are attracted to someone else.*

° *Expect a Six to identify with the problem areas of relationship, which become the focal points of attention.*

° *A Six wants to affect you (for example, through warmth, by a dutiful alliance, or through sexual power) rather than be affected. Sixes find it frightening to have their own desires aroused, to realize that they are vulnerable to what others do. They prefer to show strength by assisting others to attain their goals, are capable of significant self-sacrifice.*

° *Don't count on Sixes to be able to locate the source of tension in intimacy. "Am I afraid of showing weakness? Am I sensing a possible betrayal?" They expect hurt when their guard goes down.*

° *A Six searches for clues in your behavior. "What's going on underneath the surface? How do you act toward other people? What do you really think of me?" They need reassurance.*

Intimacy

Sixes are strong in ideas and imagination and weak in follow-through. A romance that initially seemed interesting suddenly becomes doubtful. It's a bind. If you go ahead, you're going to be hurt. If you don't, you'll miss out. Desire is frightening because you want something. You want the connection, but it might not last. You'd like to try, but it makes you afraid. When thinking replaces doing, good ideas are reduced to vague possibilities. You want, but a multitude of things could go wrong. It's safer not to want when you couldn't have it anyway.

From an outsider's position Sixes look ambivalent, because they waver between belief and doubt. From the Six's perspective, what you want is clear enough, but getting it seems unlikely. You're ambivalent about a positive outcome. Doubt is also a safe fallback position. You have feelings, but you also doubt them. You can be fully committed to a relationship in all ways—physically, financially, and emotionally—and still have doubts. The beauty of the position is that you can commit yourself to a partnership while fully realizing the negative possibilities. You take pride in seeing through image and facade and aren't usually taken in by glamour.

Periodic doubt does not mean that a Six is leaving the relationship. Oddly, doubt can be a way to stay in, because it relieves the tension of wanting someone and feeling threatened by that desire. Doubt is a way to coast without feeling anxious. Doubt reduces fear. You're not totally sure. You can see the pitfalls, so it's not threatening. Problems are familiar territory. There's something to question and refine.

A long-term relationship is going to include periods of questioning. These concerns must be aired, or they become fact in the mind of the Six. Expressing doubt is a way to gain trust, and it can be a real pain to a partner. For example, when a Six says, "Will you always love me?" it sounds like a question that doubts the partner's commitment. If the request for reassurance comes at a time when the partner is fully committed, quite correctly the partner will wonder about projection. Yet another way to hear the Six's "Will you always love me?" is "I love you now. Is it safe?" The Six has felt a surge of love and is getting scared. Rather than becoming irritated at the Six's dependency needs, a partner might simply restate the basis of his or her commitment. Knowing that falling in love is fraught with doubt to Sixes, a question like "Will you always love me?" might simply mean "Have you changed your mind since this morning?"

A partner can function as the couple's memory during a doubt attack. Feeling endangered by love, the Six doubts that things will turn out well. "I can't believe you. When will you let me down?" A partner can help by holding ground, by restating the exact terms of the commitment from his or her side. Don't exaggerate. Don't plead. Don't coax. In a crisis of faith, Sixes need a consistent story. They are afraid to love others without the shield of doubt.

The endearing aspects of this insecurity produces many stable, long-term marriages. Once reassured that the marriage will last, Sixes commonly carry more than their own share of responsibility. They are usually low-maintenance mates. They don't demand a lot of attention and are unusually loyal to the people they trust. They attach their safety, and therefore loyalty, to a particular person. "Someone who's like family," "One of ours." Sixes become attached to an individual, not to an image, or to status, or what another can produce or provide. The remarkable extension of this devotion is sacrifice. Loyal Sixes put their loved ones first.

A scared Six is galvanized into action. When paranoia peaks, it's fight or flight. Any fight is compounded by a Six's own fear of aggression. People look threatening. What another says sounds more ominous than what is intended. Fighting Sixes are angry because they were fooled. "I believed you." They forgot to doubt. They were unprepared. How stupid. "You see? I should never have trusted you."

Anger fuels a nervous grandiosity. A show of power. Mustering up. "I'm strong. I'm not afraid." Sixes can be bullies if they're threatened. Aggression covers inner doubt. Their imagination magnifies the extent of your power. Sixes expect the worst. They may be testing the extent of the danger. They may bait the people. "How angry will you get?"

Without realizing it, Sixes now offer their partners the best possible opportunity to chip away at doubt. To take advantage of the moment, a partner should quietly reaffirm faith in the relationship. "I loved you last week. Nothing has changed from my side. I love you now and I will still love you in the same way when this fight is over." Now the partner is not so dangerous. The Sixes went full out. They got angry, and the worst didn't happen.

The Signals Sixes Send

Positive Signals

Sixes exhibit strong loyalty to the trusted few, the cause, the protector, and friends. They keep faith with the powerless, with those who are afraid. The Six plays the devil's advocate; daring to question. You'll find Sixes creative thinkers, with discriminating minds and refined powers of imagination. Troopers can be steadfast in their commitments while remaining fully aware of their partner's negative tendencies. They love who you are, not your image.

Negative Signals

Sixes tend to engage in projection—reading things into relationships that aren't there; to control through overprotectiveness—securing the bunker, wanting to be safe; not to inform others about changes in thinking or to report doubt attacks. They're ambivalent about things turning out well, which leads to procrastination, avoidance, and a history of incompletion. Difficulties with authority are expressed in both submission and rebellion. Expect contrary thinking: "Yes, but . . . "; taking the opposite view.

Mixed Messages

Unexpressed doubt produces inconsistent signals. You can't always tell if your Six likes you. Sixes question the relationship but don't want to pull out. You seem welcome, but then it changes. Troopers are obviously interested at the beginning and planning stages of a relationship. Suddenly their minds flip when it's time to act, and everything's uncertain. "Are you sure this is going to work? What do you think? How can we be sure?"

Inner Signals

It's hard to compliment Sixes. Positive feedback doesn't sink in. Their thoughts say: "You're hearing something good about yourself. Remember this." But their feelings contract. They think: "This sounds sincere. It may be true." Suddenly they doubt. Doubt discredits perception. Sixes hear the words, but they don't fully believe them because it doesn't sink into their feelings. The thoughts say: "You're just being polite. When will you let me down?" It's not that Troopers think you're lying, it's that your compliments sound partial. What hasn't been said? What's the full story? "Why don't you express your doubts?"

Sixes do well to ask for clarification, to check. It helps for Sixes to focus on the exact words that were spoken and let the feelings sink in. A reality check is imperative to counteract doubt. It helps to go back over the conversation, to ask people to repeat what they said, to voice any doubts out loud. "What did you really mean by that?"

Six at Work

In the Workplace

° *Has strong analytic powers. Attention shifts to questioning and examining the opposite position. Doubt and a suspicion of the obvious develop clarity.*

° *Overvalues authority's power. Invests those who project an authoritative image with far more power than they actually possess. Feels weakened by comparison.*

° *Reacts against own weakness by either seeking protection from authority (loyalist) or attempting to bring it down (rebel). "At your feet or at your throat."*

° *Tries for superhero status as a compensation for inner anxiety. Has to prove self to others. Self-mastery. Toughing it out. Braced against fear.*

° *Able to act, to go full out when up against the odds. Will compete when the odds are against a win. Defends the underdog. A business turnaround.*

° *Tests an argument. Sensitive to the weak spots in any position. The loyal opposition. "Yes, but . . . " The devil's advocate. "Let's consider the other side."*

° *Action paralysis. Finds it hard to keep moving forward effectively when success begins to materialize and hard to focus when there is no opposition. Doubt sets in until positive options begin to seem unreal.*

° *Has tendency to diminish a powerful success. Blowing it, losing time, losing the critical file in a computer crash. Sense of endangerment arises in the exposed successful stance. Backlash from the belief that nobody likes authority.*

° *Has difficulty locating the source of tension connected to success. "Is it that my subordinates do not like authority?" "Am I sensing a behind-the-scenes attack? Is a takeover likely?" "Why don't I feel the pleasure of a win?"*

Leadership Style

Oddly, Sixes can come alive under adversity. Watch out for Six executives when the company's headed for Chapter 11. Watch out for the quarterback who's down fourteen with two minutes to play. Sixes often lead with more clarity and strength when the business has to be turned around than when it's an easy win. Doubt disappears when you can measure yourself against a known difficulty instead of an imagined worst-case scenario. Launching into focused action calls out reserves of strength and intelligence that are far beyond ordinary capability. Fears vanish when you're fully engrossed in activity, because fear is largely in the mind.

The inner situation alters when conditions are ripe for a win. Paradoxically there's less vitality and interest. Procrastination develops in the absence of opposition. Organizational matters take precedence amid an attitude of overpreparedness that didn't exist during the crisis. Delays occur in decision making. Several courses of action emerge for consideration. The leader wants certainty before moving ahead. It helps immeasurably if honest feedback can be obtained directly after a successful completion. "Honest feedback" to Sixes should include moderate, intelligent opposition. Which part of a successful presentation fell flat? Who made what criticism at lunch? Untempered compliments do not sound genuine. Others don't sound astute unless they have something constructive to say.

Sixes are ambivalent about visible success. They are often leaders who rally around an underdog cause. Their own belief is sparked by focusing the faith of others. Their own convictions are strengthened by the agreement of students when they teach. They lead well when the success of the cause is defined by obstacles. The obstacles focus attention. You're up against it. Remove those obstacles, and suddenly you're visible.

When you're an identified underdog, it can be shocking to see yourself as an authority. To stay in leadership, you have to keep the underdog momentum going. It's a lot harder to chart a course of action in the absence of opposition. You pay more attention to areas of difficulty than to positive alternatives. Success depends on a reliable follow-through system, so that momentum doesn't decrease. Steady feedback from a respected mentor or knowledgeable person in the field helps you immensely in cutting through doubt attacks.

It's important that all negative expectations be aired before attention turns to positive alternatives. Plans for expansion should be immediately set in motion in such a way that the delicate transition from success to expansion is protected by a structure that cannot be changed. Once the new phase is in operation, the Six leader will be back in position as a troubleshooter.

The up side of doubt is that it can keep a leader honest. Successful Sixes usually don't get inflated. They see themselves as having mastered many fears and are attracted to troubleshooting the next difficult problem. Like Ones, the Perfectionist of the Enneagram, Sixes focus on the flaws. They keep refining and improving and can work with great fortitude and endurance for a long time. They do not need immediate gratification.

Classic Conflicts

Classic conflicts concern Six doubt. "Yes, but . . . " is a common position. If there's a rush of enthusiasm, the Six becomes cautionary. "Yes, but . . . " "Have you considered . . . ?" "What about the other side?" Like the Perfectionism of Ones, this thought process is perceived as negativistic. No one wants to think about the hard questions when enthusiasm is running high. It helps to state ground rules for discussions. A brainstorming period where anything goes and equal time for troubleshooting.

Antiauthoritarianism is a potential conflict area. Some Sixes just hate being told what to do. Sixes do well on a team with non-threatening people who can hear them out without having to agree. Antiauthoritarianism often diminishes when the Six feels safe and has a success or two to look back on.

Conflict Resolution

See Part III, "The Directory of Relationships," for tips on mediation between Sixes and others.

Employee Participation

Sixes are either "one of us" or rebels. The loyalist stays safe by being dutiful and pleasing to the group. The rebel uses an aggressive style to determine who is safe. Rebellious Sixes are provocative. They challenge the status quo just to see where everyone stands. Any overture of acceptance reduces their anxiety. A move toward a Six with anything resembling friendship is usually welcome. Known quantities are safe. Troopers want to know what you're thinking.

Security is key. "What will happen in the future?" is a major preoccupation. Any way of assuring the future is a relief. Sixes respond to clear guidelines, clear penalties, and a clear chain of command that does not depend on favoritism or who one knows in the hierarchy. They are highly creative and cooperative if their ideas and efforts are recognized, especially if their work is building toward a secure future. They can postpone their own gratification, and they willingly support others when they feel safe. When management is perceived to be loyal, Sixes are unusually loyal in return.

Safety lies in full information. Bad news is preferable to doctored or withheld information. Error is easily forgiven when the error is known, but secrecy feels like manipulation and makes Sixes rebellious. Any unequal power arrangement triggers fear. Sixes want details when their security depends on the goodwill of authority.

Troopers are extremely uncomfortable when they have to compete with the people they see on a daily basis. It's a lose-lose situation, and one that triggers paranoia. They feel guilty about winning out over someone else; they feel bad if they don't do their best. Either way they're thinking about the fact that someone else's interests have been set against their own. Sixes have been known to quit promising career opportunities simply because they could not produce consistently good work in a competitive environment.

Controlled competition, however, is good territory for the doubtful Six. Focus improves when there's a known adversary, clear ground rules, and time to prepare. Courtrooms are a good example. Trial lawyers engage in a short, strictly monitored, and highly aggressive mental competition; and when it's over, they go their separate ways.

Team Building

Sixes are heavily focused on interpersonal relations in the workplace. Your sense of security depends so much on acceptance that who you work with can seem as important as the job itself. Being liked means fitting in, being recognized for your own contribution, finding points of agreement, knowing that you're on the same side, that you're playing the game together. Good teamwork is a natural extension of that security, whereas competition stresses separate effort. Intense interaction among a few people can be the ultimate reality check. Paranoia dies when there's certainty.

The Six has to learn how to handle public recognition well. If the Six is a star, it works best if she or he is applauded in that area and otherwise treated as an equal. A Six in difficulty should be encouraged privately by an authority and not exposed to "public ridicule." If the team includes aggressive stars, the Six will either challenge them in order to equalize power or, feeling dominated, may instigate an "us against them" alliance with other players.

Troopers are focused on power relationships. The preferred positions are the team against management, the team competing as a unit against other teams, or a team of noncompetitors who get along by mutual agreement. The most uncomfortable position is a team of competitors who have to see one another on a regular basis.

Given the security of a consistent environment and a reasonably secure future, Sixes are natural team players. They are weak in follow-through; but they are highly creative, they initiate ideas well, and they are great troubleshooters. They do not flourish in an uncertain environment. They find it easy to doubt the good intentions of people. Mixed messages, covert alliances, and having to compete for attention are guaranteed turnoffs. "Why put out good ideas that are going to be ripped off?" "Why let yourself be exploited?" "Who can I trust?" Focused on safety with other people, Sixes are going to be either creative, loyal players or, if they feel disadvantaged, a disruptive influence.

Seven ⬠ The Epicure

	PERSONALITY BIAS	ESSENCE QUALITIES
MENTAL	*planning*	*work*
EMOTIONAL	*gluttony*	*sobriety*

SUBTYPE FOCUS	
FASCINATION	sexual
SOCIAL SACRIFICE	social
LIKE-MINDED	self-survival

The Seven Bias

Worldview

The world is full of opportunity and options. I look forward to the future.

Spiritual Path

Work is a word in common usage that can be used to describe an aspect of essence involving single-pointed attention. Spiritual work depends on the ability to shift inward and to tell the difference between outer and inner reality. If the mind becomes fascinated with the delights of outer life, then spiritual work deteriorates to pleasant *planning* and *gluttony* for life experience. *Sobriety* is another word in common usage that points to a return to essence through the route of moderation, concentration, and commitment.

Concerns

- Seeks stimulation, peak experiences. Avoids limitation.
- Wants to keep the energy up. Leaves the party while it's still interesting.
- Experiences joy of the mind. Options, plans, and possibilities. Images and ideas.
- Replaces deep or painful feelings with positive alternatives. Talking, planning, and imagining.
- Acts out gluttony in three key areas of life:

    FASCINATION in sexual or one-to-one relationships.

    SOCIAL SACRIFICE, acceptance of limitations imposed by obligations to others.

    LIKE-MINDED DEFENDER, secure in belonging to a group of like-minded people.

- Confuses ideas and actualities. Mentally it's already done.
- Focuses on self. Doesn't notice people's needs or pain.
- Feeling confident and OK supports overvaluation of own ability. "I can do anything," "People think well of me." Narcissistic.
- Equalizes authority. "I'm the same as authority." Expects recognition.
- Feels either superior or inferior in the hierarchy. "We're all equal" really means "You do your thing and I'll do mine." If unchallenged, feels superior in own giftedness. If challenged, feels punctured and inferior. Uses charm to regain superior status.
- Avoids conflict with authority. Goes through the cracks.
- Diffuses fear. Charms and disarms. Talks way out of trouble.
- Sees charm as the first line of defense. Sevens are fear types who move forward into friendly contact with people.
- Practices chicanery. Fakes it. Skates and slides over the hard parts.
- Masks own fear by boredom. "This feels limiting." Boredom also masks unwillingness. "People are limited."

- ° *Angry when ability is questioned. Terrified when charm doesn't work.*
- ° *Values spontaneity.*
- ° *Likes open-ended agreements and multifaceted jobs.*
- ° *Likes the beginning and planning stages. Procrastinates about final commitment and completion.*
- ° *Interrelates and systematizes information. This style of attention can result in commitments with loopholes and backup options, and:*
  - ° *Rationalized escapism from difficult or painful events, or it can lead to:*
  - ° *Finding connections, parallels, and unusual fits. Has a talent for nonlinear analysis, remote associations, and a synthesis of different systems.*

Personality Bias

A Seven's world is full of options. Ideas and adventure, plans to make the future bright. Life calls out, but the real pleasure is mental. A Seven's mind hungers for experience. It anticipates the future. It feasts on associations and savors time and space.

Sevens often recall the pleasures of childhood. The good times are remembered and the bad times seem to fade. So long as the mind is free to explore and imagine, the movement into pleasure is a move away from pain. Feeling extended into life and activity, Sevens are the Enneagram's optimists. Everything is all right when you're looking ahead to a good time. Life is OK when the energy starts to run.

Gluttony is a banquet of experience. Stuff the weekly schedule and fill the mind with plans. Disappointments barely surface. Other options look appealing. Suddenly there's a whole new idea. Buoyed by a sense of personal worth, Sevens follow their interests. They go where they're welcomed and gravitate to people who appreciate them. Sustained by feelings of inner worth, they can move through life without much awareness of other people's

pain. People are fascinating, and each day brings its own experience. Attention shifts to the next event, and life moves on.

If entitlement becomes automatic, self-observation stops.
You don't see the over-positive spin on your thinking. You blur
potentials and fact. All you know is that being told what to do
is irritating, that limitations are the product of small-minded
thinking, that rules are annoying and probably unimportant, and
that it feels like dying when your options shrink.

Sevens grow by staying instead of leaving. They grow by
dealing with pain. You have a choice when you've made a commitment and can watch your attention fracture. It helps to stay
for one more minute instead of going away.

They are helped by significants who accept both pleasure
and pain in relating, who notice the needs and value of friends,
who see when interests start to spread, and who set a framework
for emotional depth.

Subtype Focus:

Gluttony Affects Sexual, Social, and Survival Concerns

Fascination in Sexual and One-to-One Relationships

Gluttony for stimulating one-to-one contacts is acted out
with charm. People are a source of endless attraction to Sevens.
The first sparkling hit is the best. There's a rush of initial attraction. Think where this could go! Imagine what it would be like!
"This is it!"

Sexual Sevens can be riveted by brief encounters and magnetized by people's stories. The discovery phase is delightful.
Fresh characters and a brand-new plot. Sevens are outer directed
and can meet people easily. They love new information and are
remarkably nonjudgmental. They're likable. You want to tell
them about yourself. You want to tell them your dreams.

Fascination Sevens fall right into your picture. They're in your story. They're planning. There's click. The immediate intimacy of shared imagination makes it seem as if you're in it together. At the time it doesn't seem like a suggestion. It sounds entirely possible. "You've been to Hawaii? I see that you loved it. Going back? It's a place I'd visit." The possibilities are fabulous. "What's your favorite place on the planet? I'd like to go there." It sounds like fact.

These are the Don Juans and Juanitas of the Enneagram. They are people who materialize from your dreams. Focused on their own opportunities, and how your story fits in with them, Sevens are often unaware of their impact. They expect to be liked. They are sincerely interested, and then it's time to move on. Suggestible Sevens in long-term, monogamous marriages say that they have had to cope with feeling limited by only one relationship. Commitment is the C word, and it's usually associated with pain. "This is it?"

Social Sacrifice

A Seven's group interests often reflect an idealized social order. They sacrifice immediate pleasure to materialize a future dream. They form long-range interests in the cause, the commune, and the church. Gluttony touches the social arena through like-minded affinity groups. Sevens like people who mirror their sense of inner worth, who share the same philosophical ideals, and who enjoy the same activities. It feels good to be around people who like one another. Their goal is to have stimulating company while they pursue the same activities they would choose to do on their own.

Social Sevens see strength in numbers but are also keenly aware of the limitations that people bring to group process. It's hard not to feel martyred when people struggle and blunder. What a waste of time. You can't go solo in a group enterprise, but you wish that you could. Sacrificial Sevens are hostage to their peers.

Equalizing authority is a big social consideration. No leaders and no followers. No one above and no one below. Sevens hate the limitations of rules. They eliminate authority by making everybody the authority. They like an egalitarian power structure, because it guarantees their personal freedom but also because they don't readily empathize with people who have different needs. Sevens do not want to be controlled by other people's ideas and difficulties. They hate to be dragged along on someone else's idea of a good time.

Survival Through a Family of Like-Minded Defenders

Sevens soften their survival fears by forming a chosen family—people who appreciate the same possibilities, friends who share the dream. Sevens feel comforted by having their own positive beliefs reflected back by people who share the same values and sense of pleasure. The like-minded are not the family of birth; they are the trusted few who can be counted on to bring their piece of a perfect future life to fruition. You can turn to friends when your dreams have been shaken. They come to your aid when you feel discouraged. They are defenders of the dream.

Survival Sevens can act like old-fashioned circuit riders. They visit their friends to catch up on news and to see how projects are progressing. They feel secure when the different sectors of a future life plan are flourishing. The like-minded may well have been brought together through their common friendship with the Seven, who was attracted to them because of their place in a collective possibility. Each defender is personally interesting to the Seven, and each could contribute to the vision. A gardener, a traveler, families with children, a doctor, a dancer, a mystic, a priest. Survival-minded Sevens feel reassured when they see the different sectors of a complete life being attended to. They pick up the conversation exactly where you left off months ago, as if no time had passed. There are brainstorms, new twists of information to think about, and a gluttony for positive future visioning and companions on the way.

Focal Issues

Options

The idea is to stay excited and joyous. You have so much to do and think about that boredom rarely sets in. Epicures frequently have long-standing personal interests, like music or running or bowling or chess. Those activities are scheduled or can fill odd moments during the day. The violin comes out or the running shoes go on or a chess problem forms at the back of your mind. You make plans and lists, but not to follow or to do them. The point of it all is to be able to see and have many options.

Multiple options are your insurance against feeling stuck. You do everything you can to ensure freedom of thought and freedom of possibilities. If you must do something unpleasant, you make sure there's something pleasurable to do on the other side. Then you can maintain an optimistic outlook.

Positive Imagining

The imagination is such a powerful instrument that it can set you up for disappointment. In the mind anything is possible. The most beautiful women, the most considerate men. You can bring back treasured memories in a single reverie—a lovely home, a favorite child, and background music, like a movie set. By comparison, reality can be a crushing disappointment. Physical existence just can't match the pleasures of the mind. Consequently when ideas become manifest facts, you feel alarmed at the discrepancy between the ideal and the actual. You can be impatient with a genuine accomplishment. It just isn't as interesting as you thought it was going to be. What's next?

Procrastination

Five, Six, and Seven are the Enneagram's fear types. The hallmarks of a fear type are ambivalence about authority and procrastination. Sevens procrastinate because they take on too much. A good idea will stimulate a tree of mental associations.

The possibilities are endless. There's a welter of spin-off plans. Leading ideas get sidetracked. "Why was this meeting called?" "We're back at the beginning," "I forget."

Procrastination has to do with preferring the shining world of possibilities to the critical glare of fact. A finished project invites commentary and criticism, whereas preliminary ideas can be freely circulated and enjoyed. Force of imagination can compound the problem. Imagination imbues ideas with grandeur. When you're sweating in real time, things always take longer than you ever imagined. Broken equipment, angry competitors, and back pain are never part of the plan.

Self-Referencing

Several types in the Enneagram system have narcissistic tendencies. Eights, for example, could be seen as hard narcissists— "My way or the highway." Sevens are soft narcissists—they go where they can get their way. Both types are self-referencing. They know what they want and are less in touch with the needs of others. Sevens assume that what pleases them would please anyone. How could it be otherwise? This is fun. Anyone in the same position would think so. "They would feel the same way that I do, or at least they would if I could explain." Sevens are often shocked when their actions are called into question. "You don't understand. You weren't there. You would have done the same."

Sevens often think of themselves as sensitive to people's feelings, but the truth is that people who disagree with them seem limited. Sevens are fascinated with whatever takes their interest. Moving from one positive experience to another reinforces the belief that the people around them share their vision. "Someone who loves me would want what I want." If others don't, it's because it wasn't explained properly.

It's initially difficult for Sevens to see how pleasure could be destructive. Pleasure should be idyllic, intimate, supportive, and mutually empowering. If it's not, then the right course of action lies elsewhere. Guilt rarely enters the picture. Positive goodwill stands on its own merit. Whatever is done with love in the heart ought to be OK.

Reframing

Reframing means putting a new frame or context around a static event. The technique can unveil new elements in an old problem and produce vital new directions for action. Reframing can also be used for escape purposes if the context of an agreement is reframed to include loopholes that let you off the hook. An Epicure's point of view on life lends itself to positive reframing. It's a mainstay of their optimistic outlook on life, and the mind-set is well worth considering. I once talked to a Seven about the pollution of San Francisco Bay, and this was his answer:

> I see the butterflies on a trash pile rather than the pile. A trash pile isn't permanent, so I start planning what to do with the garbage. The pile itself becomes instructive, and the message interests me. It's compost. It plays a part in the cycle of creation and destruction. It links butterflies with this conversation, and with humanity and the rest of life. Composting is a task that can rally people; the community could focus here. It's not that garbage has suddenly become sightly, it's that, in my mind, it has become a reason for people to get together.

Entitlement

Sevens follow their interests. Life should be an adventure— "Don't we all deserve a good life?" "I'm here to grow," "Don't we all deserve to learn?" Focused on the sectors of experience that are pleasurable and life giving, they like to be challenged, and they expect to profit from new experience. They are genuinely interested in people who have something to offer, and they reduce their authority by finding a neutral common denominator of interest. "Where have you traveled?" "What sport do you play?" "You seem to have an interest in art." The world seems to provide when you place yourself in hospitable, friendly environments. You learn so much by opening yourself to life. The flaw in this reasoning is the expectation of bounty. Open to life means open to learning and adventure. Sacrifice and pain are simply not of interest.

Avoiding Pain

Sevens commonly describe these techniques for avoiding painful experience: reframing the painful event as a learning experience, making another plan, distracting attention to something pleasant in the environment, or seeing the event as "interesting" and to be entertained for its instructional value. Any reframing, including "this pain is a growth experience," places a painful event in the mind as a teaching, rather than a felt, emotion.

It doesn't feel like avoiding pain to put it on the back burner. Don't dwell on it. We'll deal with it later. This ability to shelve negative experience has its pros and cons. On the positive side, Sevens can raise people's spirits by seeing the positive possibilities of what can be accomplished. They can also forgive more easily than most, because they remember the happier moments. On the negative side, Sevens often refuse to be found wrong or to deal with difficulty.

When pain comes off the back burner, Sevens will usually discuss that single event rather than the whole context of events leading up to the incident or the fact that discussion was long delayed. It's almost impossible to pin Sevens into a "negative discussion" about the way others see their character. Yes, you can spend a few minutes discussing a specific incident, but don't ever try to make a Seven look wrong as a person.

The Con Game

It's important to feel good about yourself, because any questioning of self-worth opens the door to pain. It's easy to support an idealized self-image when you live in the future and in your possibilities. You can easily see yourself as already there instead of just potentially there. Feelings of self-worth can either be legitimately earned or they can be produced by focusing on ideas like "I could do that if I tried" or "I'm almost there."

It's important for Sevens to have relationships that are dedicated to real work. They can be so charming that it's easy to keep life interesting and light. Surface relationships can be a lot more fun than those that demand emotional engagement. A commitment to depth has to produce periods of growth and pain. If you're already "there" as a person, then you have no need to question yourself or to grow psychologically. Growth can just as easily be defined to mean developing new skills or challenging yourself in areas like sports. You love to learn and you are attracted to new experience, but it takes maturity to see that the direction of growth may involve questioning your self-image.

It doesn't seem productive to question a positive outlook. Sevens choose activities that they like and gravitate toward people who find them likable. The superior stance of being there or at least almost there is supported by a positive feedback system that confirms self-worth. It takes a blow to self-image to bring up feelings of inferiority. That blow is typically delivered during a midlife crisis or when fortune smiles on someone else. The game is to keep feeling OK about yourself, but if feelings of inferiority develop, you may attempt to charm and disarm, to rationalize and reframe, and to pass off excuses as justifying explanations. The game can turn into a con game when your idealized self-image is questioned.

Security and Risk

DYNAMICS OF CHANGE FOR POINT SEVEN

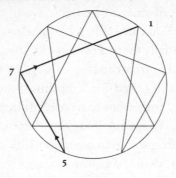

Security

Sevens never "turn into Fives"; rather the stance of withdrawal appears from a Seven-like perspective. Pressed for commitment, Sevens often withdraw into themselves to consider their options. Sevens who are offered the security of a good choice may look contracted and somewhat miserly. Secure life situations can, paradoxically, create a crisis of choice. Even a good choice feels terribly limiting in comparison with all the possibilities of imagination. Sevens never look angrier or more depressed than when they have to make a strategic choice.

Commitment feels like giving away all the other options. To settle for so little feels like a terrible limitation. Five appears when Sevens are pressed to choose. To do so, they have to make the choice their own rather than feeling pressured by someone else's needs. It's a time of quiet and deep self-evaluation, and it commonly appears in midlife, when choices begin to disappear.

The high side of the security point appears when Sevens get to withdraw from sensory overload and from an overstimulated mind. It's a time to center and redirect attention to priorities.

Sevens say that nature, or some other physical setting that can impact the senses, helps turn off monkey mind and usher in the relative quiet and even-mindedness of Five.

Risk

Under pressure, Sevens move to One, which is called Judging Mind in meditation practice. Attention turns toward comparing oneself with others. "Am I better than, or worse than, in comparison with other people?" The Seven version of Judging Mind is centered on deprivation. "John's wife will let him fly around the country, mine won't," "My wife earns money and helps to support us, John's won't." The focus is on enjoyment, on having or not having, rather than the One preoccupation with matters of right versus wrong. Judgments appear with any sense of limitation, and they quickly disappear when Sevens feel satisfied. Seven judgment concerns curtailment of pleasure rather than ethical considerations.

The high side of the risk point produces clarity of purpose and moral dedication. Sevens don't waffle or look for loopholes when they are fully committed to a difficult task. This is actually one of the best positions for Sevens. Things get finished, and perfectly finished. Every *i* gets dotted, every *t* gets crossed, and pleasure comes from the accomplishment of a job well done.

Seven in Love

Living with Sevens

○ *The main problem is getting a Seven to see the problem.*

○ *An ideal mate is someone who adores the Seven and will keep the Seven company while he or she has a good time.*

○ *Sevens want high levels of stimulation, adventure, and multiple options of activity. Because they have great difficulty staying with negative feelings, they'll want to diffuse disagreement and sweeten the situation. "Shouldn't we go to dinner and a show?"*

○ *Sevens want to be with partners who mirror their own high self-image.*

○ *Sevens are pleasant when you admire them. But they'll ridicule or discount you or the situation when they're challenged or placed in an inferior position. They make nice or make fun of.*

○ *Acutely sensitive to boredom and repetition in relationships, Sevens can adopt new interests and maintain a charming lifestyle to keep the spark alive.*

○ *Sevens go with the flow. They want to cycle in and out of encounters with people, to arrive on a high note, to leave with good feelings, to return when the flow brings you back together again.*

○ *Expect Sevens to get angry when the flow is interrupted. They don't want to be brought down by someone of lesser mind.*

○ *Sevens become acutely aware of the limitations when you call for commitment. They can live in committed relationships for decades and still be uneasy with the concept. Long-term commitments are "a process" and an adventure.*

○ *Sevens take a multidimensional approach to intimacy. They'll be fascinated by your various aspects. They'll want to do many different things with you and will support your dreams and activities.*

Intimacy

Sevens are described as upbeat in partnership. They are independent, self-directed people who pursue many interests. Mental lists often come into play. "That's an interesting possibility," "Let's try to fit that in." The list of options is fluid. Priorities can change at a moment's notice. If an activity sags, they can move on quickly. When a project gets boring, it must be the wrong approach. The escape route from difficulty lies in the direction of pleasure.

Sevens have trouble staying with negative emotions. It's almost impossible for them to sit down and feel bad. The mind immediately goes away to a positive option—something pleasurable to move them forward, something interesting on the mental list. It's not important to actually do that item on the list, it's just that the possibility makes them feel better. When their partners insist on discussing negative impact, Sevens feel as if they are being forced to stay with something unpleasant. If they can't get out of it, Sevens can get very angry. "It feels like I'm fighting for my life. My freedom is being taken away. That someone could actually limit me and make me stay and not let me go where I want to go feels like a huge waste of time."

Sevens will typically try to find many different solutions and many different exits before they reach the point of anger. It's hard to pin them into a corner when they're looking for a way out. They're committed to a positive outcome, they're committed to feeling OK about themselves, and they're verbally slippery.

Sevens can bend your mind. It's not that you're wrong— you just don't get it. You're imposing limitations on yourself. Caught with their hand in the cookie jar, they'll accuse you of having a small-minded attitude about those cookies. You haven't considered the larger issues of sustenance and the sweetness of life. Reframed in a broader context, the discussion takes on a more evolved and sophisticated meaning. Once the definition of terms is widened to the true meaning of nourishment, a handful of cookies is going to fall through the cracks.

Young Sevens can define their own reality. They commit themselves to a process but not to specifics of that process. They can reframe fiction to be an appealing fact. They can redefine key words like *authority* in ways that are out of line with their actual meaning. To Sevens, authority may mean "knows something about" rather than "masters in." In this redefined context, beginners are really authorities if they happen to know slightly more than the people around them. Committed to feeling excited and joyous about life, Epicures put a strong positive spin on reality.

Spontaneity is absolutely essential. The adventurous approach involves the option of picking up and trying something new at a moment's notice. They can put themselves in the position of having to make a final decision at the very last moment, not out of irresponsibility, but because they treasure the possibility of changing their minds. Intimacy often involves the spontaneity of shared imagination. We're in each other's future, brainstorming the possibilities of a full life together.

Strategic choices may be difficult. Choosing means leaving other options behind. Choice reveals that you can't have it all, and choice jeopardizes future contentment. An Epicure's mind fixates on the disappearing option. "Think of what that possibility might have led to," "I just lost a piece of the dream." Being caught between options can be paralyzing, and Sevens often procrastinate about final decisions. A choice doesn't feel final, even when you're on the plane.

Choices that limit options are met with grudging acceptance. The Seven will be angry or depressed. Anger means pointing the finger. "It's your fault that I feel bad," "You got me into this mess." Being limited feels demeaning. It feels like being trapped. Sevens see limitations when they feel troubled. "Someone's holding me back." Accusations are a statement of struggle. The Seven is in pain. One more minute could open the door to failure. This choice could lead to permanent stress.

Young Sevens want to experience everything. Many do not reach their capacity until later in life. Dissatisfaction can be a good sign. "I'm repeating myself," "I've done this before," "I know how this story turns out." Crisis commonly surrounds the decision to commit themselves with real dedication. A "sober" or single-minded Seven still has the pleasant diversions of a complex mind but can also remain steadfast during the limiting and painful phases of commitment. They can be helped to deepen their relationships by significants who note the signs of rationalized avoidance, who bring attention back to the present, and who welcome so-called negative emotions when they are appropriate.

The Signals Sevens Send

Positive Signals

Playful and positive. Imaginative and inventive. Daily tasks are infused with pleasure; a fascinating approach to life. Significants are buoyed by optimistic visions of the future and encouraged to accept their full potential. Sevens can make the ordinary seem extravagant and bountiful. Simple walks in the park can become points of convergence for the cycles of nature and the seasons. The laughter of a child expands through time and space.

Negative Signals

Sevens' narcissistic preoccupation with personal agendas and pleasures makes them seem uncaring or unreliable. You begin to feel inferior to a Seven. The Seven is open-minded and spontaneous, but you're narrow-minded and attached. Anger, depression, and other so-called negative emotions mark you as a lesser being; if you were more evolved, you wouldn't feel that way. When Sevens feel threatened, they take a superior stance. Your opinions are a mark of lesser vision.

Mixed Messages

A multioptional lifestyle sends many messages. Sevens may make apparently opposing commitments, but, focused on the similarity of the intention underlying those options, they feel internally consistent. For example, if young Sevens fall in love and then feel that it's time to leave, they may feel no guilt in doing so. The next love is also part of the process of learning how to love, so both love affairs are directed by the same high purpose. Because both affairs serve the same purpose, in a way they are both the same. No one was abandoned and no one was chosen, because they both sprang from the same good intention; and because no one was chosen or abandoned, the options of picking up to leave or sitting down to stay are still open, and it's still quite possible to reengage the first affair if that interest should develop again.

The message to significants is "I'm here when I want to be, and I will go without feeling bad." The way to cope with this is to focus on the permanent needs of the couple, such as raising a family or sharing a deep common interest. Attention will always cycle in and out of connection, but Sevens will be loyal to a genuine commitment.

Inner Signals

Sevens say that it's difficult to tell the difference between a genuine direction and a tangent. They get caught between options and find it difficult to decide which route to follow. Attention shifts dramatically to what would have to be sacrificed by choosing one option over the others. The decision gets stuck. Think of the possibilities that would have to be jettisoned. The future seems bleak when you throw away part of the dream. You might have prematurely discarded a good option. The thoughts say: "I'm being pushed into this. This is for someone else's benefit. I'm being held back." An outsider will see paralysis of action, an inability to move ahead. The feelings say: "I may be losing the opportunity of a lifetime. Think of the sacrifice. I have to wait on this." Sevens can be confused about the way in which people react to their indecision. Don't they see that the context could change? Sevens have a hard time discarding any viable option. The thoughts say: "People should be committed to the process of their own development. You have to be true to yourself. People are always growing and changing. The specifics are incidental."

Seven at Work

In the Workplace

° *Offers a sweet solution to authority problems. Wants to equalize authority, which can come out either as a fair peer arrangement or as a situation engineered to ensure that no one is allowed to* give orders. If no one gives orders, then people get to do as they please.

○ Can become insistent about impractical ideas and inefficient approaches. Prefers ideas and theory to implementation. Will open a task to new approaches rather than face routine.

○ Goes through the cracks rather than confronts. An antiauthoritarian stance that gets around the rules by broadening the definition of terms.

○ Excellent performer in open-ended projects that do not move into routine. Networks, plans, synthesizes ideas and approaches. Aligns the project with other areas of interest.

○ Has an inner sense of capability and high self-worth. Measures self against others to keep this sense of self alive. "Am I superior or inferior?" "Do I stand above or below?" "Am I on top of this project, or will it get me down?" Positive self-image can be punctured by negative feedback.

○ Has a tendency to bend people's minds in order to get their support. Reframes objections. Puffs the possibilities. Puts forward a lucid idea without considering backup. Offers convincing generalities with lots of little loopholes. Offers suggestions that sound like promises.

○ Delightful to work with. Can be forgiving and creative during hard times. The office person who wins the popularity poll.

Leadership Style

Their strength lies in being able to correlate different kinds of information into a coherent pattern. Seven leaders are strong on positive future visioning. They see points of coordination in different systems and bring data together in highly original ways. Successful Sevens are often found in professions that depend on ingenuity, invention, and thinking ahead of the pack.

Often verbal and convincing, they can voice the aspirations of those who are involved in a project and rally idealistic support for their goals. They are at their best in a fast-paced, quickly changing environment that depends on planning and the synthesizing of data. Best used in the early phases of a project, they can think and act quickly under pressure. These are planners rather than implementers. Quick-change artists and idea people. They typically have several projects going at the same time or are active in several aspects of a single effort. Sevens are people who like to read more than one book at the same time. A book for every room in the house.

Decision making can be chaotic. The Seven leader will be most effective at the planning stage and will do well to delegate immediately after the plan is positioned. It's best to relieve Sevens of repetitious responsibilities. Easily bored, they may change their minds or go off on tangents. Suddenly the priorities shift, and staff has to pick up the pieces. If you work for a Seven, be prepared for scheduling changes that do not seem related to business needs. There may be indefinite or conflicting directions and a lack of supervision. A crisis occurs and the Seven leader goes on vacation.

Unless they are informed, Sevens may assume that things are moving ahead. They can also make the bearer of bad news guilty. They really want someone else to make the ideas happen and can be quite willing to find fault when they are trapped by difficulty. Sevens find it hard to see their own mistakes. Supported by an idealized sense of themselves, they feel hampered by other people's limitations. The plan looked flawless. If it went astray, then someone who carried out the plan must have blundered. Rather than see their own part in a failure, Sevens rationalize, reinterpret, recontext, and reframe. The reworked version of what really happened will definitely sound better.

Managers may have to wing it. Success is going to depend on steady follow-through and on terminating impractical directions. A manager's own personality type may become more pronounced, as she or he tries to find solid ground in a Seven's unpredictable environment. In the absence of a clear signal from leadership, a One manager can become more rigid, a Two more other referenced, a Three more assertive, and so on.

Classic Conflicts

Short-term gains achieved by escaping limits invite the long-term pain of missed opportunities—no pain, no gain. Sevens' desire to equalize authority and their unwillingness to accept their actual level of ability, can create conflicts with other people. Sevens can find themselves repeating the same mistakes. "I've been here before." They have a tendency to avoid conflict and especially to avert criticism that could tarnish self-image.

The classic conflict involves exaggerated, promissory plans that terminate in poor follow-through. The results are rationalized. The results are really OK. The results were what we should have expected in the first place. Sevens run into trouble in the nitty-gritty of detail. They are accused of not carrying their share of the load.

Conflict Resolution

See Part III, "The Directory of Relationships," for tips on conflict resolution between Sevens and others.

Employee Participation

Sevens can be a lot of fun to work with. They love the process of working and the mutual respect and involvement that occurs during a project. Product can be less important than process, because most of the excitement comes from seeing the directions that arise from a single idea. What authority does or doesn't say may be of secondary importance. Sevens like to hear a co-worker say, "That was great. You did a great job and I really enjoyed working with you." What really matters is peer acceptance.

These are people who look to themselves for approval. They are self-motivated, especially in the early and exciting stages of a project. There will be a trend toward equalizing authority, which can come out as difficulty understanding organizational limits. It's easy enough to go through the cracks or around the authority or to seem compliant while actually bending the rules.

Equalizing authority is a natural social expression of the Seven's desire for unlimited freedom. "Someone who's the same as me won't tell me what to do," "Someone who's the same as me will want the same things that I want." Like-minded people will be the Seven's independent, emotionally autonomous mirrors, and they won't inhibit the Seven's actions.

Sevens are quick studies. They like fast-paced, interesting tasks that allow them to pull in many options for action. They like to work from a general scheme, and they can learn on their feet through experience. They tend to be less effective in routine, predictable environments.

Team Building

A Seven on the team is going to ensure creative ideas and an awareness of new developments in the field. They keep the flow of information coming. They stay on top of possible applications from new technology and related areas of interest. They like to act as liaisons with other groups doing similar work. Sevens are good representatives. They can put the product in a positive light and are sincerely interested in enrolling the goodwill of others.

They move quickly from idea to action and can be examples of useful risk taking. They like new options, new directions, and a novel approach. They can see the possibilities in ways that are not apparent to more literal thinkers, and they are usually drawn to experimentation. They are useful in consultation with other sectors of a project, often finding an ingenious way around apparent obstacles. Difficulties typically appear when the Seven becomes insistent about an untenable approach and obstinate about routine. The completion phases of a project may signal the onset of several brilliant new possibilities.

Difficulties with team players typically center on the "unreal" insistence that possibilities are actually responsible lines of investigation and on the Seven's habit of splitting attention between several different interests. It helps for the Seven to feel comfortable enough to voice difficulties and to ask for assistance. You can tell that Epicures are becoming committed to the effort when they begin to complain, when they fight for what they believe in, and when they do not have to be the life of the party.

8

Eight ⬡ *The Boss*

	PERSONALITY BIAS	ESSENCE QUALITIES
MENTAL	*vengeance*	*truth*
EMOTIONAL	*lust (excess)*	*innocence*

SUBTYPE FOCUS	
POSSESSION/SURRENDER	sexual
SEEKING FRIENDSHIP	social
SATISFACTORY SURVIVAL	self-survival

The Eight Bias

Worldview

The world is an unjust place. I defend the innocent.

Spiritual Path

Eights' preoccupation with justice points to a search for *truth*. If undivided truth prevailed, control would be unnecessary. From a spiritual perspective, the child saw how truth could be distorted and *innocence* betrayed. Eights were once such innocents, vulnerable and without protection. The Eight child found that innocence was seen as weakness, that the strong dominated the weak, and that good things in life went to those who took control. The inevitable confrontation fueled *vengeance* and mobilized power, energy, and *lust* for the satisfaction of needs. Eights confuse their own subjective needs with objective truth. Maintaining a personal power base is confused with protective acts and mimics serving the objective truth. It is a child's attempt both to ensure fair treatment and to protect a connection to the undivided truth of essence.

Concerns

- *Concerned about justice and fair use of power. Avoids weakness.*
- *Controls possessions and personal space. Controls the territory.*
- *Excess is a life stance. Has easy access to energy and anger.*
- *Lusts for life. Has an appetite for satisfaction. "If something's good, let's go for it."*
- *Lust is acted out in three key areas of life:*
  POSSESSION/SURRENDER *tactics in one-to-one relationships.*
  FRIENDSHIP *in social relating.*
  SATISFACTORY SURVIVAL *in self-preservation.*
- *"My way or the highway." Finds it hard to take in other points of view.*
- *Intolerance of differences masks a fear of being disadvantaged.*
- *Larger than life—too much, too loud, too many.*
- *Sets boundaries. Sees others as controlling and acts in self-defense.*
- *Sees rules as controlling. Tests limits and consequences.*
- *Confuses self-serving versions of the truth with objective justice.*
- *Softer emotions and dependency needs appear when it's safe.*
- *Has an all-or-nothing style of attention, with a focus on extremes. Either fair or not fair, warrior or wimp. No middle ground.*
- *This style of attention can lead to a denial of personal weakness, or:*
  - *An ability to exercise appropriate force in the service of others.*

Personality Bias

We all enter the Eight perspective when we see the truth with complete certainty and act accordingly. A force of power and fortitude wells up that cannot be compromised. The mind stops questioning. Emotions are swept away in the forward rush of action. We find ourselves in motion before we know what we will do, and we hear ourselves speaking before we know what we will say. It's not a matter of courage. When the truth is at stake, we couldn't draw back if we tried.

Eights were respected for strength in childhood. Assertion was valued over compliance; leaders were needed, rather than rules. It seemed natural to stand up for the truth, to protect the innocent, to mobilize against authorities who took advantage of innocence.

When respect is earned through power, you learn to control your feelings. You can't be vulnerable and invincible at the same time. You can't be concerned about other people's needs while they seem intent on denying needs of your own. You can't deal with tenderness or fear or regret when you're on the line of battle. The prime objective is to gain control of the territory and to get there first.

Lust develops from a battle mentality. You know what you stand for, you know who stands against you, and you learn to summon reserves of energy to protect your position. Believing in the justice of your cause, you test the loyalty of comrades and protect your perimeter, your supplies, and your information. If the war is protracted, you entrench in a small, secure area, conserve your strength, and prepare to blast out at a moment's notice. You develop a full-bore approach to life. The energy switch is either on or off. When life is interesting, the energy comes on. A larger-than-life demand to be seen, heard, paid attention to. An escalating desire to get a piece of the action. An urgency to get some more of whatever's vital and good, and to get it first.

If the top-dog approach works well, you can forget your impact on people. You forget to consult, to inform, or to get consent. You are aware only of your need, and you'll use everything at your disposal to meet that need. You don't see that you've become overbearing or demanding. All you know is that you hate being deprived, that objections sound stupid, and that obstacles are incidental. The energy comes on when you think of being disadvantaged, and the energy brings speed, cleverness, and the strength of will. If this habit becomes automatic, self-observation stops. The results are predictable. You're the only one left on the field after the war is won.

Eights grow by questioning their ideas of justice, by hearing the other side of the story, by learning to wait. You have a choice when you feel secure enough to relax your own position and can watch yourself assume control by escalating the action.

Eights are helped by significants who stick to their own version of the truth, who hold ground under fire, who deal fairly, and who model the use of power in appropriate service to others.

Subtype Focus:

Lust (Excess) Affects Sexual, Social, and Survival Behavior

Possession/Surrender in Sexual and One-to-One Relationships

Eights act out lust in the one-to-one arena by a possessive attitude toward intimates and friends. Every aspect of intimate life cries out for exploration. All the secrets have to be shared. Eights want to know all. They want to advise, to be consulted, and to take part in decisions. They often take charge of a loved one's life. Sexual subtype Eights are one of the highest energy positions on the diagram. A combination of physical verve and an inclination toward domination makes them lusty in love and commanding in business. They are quick to stave off what they perceive to be encroachment on their private territories. Other people perceive them as relentless competitors.

Part of the pleasure of one-to-one relationships involves a control struggle. It's the struggle that's interesting. Winning may erase interest. The control struggle infuses relationships with vital energy and offers a way to test an associate's strength, honesty, and protective nature—all of which are fundamental to establishing commitment. Possession denotes access to the body, mind, and spirit of the mate whenever the occasion arises. Surrender involves fully possessing the loyalty and affections of a mate who will not put you at a disadvantage. When you are completely certain about someone's intentions toward you, it is finally safe to surrender control.

Social Friendship

Good times are magnified by good friends, those who can hold their ground and assert themselves honorably. Friendship is a way of relating through tested alliances; when someone is on your side, you can trust them to hear you out. Friends are a safe channel of information. You don't feel controlled when they point out your blind spots; they will not take advantage of your weaknesses; and they will not manipulate or misuse private information. Eights let their feelings out within a close circle. They can try out different viewpoints by entertaining a friend's opinion. Friendship is based on mutual regard and common purpose. You can let your guard down with the people you trust.

Eights are often loners and can be seen as testy and aggressive. Social invitations and an affinity group are therefore especially welcome. They can conduct a full-scale, ongoing quest for friendship. Their time is booked, they commandeer the volleyball court, and they have legendary stamina for carousing. They enjoy marathon talks and deep discussions about important matters, the content of which varies from baseball to Zen, depending on their tastes. The common factor in the lust for friendship has to do with camaraderie. You can go full out because you've tested each other's limits. You know you'll be protected, that whatever gets said is in the spirit of friendship, and you want to take care of your friends in return. You are generous with time and attention, because with friends it's safe to kick back, say anything, open the throttle, and let the energy rise.

Satisfactory Survival in the Area of Self-Survival

Survival Eights exercise territorial control over space, personal belongings, and a steady supply of creature comforts. It is important to have a good security system for the house, to establish a neighborhood watch, and to check every window and door before you go to sleep. These are the survivalists: people who secure a personal bunker against invasion, who want a place that can't be gotten to and possessions that can't be touched. Satisfaction depends on having the simple, uncomplicated necessities of life. Just enough is the most satisfying. The security of familiar surroundings, of knowing that your supper, your cat, and your current book are within easy reach. You can relax when you feel physically satisfied.

Survivalists hunker down in a small, protected space. They fear being deprived, lacking necessities, being out in the rain alone. They therefore develop an elaborate supply system so they'll never be in need: food clubs, a competent laundry, a hardware store that stocks absolutely everything. It's not important to hoard, but when survival lust comes on, they know exactly where to go for ten kinds of pizza, interesting talk, and a movie marathon. It's actually more fun if friends stop at the video rental store on their way over. Then a survival Eight will only have to talk until pizza is delivered and the first video goes on.

The fear of deprivation fosters a preoccupation with comfort. "Where is my pen? My favorite saucepan?" "Where did I leave my comfortable shoes?" A mislaid shoe is upsetting. The discomfort might escalate. If someone else has moved the shoes, it can feel like invasion, a domino effect where unpredictable events could escalate. If it's the shoes now, what next? You don't want your shoes put back in the closet or your mail sorted because something important might get lost in the shuffle. To ensure comfort you carry several layers of clothing in case the temperature changes and collect information about eateries when entering new territory. You get your itinerary and maps together and triple check your tickets and hotel so you'll never be stranded.

Focal Issues

Innocence

Innocence is a word for one of the qualities of higher being. It describes an open and undefended awareness that lies outside the boundaries of personality. When children reach out for contact, they go openly toward what pleases them; they sense what they need and know how much they want of it and when they've had enough.

Like all children, Eights were once in a state of innocence, vulnerable to everything and without a means of control. They quickly found it necessary to close down, to be savvy, aggressive, to be a good opponent, and to learn to oppose.

Anger

Anger is the emotion of choice. It flares quickly and is easily expressed. It's difficult to have a relationship with someone whom you can't push up against. Anybody interesting enough to excite you will be a target, because when the energy comes up, any minor incident can trigger a full-scale reaction. It takes years for you to understand your impact, to see what happens on the other side when people feel your anger. You are relieved and pleased to have expressed the truth as you see it; meanwhile the effects on others are devastating. Anger makes you feel better, but it can ruin your partnerships.

Eights feel defeated if they can't say what they think. It stays on your mind and you mentally write letters until you can voice your opinion. It's important to have the matter out on the table, not necessarily to win, but because you feel as if you're compromising the truth if something isn't said. You are on the defensive about being abused or taken advantage of. When someone cuts you off on the freeway or beats down your price in business, you take it personally. It might escalate. It has to be dealt with right now, before things get out of control. Once expressed, the anger dissipates. Everything has been said, and your attention turns elsewhere. Eights can pick up the friendship right after a fight. "Where did everyone go?"

Control

If you think that the truth comes out in a fight, you are going to be fascinated by the ways people handle aggression. Are they sneaky? Do they withhold? Do they act behind your back? Are they fair? Do they punish? Do they manipulate? Do they collapse? All of these qualities of information are vital to someone who has to know the consequences of surrendering power. If you see the world as an unjust place, you have to be certain about what to expect before you let your guard down. Eights are therefore far more interested in predicting how people conduct themselves in a fight than they are in winning an argument. They sometimes conduct a small "stress test" to see how people act under pressure. If they pass, then it's safe to be friends.

Boundaries

Eights are awake to aggressive ploys. Manipulation, passive aggression, and withholding information seem to be just as aggressive as honest anger. Eights meet covert hostility with direct confrontation. The resulting conflict looks horrifying to people who have contained their anger through other defenses, leading to the misperception that Eights are inherently violent. Most

Eights are distressed to realize that they appear to be physically dangerous. They look blank when people flinch just because they're yelling. "Why? I've never hit anybody!" By learning to modify their impact on others, Eights can build trust. A soft approach and a quiet voice work wonders because they show that anger can be controlled. Partners can help Eights by being willing to call them on their tactics. "Fight fair," "Don't punish." Set limits. "This is hurting me." Above all, agree to talk the matter through. Set the time. "I will come back and talk in an hour."

Excess

Lust is a craving for satisfaction. When something desirable comes to mind, Eights are not particularly aware of the consequences of what they say or do, nor are they sensitive to feedback from other people. Instead they are preoccupied by securing control of a source of gratification and forestalling potential frustration. Once the goal is set, obstacles seem minimal. Their task is to get what they want in the most expedient way possible.

It's actually difficult to feel pleasure when the body is too stimulated. A numbing of sensation occurs, coupled with an overcharged desire. Eights are famous for their high pain threshold and for not feeling the effects of a stimulant until they wind up under the table.

When an appetite for satisfaction takes off, substitutes seem boring. If you want something, then why not go for it? When desire takes hold, there's no limit until you're over the limit and find yourself recovering from a full-blown binge. Eights often say that they feel in control during an excess attack—driving too fast, eating too much, making intense demands on lovers and friends. Part of the fun is seeing how far you can go without being affected, how much you can take without caving in, how long you can go without feeling the strain. It follows that when you have energy to burn, and derive a sense of power from controlling your reactions, you'll need a lot of a good thing to let the pleasure sink in.

Self-Forgetting

A Boss hardly ever goes first. You would think that with all that access to energy, and all that engagement with justice and truth, they would be likely to take the initiative. But Eights are far more likely to be reactive than proactive. They more commonly find themselves challenging a known position, refining an established procedure, or improving an existing idea. Centered on the core point of Nine, the 8-9-1 triad is the Enneagram's place of self-forgetting. Eights lose priorities through excessive behavior and express anger to defend what they want. Nines replace their own priorities by merging with many points of view and express their anger indirectly. Ones replace priorities with "the correct thing to do" and recognize their anger only when convinced that they are right.

Eights' emotional needs often stem from the deeper, more submissive depths of their nature. In the interests of survival Eights can suppress their softer feelings, which makes it difficult to recognize their own needs. They find it easy to speak to an opinion, to offer protection, and to stand up for justice but difficult to remember what really matters.

Justice

"Do Eights take justice into their own hands?" is a commonly asked question in Enneagram classes. "Will they seek revenge?" The revenge motive has to do with evening the score so that Eights don't feel abused or taken advantage of. You may have lost the first round, but the game's not over yet when you're planning to even the score. It probably won't be acted out, but it feels good to think that you could. Compromise can feel like showing weakness, like showing your throat to your enemies. Compromise feels like inviting further abuse. Eights can be mollified by a face-saving solution that saves pride on both sides. If you back Eights into a corner, they will have thoughts of getting back, but an honorable opponent does not invite their retaliation. Set clear rules and consequences. Do not humiliate the loser. Be fair.

Revenge has an active and a passive component. Eights taking passive revenge may doctor information or withhold useful information from an adversary. It's not necessary that the adversary know that revenge has been taken. The idea is to even the score. If Eights take active revenge, they will usually rationalize it as a form of justice. "They took advantage of me. They acted unfairly and ought to be punished."

Security and Risk

DYNAMICS OF CHANGE FOR POINT EIGHT

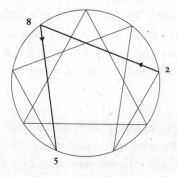

Security

Trust usually develops through toe-to-toe confrontations, and once trust is gained, Eights' defenses relax. It's safe to go toward people who accept them, and safe to develop their submissive side. Eights can be deeply touched by people who care enough to reach out. Accustomed to being loners, they are inwardly grateful when someone is attracted to them. Bosses who are secure enough to shift to the Giver strategy want to be of help. They can be excessively generous, romantic, and attentive; and they can quite suddenly withdraw support. This aggressive giving and taking makes it quite clear who's in control.

Eights are overtly possessive and secretly sentimental. They compete openly for sex and attention but often withdraw when something really matters. There's a close connection between anger and lust. The actual sensation of anger is pleasant, powerful, and cleansing. You know where you stand, your mind is clear, and you feel trustful because everything has been said. It's an intimate moment that can easily turn sexual. Eights like the contact of fighting, sex, and having adventures with people they love. The trick is to keep the horizon big enough to engage an Eight's attention. When the point of attention is a mutual interest, the survival strategy of moving against people naturally softens into cooperation. Eights make friends of their intimates. It's very common for their friendships to outlast initial sexual attraction.

The high side of Two manifests as going toward people in support rather than aggression. Eights who move to the low side of Two manipulate their partners' affections through strategic generosity. Giving is used to control someone else's life.

Risk

The first signs of stress show an increase of the basic Eight defenses. When these are inadequate over time, Eights shift to the more withdrawn and private stance of Five. When opposition fails to produce results, Eights tend to move away. A closed door, very little communication, and a period of introspection. When the issue is manageable again, Eights will emerge, often without explanation. Like Fives, Eights feel no great desire to discuss the content of private thinking. Many Eights say that they love the Five position—hours alone, often devoted to intellectual pursuits. Some Eights could easily pass for Fives simply because they do not fit the stereotype of an extroverted, gutsy Boss. They look more like contained intellectuals who prefer to be left alone.

The high side of Five produces self-awareness, Eights who observe themselves and others, looking for hidden motives and meaning in their own actions. Self-aware Eights are very powerful because they can test their insights in real life. Moving easily into contact, they have the advantage of interacting with people in a way that most Fives do not. The low side of Five is simply psychological denial acted out in a physical way. A shutdown. Lots of wall staring without any insight. Waiting out a bad time until it's less risky.

Eight in Love

Living with Eights

° *Eights like partners who are independent and strong, and they enjoy fighting, sex, and adventure as ways of making contact. Because Eights experience deep joy in sexuality, they are willing to match the partner's intensity.*

° *Their lust for life and desire for stimulation mean late hours, heavy entertainment, and binges. Too much, too loud, too many. If something's good then they want more of it.*

° *Eights' tendency toward excess, all or nothing, all work and no play, or all play and nothing gets done, may burden the partner with the task of keeping the different areas of life in balance.*

° *Episodes of strict control followed by disobedience are Eights' demonstrations of power. First they make the rules, then they break them to stimulate interest when boredom sets in.*

° *Eights need control and will therefore want to predict your intentions.*

° *Their fear of being controlled displaces into the territorial control of schedules, personal objects, and physical space.*

° *Because Eights cannot tolerate ambiguity or lack of information, your small oversights may be perceived as a betrayal of trust. They may feel that you've overlooked their options or left them out of a decision.*

° *When affected by softer emotions, can deny feelings by withdrawal, by claiming boredom, or by beginning a process of self-blame for past misdeeds.*

° *Eights rarely allow themselves to be hurt by others. If you hurt them emotionally, they will want to manipulate circumstances in order to get back. Thoughts of revenge will forestall their feelings of vulnerability.*

° *Partners will find Eights to be rallying points during difficulty, towers of strength in dangerous times.*

Intimacy

Eights' main concern is personal freedom. They hate to feel controlled. They're already encumbered by too many rules, too many bureaucrats, and too many brain-dead drivers on the road. Traffic is a small instance of Eights' inner predicament. When the energy's up, they want to be weaving through the cars and barreling down the highway, but there they are, strapped in by a seatbelt and stuck in a mindless morass.

Much of their seemingly dominant behavior is in fact an effort to make sure nobody dominates them. They fear that someone in power will seize the advantage, so Eights refuse to be denied and will not be coerced into obedience. They place extreme value on independence in relationships. Eights can work until they drop to support a loved one's interests, especially when they're not told that they have to. But being told, or having love conditioned on good behavior, provokes resistance. Rules were made to be broken. Even rules that serve their own interests are hard to obey because control feels coercive.

Convinced that dependency can make them powerless, Eights can deny soft feelings. They can mistake tenderness for dependency. Sex can be moving without being intimate. Compromise can be seen as a weakness, and acceptance equated with fear. Softer feelings are a real disadvantage if you believe that they open you to manipulation and loss of control. Eights are extremely direct. You know what they want because they tell you, and you know what they like because they invite you along. Happy Eights bring the party with them. They are generous with time, talk, and energy, and can definitely hang out for a long time. They naturally assume that other types of people have the same energy level and appreciation for pleasure. "This looks good, let's go for it," "This feels good, let's do it again." This aggressive appetite for satisfaction produces an illusion of control. When you're on to something good, it feels like you could go forever and you tend to forget more sensitive matters.

Eights are also gut-based people who feel and act in their own interests, often without considering the consequences. They respond to their own needs. "Doesn't everyone act from self-interest?" "People should look out for themselves." You have to question Eights bluntly because they seldom question their own motives. Focused on personal goals, they may not be aware of your feelings. They can be inadvertently selfish, simply because their habit of mind moves toward their own goals with little attention given to people's reactions.

Bored Eights are trouble. They will not submit to a dull evening, they won't be charmed into cooperating, and they won't be bribed to be good. Be prepared. The evening can slide from stony silence to stories that polarize the guests. Eights nudge you publicly; they will slouch and yawn and point to their watches. "Can't we leave yet?" The solution lies in independence. You can't drag them along, but if the door is left open Eights join when they want to. Do your own thing.

Relating to Eights has to include confrontation. They have to test your limits, they have to know that it's safe to surrender control. Anger can erupt about trivial issues, because conflict is often a test of power. Fights can be a way to draw closer. Are you fair? Are you truthful? Do you cave in or stand up for yourself? These questions are of great interest to someone who is afraid of emotional dependency. Eights can invigorate their relationships through conflict, activity, adventure, or sex; but they are inexperienced with softer feelings. Like Twos, Eights in relationship are sensitive to rejection. They can be helped to deal with softer feelings by significants who are bluntly honest, who can stand firm in an argument, and who do not manipulate, withhold information, or make their love contingent on good behavior.

The Signals Eights Send

Positive Signals

Eights can offer incredible support to their loved ones. They want to empower people, to test and to trust; to trust you enough to become a part of their lives. They bring excitement and intensity to a relationship. They invite you to the life force, to plug into the juice. They move forward into contact and are willing to explore the domains of pleasure and satisfaction. They are courageous, determined, and persistent, fair minded, truthful, straightforward, and unpretentious. What you see is what you get.

Negative Signals

They defend their excessive behavior by denial and anger, often with a counteraccusation to the significant—"I'm not a controlling person, but you are," "I don't make trouble, but you do." Eights can take over through intimidation and intrusion. They can transgress boundaries when their misdirected sense of justice leads to violations of rights and property. Eights can punish the people they love, and when denial lifts, they also punish themselves without mercy. Blame turns inward when they see their own role in their difficulties.

Mixed Messages

A Boss can seem like two people: a tough persona that covers a soft heart. The Eight–Two crossbrace of the diagram indicates a conflict between going against people and wanting to move toward them. An emotional Giver is protected by the domineering Boss.

Eights in relationship want to protect the people they love; they also need to protect themselves against those tender feelings. It feels threatening to trust, to become dependent, to care about what people think. The intolerance for weakness supports an obsessive need to right wrongs, to protect loved ones, and to even the score. Their partners in love and work are often beset with confusion. "Are you loving or angry?" "Are you with me or against me?" The truth of the matter is, both.

Eights can be utterly open and sensitive to others when the denial of soft emotions lifts. But, easily startled into vigilance, they can be punitive and uncaring toward those same people at the least hint of being disadvantaged.

Inner Signals

Like Nines, Eights' energy follows the principle of inertia: A body at rest tends to stay at rest and a body in motion tends to stay in motion. Inertia for Eights is an all-or-nothing phenomenon. The switch is either on or off. When a physical red alert comes on, they find it hard to discriminate between action and anger and almost impossible to stop and question their own certainty. It doesn't seem intemperate to act immediately. Inaction would be foolish.

Afraid of being disadvantaged, Eights tend to act prematurely. They have practically no tolerance for ambiguity, mixed messages, or vague feelings of uneasiness. An uneasy feeling signals an immediate search for the source of distress. The rising signals are anger and blame. The thoughts say: "I feel uneasy. Who's the responsible party?" The feelings say: "Why should I have to feel uncomfortable? This feels unfair."

Without realizing it, Eights become provocative in attempting to discover why they feel threatened. The thoughts say: "What are you hiding from me? What are you thinking? Let's test you out!" A fight lessens the tension immediately. Energy is discharged, discomfort vanishes, and the mind can rest. The aftermath is shocking. Eights see themselves as having clarified the tension but find themselves facing the consequences.

The inner task is to recognize blame as a signal of vulnerability. Blame feels strong and certain, the opposite of weakness or doubt. The thoughts say: "Admit what you've done. Take responsibility and we can continue our friendship." The feelings say: "Come on strong. This may escalate. Don't show your throat." It seems to go against instinct for Eights to consider, "I might be making an assumption. Don't act prematurely. It's safe to wait." It takes maturity for Eights to reduce their impact and to question their assumptions when the mind begins to blame.

Eight at Work

In the Workplace

° *Controls the office hierarchy. Sets limits to ensure self-protection. Who's in charge? Is the leadership fair?*

° *May see compromise as weakness.*

° *Will assume leadership. The focus of attention goes to others who are strong contenders for control of the project, the firm, the loyalty of followers. Respects honest leadership. Likes a worthy opponent.*

° *Unwittingly polarizes people into factions. Wants to know where everyone stands. Will provoke to get clear answers.*

° *Concerned about justice and protection.*

° *Anger is direct. No hidden agenda. Holds no grudges if anger is expressed.*

° *"My way or the highway." Sees own opinion as the correct approach.*

° *Enforces rules that support personal advantage. Bends the rules that don't.*

° *Demands to be fully informed. Changes in details can stimulate concern about being manipulated.*

Leadership Style

Eight and Three are the dominant American business styles. Eights are direct and assertive. What you see is what you get. Much in demand as spearhead figures, they are highly valued during a go-ahead phase of operations. We all line up behind a Boss when we need a plan of battle, especially during times of expansion. We want them to lead the assault for a turnaround, rally the troops for a takeover, and hit the opposition as hard as they can. Highly effective when feelings are polarized, Eights can deny their submissive side long enough to get the job done. Armored against the anger of their opponents, they can calculate consequences in terms of real damage rather than damage to fragile egos. Secure in their leadership, they can be dynamic public figures. They prefer to centralize power rather than to delegate. There is likely to be a top-down reorganization plan that includes clearing out the deadwood, hiring and firing, and a general show of strength. They commonly become protective of a hand-picked cadre of "my people."

Bosses may be less effective leaders during a period of consolidation. Daily management is far less exciting than open competition, and the energy that so effectively matches emergency conditions can turn to trouble making. Without a constructive outlet, Eight leaders can lose interest. It's best to redirect their attention to useful projects before trouble hits. High-powered Eights with energy to burn often invest minor incidents with great importance. They can become passionate about a minor breach, and meddle in office politics. The emotional fuel that brought them into power has to go somewhere and is likely to be vented through trivia. When Eights displace anger, minor incidents can flare up to major proportions, and small matters of procedure can trigger a full-scale war.

Self-disclosure is the key to working with Eights. You don't have to agree with their opinions, but you must make your views known. Do not soften or doctor information for fear of drawing fire. Do not withhold. Do not act on your own initiative. Consult whenever you're in doubt. Constant reportage is critical to building trust with Eights. It's OK to bring bad news to this leader. Bad news can be handled, but no news is death. Sensitive to being disadvantaged, they are primed to see the seeds of betrayal in an innocent oversight.

Bosses hate to be blindsided by poor information. They will feel set up by procedural breakdowns. "Is this the tip of the iceberg?" "I want the facts." Blame is the first line of defense. "Who's responsible for this?" "I want a report." Blame shifts easily to contempt. Inaction on your part looks like admission of guilt. Bosses want to be sure that the problem won't escalate. If you're blamed, assume the burden of responsibility. A Boss is going to be interested in the way that you handle yourself under fire. Have your position well documented. Eights definitely check details. Do not make excuses or shift blame. Take the spotlight. Put your explanation on the table. Define the perimeters of the problem so the Boss knows it won't spread. State your recommendations and append a direct report system, so that the Boss can personally check on progress.

Eights find it difficult to delegate, and when they do, they keep an eagle eye on the results. Delegation is difficult because the Boss wants control. You may not know you're being tested when they observe your work. If you do a piece well, then the next piece may be forthcoming. They will observe your ability to handle all the pieces before you're given control.

No news is good news. You hear immediately if there's a problem. No news means stay on course. Eights are sparing with compliments and praise. A spot check that does not generate a memo signals full steam ahead. You may blast past a major objective without realizing that you've succeeded. You'll be likely to hear the good news secondhand. Approval is sparse: "We're doing better" may mean we've gone over the top.

Classic Conflicts

Unfair and *unjust* are buzzwords. It's important to tell the difference between a personal gripe and whether the angry Eight is an early warning sign of widespread organizational discontent. Eights must take action when they feel threatened. They are often perceived as troublemakers when they are simply spokespersons for other people's battles. Eights often voice the dissatisfaction of people who are unwilling to go public and are sometimes quite unfairly cast in the role of a crank. Having little interest in delicacy of presentation, they can be seen as aggressive complainers, which often damages the credibility of the issues they raise.

Ambiguity and mixed messages are red flags to Eights. They will push for clarity and not stop until they get it. The classic conflict is fight technique. Eights fight to win. If they sense ambiguity or deceit, Eights can move into character assasination. Why discuss goals when you're dealing with wimps and liars? A disgruntled Eight will go over your head and manipulate every avenue of influence. "Who do you report to? What's the grievance procedure? Who do you know that I know? I'll inform them about this!" Eights escalate when you expect them to concede. To them compromise feels like capitulation. Mediation is for wimps. They want a clear avenue of rewards and punishments and will probably push the limit to see if you enforce the consequences. "It looks like I lost but I got concessions" is a key phrase.

Conflict Resolution

See Part III, "The Directory of Relationships," for mediation tips between Eights and others.

Employee Participation

Eights are really the boss even though you have the title, and that sense of entitlement either makes or breaks their relationships. Developed Eights are natural leaders, but their immature counterparts are workplace disasters. The focus will be on the power structure. Who has authority, and will they be fair? Highly practical in their approach, Eights are real-world people who think in terms of livelihood, security, and benefits. They want a fair exchange for time and labor and offer strong support for systems they deem fair. A mature approach shows Eights marshaling protection for the innocents of the organization, which often produces good communication with management. The same maneuver can also become a platform for personal power.

Immature Eights will be antiauthoritarian. They lead by intimidation and are focused on inequalities of status, money, and power. Their desire to dominate produces counterattack, leading to potential trouble with authorities. They have illusions of invincibility. Young Eights are prone to excess and self-abuse, which in the workplace can translate to a denial of physical limits; this can eventually exhaust or damage them. Self-defeating behavior can impair their productivity. Don't count on cooperation from a disgruntled employee. They will work the system to their own advantage. Whatever works: a slowdown, a walkout, a petition, a strike. Do not be ambiguous in dealing with recalcitrant Eights. To be respected, you must set limits and you must enforce penalties. This is one position on the Enneagram where boundaries and penalties can improve participation.

Team Building

Bosses can be great players. They are dedicated competitors and work until they drop when they're interested. They embrace difficulty rather than shun it and often wind up in key positions simply by force of personal presence. Eights have a notoriously low tolerance for meetings. "Another form for us to deal with?" "Get those administrators off their butts! Make them earn their pay!" Eights control details when they feel out of control on the larger issues. State your business, give your opinion, and get out. Paradoxically they can be terribly hurt if they're left out of a social event. They may not come, but they must be invited. The social relationships among team members are a big deal for Eights. The easiest route is a weekly Thank God It's Friday lunch. Something to look forward to. For Eights, friendship equals safety.

Give them a designated area to control. These are solo performers rather than cooperators, and they take over without realizing it. They keep going until someone says stop. Set clear boundaries of responsibility. Eights are cooperative when there's no threat to their own sphere of influence, but they are highly territorial if space, equipment, or information has to be shared. They will have to adapt to the consultations and constant information flow of a team. Eights in action head for the goal following a predetermined plan of action. They do not shift easily once they are in motion. It's a dead-ahead approach, with very little attention given to new developments once the plan is conceived.

The trick to getting cooperation is a clear statement of objectives, incentives, and who gets the credit. Eights are excellent support players in a fair arena. Do not place them at a disadvantage or make them prove themselves.

Eights can appear to be aggressively invested in an idea when in fact they're just thinking out loud. They like high-decibel discussion, which can appear to be argumentative. Types that retract from anger are likely to back down or, worse yet, confer behind the Eight's back. Sincerely interested Eights have a way of trying to be helpful that covers their own vulnerability. They prod and urge. A show of interest is an excellent sign. Eights won't bring their enthusiasm to the table unless they're invested.

9

Nine ◈ The Mediator

	PERSONALITY BIAS	ESSENCE QUALITIES
MENTAL	*indolence (self-forgetting)*	love
EMOTIONAL	*sloth (laziness)*	right action
	SUBTYPE FOCUS	
	UNION	sexual
	PARTICIPATION	social
	APPETITE	self-survival

The Nine Bias

Worldview

The world won't value my efforts. Stay comfortable. Keep the peace.

Spiritual Path

Babies "are" essence, in that their awareness is permeated by *love*, or the unconditional pleasure of pure being. When personality formed, attention turned to momentary comforts, and the child became *indolent* or forgetful of the self-perpetuating pleasure of essence. *Sloth* is an overaccommodation, a desire to remain comfortable and undisturbed. It feels more comfortable to go along with others than to oppose them. Sloth is a failure to initiate, to take *right action* toward the essential features of life. Nines avoid conflict and merge with the agendas of others, which mimics the comfort of union with the environment and all beings.

Concerns

- *Maintains the comfort of neutrality. Avoids anger and conflict.*
- *Replaces essential needs with unessential substitutes.*
- *Ambivalent about personal decisions. "Do I agree or disagree?" Sees all sides of the question. Personal decisions are hard. Decisions are easy when not personally loaded, for example, emergency action or political opinions.*
- *Postpones loaded decisions by repeating a familiar solution. Acts through habit. "Seems like there's endless time. Why act now?"*
- *Inaction or sloth. Goes along with others. Follows the program. Finds it hard to initiate change. It's easier to know what you don't want than what you do.*
- *Acts out sloth in three key areas of life:*
    UNION—*the desire to merge in one-to-one relationships.*
    PARTICIPATION *in social groups, organizations. Affiliations.*
    APPETITE *for material interests.*
- *Can't say no. Finds it hard to separate, hard to be the one to go.*
- *Damps physical energy and anger. Diverts energy to trivia. Has delayed reaction time for anger. Passive aggression. Anger equals separation.*
- *Controls by going stubborn. Waits it out.*
- *Pays attention to other people's agendas, which leads to:*
    - *Difficulty in forming a personal position, but also develops:*
    - *The ability to recognize and support what is essential to other people's lives.*

Personality Bias

We all enter the Nine perspective when we feel inseparable. Boundaries go down. Someone else's life becomes the motive for our own. Once merged, it feels like one skin and a single being. We have energy for a partner's agenda. Their interests feel vital.

Their opinions seem valid. We feel enthusiastic about their life, which has become the focus of our own.

Nines felt overlooked in childhood. They blended in and learned to merge with other people's lives. They shelved their own agenda so they wouldn't be forgotten; it was either agree and lose a position or oppose and be left behind. A tension develops between wanting to comply so as to be loved and wanting to defy, to assert your independence. The question is, "Do I agree and go along, or disagree and create conflict?" Agreement feels like giving in, but it's hard to say no. You are merged with someone else's life, and choice no longer matters. You can see the worth of their position more easily than your own.

Sloth means being lazy about life. You can see all sides of a question, which overwhelms your own agenda. Decisions are difficult. Conflicting opinions appear to have equal merit. Attention cycles from the central issue to secondary matters. You get sidetracked to chores and backlogs of unfinished business. Your energy gets diverted from the essential task of the day. Your momentum slows. Without your realizing it, a holding pattern develops. Energy for primary goals gets siphoned off to secondary pursuits.

If shelving your own agenda becomes automatic, self-observation stops. You forget yourself. You become absorbed with what other people are thinking. Life is overlaid with other people's ideas. Unfinished business mounts when you don't pay attention, and it's hard to remember what's important when there's so much else in the way.

Nines grow by paying attention, by structuring their own agenda, by staying on track. You have a choice when you can watch yourself absorbing a new position. You can learn to separate and pay attention to yourself.

They are helped by significants who encourage separate goals, who provide solid reinforcement for progress, and who remind them of deeply held purposes that can be attained only by paying attention to themselves. Because Nines merge with others, partners can help them to express a position and to move through the discomfort of separating and having to choose for oneself.

Subtype Focus:

Sloth (Laziness) Affects Sexual, Social, and Survival Attitudes

Union in Sexual and One-to-One Relationships

Sexual subtype Nines want total merger. A beloved figure becomes the focalizer for life. Union is the sense of a mutual existence rather than being a separate individual. Nines can absorb another's life into their own.

Feelings of being overlooked and disregarded vanish in a psychologically undivided state. It's as if awareness can stretch when you think in the way that someone else might be thinking and try to enter the other's point of view. Thoughts and feelings seem synonymous rather than separate. Identities merge. Moments of "we-ness," "We are the same being," "Who has this face?"

Union provides focus and energy. Lazy about their own direction, Nines' partners can focalize effort and become the reason for being. Now the Nine's is a mutual life rather than a separate existence. Nines can be swept along by other people's enthusiasm and can merge with a partner's agenda without conscious awareness. All they know is that they hate feeling discounted, that they like being connected, that they can see equal value in many different perspectives and feel better when they do.

Social Participation

In the area of social interaction, participating in group activities can be a comforting way to feel included and loved. It can also be the place of greatest laziness for a social Nine, because the energy that could be spent in meeting personal agendas is shunted instead to taking part in social activities.

High-energy feelings are molded and contained by familiar group activity. A defined activity presents goals, procedures, and an ongoing timetable that demand predictable expenditures of energy. You know what you're going to do, how long it's going to last, and who will be there with you. You gravitate toward groups with meetings and agendas that allow members to participate at a low level of energy or to take responsibility and leadership when they have energy to burn. Social Nines are inclined to join groups and to attend on a regular basis without making a full inner commitment. The question stays open. "Do I agree or disagree?" "Do I belong here or not?" "Do I like this or not?" Ambivalence is constant.

Self-Survival Appetite

For Nines attention readily becomes fixated on secondary sources of gratification. You neglect real needs in favor of substitutes, most commonly food, travel, TV, or collecting. Cutting off the substitute feels threatening because it represents the crux of a holding pattern that expends surplus energy in a predictable way. You develop a strong appetite for the substitute when there is time and energy for your personal agenda.

All Nines have a tendency to replace essential goals with unessential substitutes, but Appetite Nines can develop a voracious attachment to the replacement. Survival substitutes are an automatic source of comfort and a temporary replacement for love. You find immediate relief in zoning out on food or mystery novels. You easily become a couch potato, vegging out with your newspaper, chips, and beer. Security-minded Nines don't realize that they're shelving a personal agenda when they're gripped by an appetite like shopping fever. The rising interest in indulging an appetite doesn't feel lazy. It feels exhilarating. Something interesting to do that pulls you out of ambivalence, even though it means a lack of commitment to yourself.

Focal Issues

Comfort

Nines like the inseparable feeling of merger. They don't like a divisive influence, and they tend to act as mediators rather than taking sides. They are attracted to familiar, known, and pre-dictable ways of doing things, because attention is free to wander when there's no pressure. Nines like to reflect. They like to muse and consider things. They like time off and the pleasure of a day without goals. It's described as liking to cruise on energy rather than having to mobilize for action, liking to expend energy in a comfortable way. A great deal of energy can be extremely disori-enting, unless it's called forth for a predictable activity. Energy wakes you up. For Nines, that knowing can be uncomfortable. Things get worse when you know what you're missing. It doesn't hurt when your foot falls asleep, but it really stings when you start to walk again.

Avoiding conflict is part of a larger pattern of diverting en-ergy from important matters. Nines are clever about energy man-agement. They don't have to be couch potatoes to contain their energy. High-powered activities are comfortable as long as there's no juice left to fuel the search for a personal agenda.

Acceptance

Everybody wants to be accepted, but Nines need to have their position spelled out, underscored, and directly acknowl-edged. When your own position feels tenuous, and another's po-sition is stronger, you look to that person to validate your own. You see yourself as accepting people as they are. The actuality is that if you merge with another's agenda, you'll blame that person when things don't go well. "This was your idea, not mine. I just went along." Because you are willing to go along with others, you expect similar acceptance in return. It takes great effort for you to shape a personal agenda, and when it does happen, you expect other people to accept it. "I took you as you are. Now you should do the same." It feels unfair to you that the same merger and sup-port that you offer is not reciprocated.

A Mediator's newly discovered priority may sound small and uncertain to the average listener, but it sounds loud and defi-nite to the Nine. A partner will have to listen carefully when an agenda does emerge, because the Nine is counting on the partner's acceptance in order to proceed.

Saga

Nines are famous for making 360-degree changes in life without prior notice. Others don't know the steps and stages along the way and then suddenly the Nine does something completely different. The reason is that a decision has to be fully formed before you can bring it out with enough strength to withstand counterargument. Once it's strong enough, you can become stubbornly devoted to your point of view, resisting any contradiction. Once you're sure, you hold on tight. Sometimes you filibuster to make certain you're heard. The Nine version of a filibuster is to tell your story at great length while tuning out the opposition. You tell sagas to hold ground while not letting anyone disrupt your concentration. You have found a position and want to tell others about it at great length.

Another way to divert opposition is to bring in as much detail and support as possible. You can give all of the details without distinguishing between triviality and the salient points under discussion. The central point seems equal to the details, as if you can't get to the point. It's true. The point may be a point of potential controversy. It's delicate, and you need to justify it at length.

Decision Making

You have no difficulty deciding about unloaded "neutral" matters, such as political preferences or practical needs; but a personal decision entails separating your thinking from everybody else's agenda. Obsessive thinking about personal decisions is a hallmark of the type. "Should I, or shouldn't I?" "What do you think?" Knowing what you want can feel isolating and threatening rather than energizing. Acting for yourself is unfamiliar territory. It brings up loneliness and disinterest.

You mull a decision from all possible points of view. When the sides seem equal, there's no reason to act. It's easier to be presented with a choice such as "Which one don't you want?" It's much easier to know what you don't want than what you do want. A starting point can be discovered by process of elimination, which can then be reinforced with a structure and approval.

Acting from Habit

Nines often fall into a kind of ritualistic routine. Familiar routes are comforting because you know just how much energy to let into your system, and the outcome is predictable. Conflict, separation, and discomfort are minimized, and the decision-making quandary is dominated by the needs of the routine. Once a groove has been established, it's difficult to move a Nine out of acting habitually. To help Nines change, set a priority list and begin slowly to build a routine that supports the new priority. Partners should offer unconditional support for the new program. Personal presence and encouragement helps. If possible, do the activity together until the habit sets. If Nines lose focus, remind them that this was their own priority. They may have forgotten. Reestablish their enthusiasm by being enthusiastic yourself. If they lose track of themselves, just start over again without recrimination. Mediators absorb positive regard and believe in themselves when others believe in them.

Cos

"Are Nines codependent?" is a commonly asked question. Like Twos, they identify with others' needs more strongly than their own. It seems to me that anyone can become codependent, but the way in which the dependency is acted out varies according to type. The same external behavior can be produced from a variety of different motivations. If a Nine is codependent, it takes the form of merging with another's life and abandoning oneself, but many Nines act out seemingly codependent merger while remaining internally separate and uncommitted. We must look to individual motivation and take each case on its own merits.

Passive Aggression

Conflict is frightening, and Mediators will do everything possible to avoid open anger. Conflict leads to opposition, separation, and aggression, all of which create discomfort. Their anger is expressed in indirect and passive ways. Slowing down, sidetracking into other projects, tuning out, outwaiting the enemy, and going stubborn are common tactics. The actual awareness of anger is usually delayed until long after the provocation took place. Nines are famous for waking up to the fact that they're angry days after the actual event. Going stubborn is preferable to open anger. Feeling coerced or angry, Nines can literally sit down, tune out, and do nothing. No argument. No threats. No physical withdrawal. Only a deafening, stubborn silence to inform you that things will not go your way.

Nine stubbornness can be provocative. The partner explodes, which follows the pattern of making other people the active agent in relationship. By not doing, when action is clearly expected, Nines goad others into looking foolish or exploding in frustration. When others want action and someone holds out on them or forgets or fails to initiate, others quite correctly perceive this as highly aggressive. Partners want to know where the Nine stands. Are they in this relationship or not? If it bothers them enough, the partners are likely to feel insulted and are also likely to hear, "But I didn't do anything."

Inertia

The principle of inertia states that a physical body at rest tends to stay at rest, and a body in motion tends to stay in motion. Nines say that they need a jump start to get rolling, and that once they get into gear they're unstoppable. A good structure, coupled with a good example and a high-energy environment, guarantees participation. The least effective method is to leave Nines on their own to initiate their personal priorities.

Once in gear, Nines need to pay attention. They can lose awareness of themselves in what externally looks like highly productive activity and internally feels like falling asleep. At the high-activity end of the inertia principle, Nines can perform intricate and complicated maneuvers while remaining oblivious to their real priorities. What that means is that just enough energy is sectioned off to accomplish a difficult task, while attention spreads to secondary considerations. The net effect is to get a lot done while managing to divert energy and attention from yourself. If a Nine is asked how it felt to be a winner, she or he may answer, "I don't know, because I wasn't there at the time." The trick for a Nine is to stay attentive while at rest and to keep paying attention when the action begins to roll. In this way you can build a tempo in which you remain in touch with yourself.

Nine Ambivalence/Six Doubt

Ambivalence about a personal commitment can look like Six doubt from an outsider's position. The availability of so many viewpoints makes it hard to activate any one of them. The inside story heard from Nines is more a sense of being overwhelmed with input, seeing the many sides of a situation and the different contexts in which the same situation could be played out. Not only do Nines see all sides of an argument, they also see how context affects a decision. Even a clear-cut argument can change when the context expands to include more information. There's also the time element to consider. Everything changes with time. How can you come to a conclusion when all these inputs have merit? You can see all the points on one side of an argument and how they intermesh with all the points on the other side. How can you take sides when you're operating from a global perspective? Everything seems so interrelated with everything else that it feels like taking sides on the surface of a ball rather than standing on one side or the other of a clearly drawn line of opinion.

Six doubt also produces procrastination, but the placement of attention is quite different. An idea is proposed and then doubted. Attention shifts from belief to doubt and back to belief again. It's more like questioning the validity of a single idea rather than seeing the equality of different ideas. Finding the significant position isn't the problem for Sixes, but they have massive doubts about the feasibility and the potential hazards of implementing something significant. Sixes take a definite position but become vastly preoccupied about who or what might interfere with their activities and the potential negative consequences of taking action. Implementation is the main point of concern. Will an authority be upset? Will the idea be attacked? In a doubt attack, attention goes to the contrary, or opposite, point of view, as if to anticipate the objections and interference that Sixes expect to encounter from other people. In the devil's advocate stance, the mind proposes an idea and then takes the opposite, or contradictory, point of view. The Six mind is contradictory rather than ambivalent in the Nine sense of weighing the different sides of a question.

Security and Risk

DYNAMICS OF CHANGE FOR POINT NINE

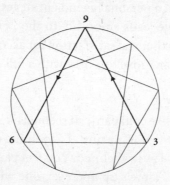

Security

The antidotes to laziness are high-level energetic habits. Secure Nines are usually established in a productive routine, and they enjoy the same degree of acceptance and regard as any hardworking Three. The agenda is similar to Three—recognition for performance and task—but Nines in their security also want to be loved for themselves. They can tell the difference between task-related attention and real acceptance. They want acceptance but go about earning that acceptance through product and image. The energy is up, they are operating on the high end of the inertia principle, and they like success. Nines in Three can develop real powers of concentration for a personal agenda rather than going on automatic at high speed. Secure Nines are in a good position to tell the difference between automatic habit and an authentic choice about how to live life. At the low side of the security point, Nines are still subject to the start-stop syndrome of inertia, where they depend on deadlines and other people's agendas to ensure the completion of goals. The image may be in place, but internally it's a struggle to keep going. The world at large wouldn't notice, but Nines feel the stress of constantly fighting low energy and having to reset, restart, and reengage when attention wanders.

Nines can work incredibly long hours in an efficient manner to meet a deadline, but with the completion of the task, energies slow and eventually halt. To activate the high side of Three, it helps to implement a personal agenda in stages, so that the completion of one stage leads smoothly to the next. The beauty of Nines in security is that real satisfaction for accomplishments can take place. Nines can move to Three with a full set of feelings.

Risk

This can feel like cold panic. It seemed like there was endless time, but suddenly you're staring at a looming deadline. There is no time, and you're overwhelmed. You feel panicky about alienating other people. Time's up and everyone will be angry. Nines typically report this as a feeling of paralysis. There is so much to do that you can't do anything. Under severe pressure, Nines stop and cannot move. The low side of stress is frozen panic.

The usual stressors are deadlines and having to oppose people openly. It's so easy to identify with the other side that you lose your own position over and over again. So you don't confront, and you lose more time and get more paralyzed. The usual buffers of distraction don't work. This can be a dangerous place. A kind of inactive, armchair depression where attention is immersed in a television set or rerunning the problem situation mentally. Externally Nines may look comfortable; inside they're numbed out. Any small encouragement and an offer to help them initiate first steps can break a depression cycle.

In depression, obsessive thinking centers on a worst-case scenario. Nines become afraid of consequences and blame themselves for inaction. Blame easily shifts to others. Nines feel victimized; it's authority's fault. They were taken advantage of by more aggressive people. Someone else should be blamed. Blame and rising emotion can be turned to advantage if it allows real values to emerge. Nines know exactly what they don't want when they're in stress. A real agenda can be set. Sometimes Nines will act for themselves and their own interests against the will of others when they are afraid, rather than diverting, distracting, or diffusing their attention. Fear gives them access to the single-pointed focus of the Six.

The best feature of stress for Nines is that they find their anger, and that charge of anger can be redirected to constructive purposes. The energy is there to be transformed to its higher opposite, which is faith in oneself and the ability to carry on alone.

Nine in Love

Living with Nines

° *Once a Nine merges with you it is hard to separate. Relationships can continue for years beyond the natural stopping point. Nines find it hard to give up memories of old relationships so that new ones can develop.*

- *You'll find that Nines divert attention from feelings by becoming preoccupied with unessentials. They search for alternatives to fore-stall arguments. They are often laconic and uncommunicative about what they really feel: "Let the unspoken remain unsaid."*

- *Nines retreat into habitual patterns and trivial concerns ("lots of little things to do") rather than really engaging in the relation-ship. Energy spreads to the mechanics of living together: the house repairs, the mortgage rate. As a Nine's partner, you will find yourself being the active agent for change.*

- *The Nine will say back what you want to hear. This does not imply that the Nine agrees with you. It's hard for Nines to say no because your needs sound louder than their own.*

- *Nines fantasize about merging with ideal partners and being swept into a new life. The flip side of merging with the lives of others is that the Nine blames you when things go wrong.*

- *Relationships deepen when the Nine can merge with you without any loss of personal identity.*

Intimacy

Nines can know other people's wishes more clearly than their own. It's easy to step into someone else's shoes, and to see through their eyes, but difficult to decide for yourself. A personal position is fragile when it's so easy to take on other points of view. "Why do things my way rather than your way?" "Look at the similarities be-tween them both." Decisions seem arbitrary. Why choose when each opposing opinion has its own validity? By weighing each side so carefully, Mediators can lose a clear sense of their own position.

Having a position means having to defend it. Is it worth the effort? Is a fragile position worth the risk of alienating the people you love and feeling separated from their interests? It's easier to keep the peace. Time slips by if you're not focused on your own essential priorities. Seems like there's plenty of time when you're not engaged in critical work. Deadlines and the needs of family members create a structure for action. Their agendas set the pri-orities, and deadlines ensure a wake-up call.

Participation may not indicate commitment. From the outside it may look like Nines support the program, but internally they can be going through the motions while remaining uncommitted. Without the counterforce of a strong personal position, Nines move along in the flow of activity because they see no reason not to. It's important for partners to draw out the extent of a Nine's actual interest, because it's all too easy to look agreeable, to say back something acceptably neutral, and to be carried along on someone else's enthusiasm. When they're in your presence, Nines can be genuinely buoyed by your eagerness. They merge with your intensity and may indeed be attracted to your interests, confusing them with their own. The truth of the matter may be different when they're alone, and the momentum dies without your vitality.

Nine indecisiveness can be a challenge for partners who want leadership. Decision making can become obsessive. "Should I, or shouldn't I?" "Will I, or won't I?" Attention spreads to all sides of the question until the sides are intermeshed, so no side can be taken. Nines often have the feeling that they fall into goals rather than make choices. They fell into their career or their livelihood or the place where they live. They have a sense of "this is happening to me" rather than "I choose." It's not usually effective to force the Nine to choose, but it does help when a partner activates his or her own direction without requiring the Nine to join in. Do your own thing. You can draw Nines into activity, but you can't make them go first. You can help them most by setting the example of being a good self-starter. Oddly, Nines can assert their agenda in ways that are hidden even from themselves. They may not know what they want, but they know what they don't want when they're uncomfortable. They complain, without realizing how they chart a direction by process of elimination. "Not that, not that" is a path toward clarifying real goals, without having to know exactly where you're headed.

Embedding in a familiar activity is another way to eliminate choice. Nines can set up a high-powered routine that takes time and attention to maintain and eliminates decision making. When you're up early and immediately into a structured schedule, there's no time to consider new directions. Nines can go on autopilot at high speed and finish a complex task without really being present. You do well to put decision making on a timetable, sandwiched between structured, familiar activities, so the energy doesn't die when you ask yourself what you want.

Paradoxically, Mediators resist help in decision making. They can seem poised in ambivalence. Comfortably certain about being uncertain. Sitting on the fence seems like a definite base of operations. Mediators can appreciate many positions without sacrificing their own independence. Actually taking a position disrupts the equilibrium that keeps discomfort and conflict at bay.

When Nines feel coerced, they go stubborn. When they feel pushed to make a decision, they control through nonaction. It's very difficult to move planted, stubborn Nines, especially if they tune you out. The message is: "I've gone along with you as far as I can. This was your idea not mine. Now I don't like it, and it's your fault." The subtext reads: "I'm merged with you. Come up with something I like." Mediators have great difficulty in separating their awareness from someone they love. They can fear separation and being completely on their own. There is a fine line between merging with the life of another and feeling that your own life has been overlooked. It's a close call between the desire to be inseparable from another and feeling discounted as an individual. When Nines merge with the life of another, they can feel chronically submerged, as if their private opinions are muffled by louder voices. The most intimate task of relating to them has to do with supporting decisions that come from their own being and allowing their choices to become their own.

See Part III, "The Directory of Relationships," for interactions between Nines and others in intimate life.

The Signals Nines Send

Positive Signals

You'll experience Nines supporting the lives of others as their own. They are caring and attentive, often aware of what is essentially good about other people. Giving, compromising, adaptive, and receptive. Highly productive and happy when on track. Welcoming a safe structure. A bulwark in other people's lives. Able to offer nonjudgmental regard.

Negative Signals

Nines often seem passive aggressive and stubborn, as missing the point, or detached, even out of it. Their dispersion of energy and focus makes it look like "everything" is equally important, which makes you feel unimportant. Nines will seem to be in agreement when they may not be. They want to keep things comfortable, to give what's familiar, which may not be what you really need. You'll see them space-out or move into substitutes for real needs: TV, food, habits that drain energy and slow the relationship down.

Mixed Messages

Nines develop secondary interests as a way of burying their own priorities. Therefore when they appear to be in full agreement with you, they may just be involved in a peripheral interest or not wanting to cause trouble and out of touch with what they really want. Nines manifest an inherent self-depreciation in losing focus on their own priorities. They may act as if others' interests are their own. The mixed message is outer compliance coupled with deep inner anger over missed opportunities. The overt message is "It's not important." The covert message is "I'm angry about being overlooked." You can help Nines by setting boundaries on your own interests and helping Nines to refocus on their own needs.

Inner Signals

Nines can become confused by having to choose between alternatives. They get pulled into other people's lives and then have to extricate themselves. They may initially go along and later resist. They feel overinfluenced and have a hard time saying no. The thoughts say: "I can see what she wants and why she wants it," "I can see why he dislikes that and why it doesn't work for him." It's hard to find a position that's truly your own when a position and its opposite both make sense. You get caught in the middle. You see all sides of an argument and don't have a clear position yourself. You want predictability and a safe structure; to keep life comfortable and easy. You resist change. The thoughts say: "Blend in. Don't make waves. This will pass." You have a tendency to suppress energy and anger, which delays decision making. It's hard to get too enthusiastic without coming dangerously close to taking a stand and getting angry in your own defense. The thoughts say: "It's not worth it. Wait it out. The right time will come." It helps for significants to realize that time is passing, that real needs are not being met, and to meet with Nines on a regular basis to remind them about their priorities.

Nine at Work

In the Workplace

- Relaxes in the absence of friction. Wants things to feel comfortable and to run without hassle. Wants the "job family" to get along. Has a deep desire to have good feelings on the job, between authority and employee.

- Flourishes in conditions of positive support, but avoids self-promotions. Wants recognition but will not ask.

- Likes procedures, lines of command, and rewards to be well defined. Likes to adjust own energy output to a predictable set of guidelines. No sudden surprises, please.

- Can go on automatic and produce a great deal of work. Suspends awareness of own agenda while following routine.

○ *Energized by a productive routine and other people's enthusiasm for projects.*

○ *Wants a structure to support decisions. Doesn't like to make decisions. Goes by the book; keeps spontaneous decision making at a minimum.*

○ *Cautionary in taking risks. Feels safer in known routes. Goes with what has worked in the past. Avoids risks that raise hopes, for fear of disappointment.*

○ *Forestalls a decision by gathering information. Puts off essentials while the unessentials get done. Strategic use of deadlines produces magnificent last-minute saves.*

○ *Feels overwhelmed with too much to do. Finds it hard to focus on a business priority when items of lesser importance seem like equally pressing concerns.*

○ *Often ambivalent about authority. Has difficulty setting priorities and getting going, but is stubborn about taking directions from others.*

○ *First expresses anger on the job covertly by ignoring the problem or shifting blame to the structure, to mismanagement, to other people at work.*

Leadership Style

Nine leaders can get torn between different points of view and may examine alternatives at great length, missing the opportunity for precise directive leadership. Goals are global rather than specific, because the specifics tend to conflict with each other. One department's needs may conflict with another's, so Nines have a tendency to listen overlong, to gather too much information, and to apportion a little bit to everybody. Reports will come in from every part of the big picture, and these factions will war for position if leadership doesn't narrow the vision.

Wanting a comprehensive picture, Nines are unwilling to fill in others until the plan is complete. Nine leaders assume that others comprehend the global perspective, and they may be distressed to discover that employees have assumed a private, self-interested course of action. Nines are imprecise in specifying the ways in which a plan is to be carried out.

Nine leaders will want recommendations from every sector. Big-picture thinking will either be a deterrent to moving swiftly or produce a comprehensive overview in which every sector of the project is well accounted for. Nine leaders do not move quickly, and once a workable solution is in place they tend to want to repeat the known.

Conflict is very difficult. Nines would rather fill the breach than harass an employee or face a fight. Consequently they remove themselves from difficulty and do not exert clarity of direction exactly when it is most needed. If it looks like a fight, Nines may try evasive action, which weakens their position and opens them to accusations of selling out or compromising the integrity of the work. This style works best with self-motivated employees who do not require a great deal of direction, those who can work within general guidelines and fill in the specifics for themselves. It does not work well for people who require clarity and precision or when the situation demands quick shifts and immediate decisions.

The energy can die for new directions. There will be energy for routine implementation and a known course of action. It's a trade-off between risking the unknown and having to deal with the hassle of change. This is a common mentality underlying service organizations such as utility companies and the United States Postal Service. It's a style of leadership that's appropriate for the long haul. Administrative levels have a lot of this quality of energy. The strategy is to apportion a little bit to everybody and strive for consensus.

Classic Conflicts

There are typically two phases of conflict. The first is marked by ambivalence, and the second by stubborn noncommunication. In the first phase, it's hard to know where Nines stand. Which side are they on? They seem to take too long to examine the various sides of the question. In the meantime, the various factions involved feel unheard and unattended to. In the absence of accurate information from the Nine, people feel discounted and set against each other. It seems that whoever gets the Nine's ear gets heard, and that factions have to vie for attention. People push Nines for definition. "Which position are you committed to? And when will you decide?"

Abhorring conflict, Mediators inadvertently create it by withholding information during the decision-making phase. Nine leaders are famous for not filling people in while they ponder, and for delivering the final decision without explanation or comment. Bad news may seem to come out of the blue without warning. It may seem less conflictual to send pink slips in the mail without comment rather than to face a series of difficult meetings to explain why those slips are necessary. Others often complain about feeling unheeded. They want to know if the Nine is hiding something or why the Nine won't communicate. It's as if, by not saying anything, Nines hope to avoid saying no. The nonaction strategy is infuriating to other participants, who feel both neglected and angry because they feel manipulated into taking the active, aggressive force in discussions.

The second phase of conflict shows a Nine digging in. This is when passive aggressive tactics are likely to emerge. A classic Nine tactic involves slowing down, fulfilling only the bare requirements of a job description. The sense is: "No one will listen anyway, so why bother?" or "I'll do only as much as I'm paid for." Once they take a position, they refuse to budge. If Nines can't decide which options to discard and which to support, then the position taken and defended will be "I want it all. No compromise." Commitment requires so much effort that any change seems impossible. A stubborn Nine is very slow and very angry, which the others involved construe as selfish and uncompromising.

Stubborn Nines can be willing to entrench in an unresolved conflict and outwait the opposite, sometimes for years.

Conflict Resolution

See Part III, "The Directory of Relationships," for tips on
mediation between Nines and others.

Employee Participation

Nines respond to structure. They like environments that
provide clear incentives and rewards. Sensitive to being overlooked, and easily overshadowed by self-promoting, high-profile
types, they look to a fair structure for support. They may not want
to compete or to call attention to themselves, therefore they gravitate to systems that allow them to coast on known procedures
until they decide that they want to move ahead. Nines can take
risks, make decisions, and be creative within the parameters of an
organizational system far more easily than they can attend to
their own personal priorities. It's important for them to see the
opportunity for advancement, although they may not take advantage of it immediately.

Nines take on the shape of their environment. They inter-
nalize the climate of opinions, satisfactions, and frustrations of
their fellow workers. If the climate is upbeat, it's easy for Mediators to absorb that quality of the group culture. They are likely to
merge with dissatisfaction as well. Conflict is particularly disruptive. Nines can react to unspoken emotional cross fire in their
immediate environment without realizing how much of their attention is drawn to ruminating about the sides of a controversy.
Mediators are attracted to a benign work environment. They prefer to merge with the immediate milieu rather than to carve out
personal niches for themselves.

Mediators may be ambivalent about authority. They both
want structure and security but are also stubborn about being
told what to do. The solution lies in good systems and a fair struc-

ture that can be internalized. Structure serves as a rudder to help Nines steer through the storm of conflicting opinions, and there's no reason for opposition if the structure is fair. Nines are usually agreeable in the workplace if their opinions are heard.

Team Building

Nines are natural team players as long as conflict is minimal. They take great pride in a group victory and can feel another player's triumph as their own. It's important that the team realize is dependency on all the players. Nines will back a star as long as the star is quick to recognize that team effort really won the game. Merged with the ambitions and aspirations of others, Nines can shoot for very high goals and surpass themselves in a group. They often produce more creatively and effectively on a team than as an individual contributor. Mediators can also serve as a project's glue. They are steady during difficult times because they can stick to routine under pressure.

They become confused in the midst of conflict or diverging opinions. Their natural mediation capacity usually emerges, and they become sounding boards for others players' ideas. Striving for harmony, Nines will begin to report the unifying facets of opinion to the different warring factions. They may in fact become the hub of negotiations when the factions find that their own best interests are being relayed to "difficult" members of the team. It would be well to sound out the Nine on a team when difficulties arise. The Nine will probably be in a position to sense the threads of agreement between differing positions.

It's difficult for Nines to simply chose a position and move on. They want consensus. If negotiations falter, Nines can become deeply discouraged. They will still be in close touch with all the different players, but instead of seeing points of unity, they now notice points of disagreement. It helps for a third party to consult Nines about solutions. They can produce a fountain of information when they are sought out by a neutral, safe observer.

III

The Directory of Relationships

The Directory of Relationships

Compassionate Understanding

TWO OF THE MOST commonly asked questions about the Enneagram are, "Which types are best for me to relate to?" and "How can we mobilize the most successful team?"

Dating services epitomize the "best match" approach, as do personnel departments that use psychological questionnaires for employment purposes. But the "which is best?" approach is usually less effective than it seems. On the job, for example, many of us have learned to test well and act like high-performance Threes. We have specific skills, and within that framework we are happy to stay on task, using a convenient social mask that has little to do with our real nature. Yet that performance image needs to be questioned because the truth is that teams do get stuck, and the sticking point is often the misperceptions that people have of one another.

In intimate relating, the "which is my best match?" question is underscored by the fact that our feelings about type are heavily influenced by the few significant people who have reared us, loved us, or disliked us. We generalize our feelings about a single exemplar of a type to include everyone who shares the same worldview. We find ourselves biased for or against a type because we've been exposed to someone who acted out its best or worst characteristics.

In the Enneagram oral tradition, we depend on panels of speakers to represent each type. It is typical for a panel of the same type to report totally different preferences for the eight other worldviews. For example, if a panel of Fours (Romantics) is asked, "How do you relate to Eights (Bosses)?" we might hear: I marry them, I fear them, I love them, I hate them, I avoid them, or I compete with them. The Romantics are all telling the truth, based on their personal history with the good side or the bad side of a Boss.

It would be a mistake, therefore, to categorize types according to compatibility or incompatibility. *Your best match in intimacy and team building is actually any psychologically mature person.*

The interactions presented in the directory are the most often reported findings from Enneagram students who practice self-observation. They are a gold mine of information about the hits, misses, aspirations, and agendas of the types in relationship, as depicted by people who speak with authority from their point of view. These interactions are not about the chemistry that bonds a successful team or the attractions that enliven a marriage. They are about pinpointing the concerns that inevitably emerge during the course of any committed partnership and that make or break the connection to people who are unlike ourselves.

As a general guideline, it's important, and consoling, to remember that we are not always fixated in a limited view of reality. The compulsion, or bias, of type isn't always in force. Most of us can think clearly and respond appropriately most of the time, but when the pressure builds, the "veil of illusion," or bias of type, comes into play and tends to dominate our perceptions.

To exercise compassionate understanding for people who are unlike themselves, it helps when both partners work their side of an issue at the same time. One works on change, while the other works on acceptance. Threes, for example, might initiate change by beginning to shrink their schedules. At the same time, their partners learn to accept that Threes put their hearts in their work.

Reading the Directory

The interactions are presented without regard to gender and cultural differences that can affect the manner in which type is acted out. In this context, type is described in terms of mental and emotional preoccupations despite the fact that the same concerns may be dramatized in a more "masculine" or "feminine" manner.

Two young women of the same type, for example, who have been raised in different cultural settings, will describe the same mental and emotional habits, but they will act out their similar concerns in different ways. A southern belle, influenced by her culture, may act out Four-ness in a strikingly different manner from a sister Four trained with the expectation of entering the corporate structure. Any two representatives of the same type will describe similar thoughts, feelings, motives, and styles of relating, but the way in which they personify that worldview can be influenced by their culture.

The concept of masculine or feminine characterization also varies from culture to culture. For example, I have noticed that Argentina seems to produce many males who favor their emotionally expressive side. The Gypsy culture, on the other hand, values women's organizational strengths and earning power, which seems to reinforce aggressive, or apparently "masculine," behavior. These cultural overlays definitely affect self-presentation, but they do not alter the basic preoccupations that underlie type.

The Work and Family Platform

Because love and work are merely different expressions of the same outlook, there will be obvious crossovers and similarities between the preoccupations attributed to the work sector and those ascribed to the couples. Each of us is unique, and we each demonstrate only a few of the full range of focal issues that characterize our type. Which of those issues appear at work, and which are accentuated in home life, are also purely individual matters. The wealth of diversity within a type is based on the fact that no two people act out the same range of concerns in exactly the same way.

These descriptions have been drawn from thousands of reports given in oral tradition classes, in which the types converse with one another. The couples format usually presents a panel of the same type seated opposite their spouses and significants. The conversation pinpoints the typical projections, blunders, and transformations that occur between people who operate from radically different perspectives. Rather than being divisive, such pivotal events can become the raw material, the compost, the energy source for personal transformation.

In the directory, couples are described as peers, while work interactions are framed as manager-employee relationships. In order to avoid repetition, I present the interactions between each type only once. For instance, I describe the relationship of One with Two, but not Two with One. Thus, the presentation of the interactions for each type involves one less combination each time.

Interactions Between the Types

Double One: A Double Perfectionist Couple

This couple can strive for a perfect lifestyle. Good food, good health, the right way to raise kids. They often build families within a practical framework that emphasizes responsibility and pride in earned achievement. Projects bond this couple, but teamwork favors function over feeling. Tender emotions can be easily numbed by hard labor. "No time for hugs. Lots to do. See you later." Love is demonstrated as much through effort as through sentiment.

A double One couple understands criticism. Although they can be very hard on each other, each understands that being critical toward someone you love is a way of acknowledging your investment in the relationship. Ones want the people who matter to them to be as close to perfection as possible. It's a sign of trust when Ones feel safe enough to be openly critical, and a sign of distrust when silent resentment builds. A double One fight is a slow buildup, a short explosive tussle, a long silent standoff, and then a gradual reengagement as forgiveness takes place.

Open anger about safe topics, like neighborhood politics or saving the whales, can open the conduit for letting off steam about more personal matters. A safe fight enlivens this couple. Once anger is allowed in the relationship, the bottleneck caused by choking off "bad" feelings is eased. To Ones the release of tension from a healthy fight is amazing. The feeling is: "We fought, we said everything that we were afraid to say, we still love each other, and nobody died." In fact long-standing One couples say that deeper intimacy depends on being able to fight with each other, that showing anger is an act of trust.

Difficulties can arise when Ones get involved in outside projects that demand time. Each will see her or his own project as the priority and will pull out of supporting the couple. Chores and household maintenance and care of children may become a problem. Each will blame the other for the lack of organization. "You should have done the supermarket run. It was your turn. This isn't fair." Nothing can be more irritating to a dedicated worker than being dumped with unexpected duties. Ones are compulsive about chores and are constantly pressed for time. It helps to have the division of labor clearly apportioned. Ones do well with a household job sheet. Their basic sense of fair play comes into operation when they can see a division of labor.

THE PARTY WILL BE LATE

This year we each finished a graduate thesis after carrying full programs, and we're raising a three-year-old. We earned the money for school tuition by remodeling and selling an old house, but I still do electrical work, and we live a lot out of my wife's garden. So last week she came home and wanted to have a birthday party for our son. But she thinks that we'll have to get furniture first, because certain parents who will be coming won't like floor pillows.

But we can't get furniture until I finish the inside trim. The wallboard still shows around the windows. A good couch sitting in that living room? It would be a disgrace to throw a party with wallboard hanging out. So I do the trim after dinner for a few days, and then there's the tile job around the stove that isn't right, and now it's been weeks since I had a day off, and we're so deeply into the garden and our son and studying and remodeling that my wife and I are both in the house all the time, but we see each other mostly in passing.

Double Ones tend to question, "Who is better?" This comparison of self to others stems from the childhood belief that being perfect is a way to earn love. A more subtle subtext reads, "You will look up to me if I am better. Am I good enough to be loved?" Young double Ones are more than likely to compare themselves with each other. They may look competitive, but with time they can see "comparison attacks" as a signal of insecurity.

"You go first!" is another sign of insecurity. It means "I'm afraid to initiate change." The partners criticize each other for not improving. It's a standoff. "You go first" or "Why should I when you haven't?" usually means "I'm afraid of making a mistake." Oddly, "You go first" can be a compliment in disguise. It means "I'm afraid to fail in your eyes, because I'm not lovable unless I'm perfect."

Double One Partnership at Work

Ones often seek each other out. They say that it's a relief to find someone else who cares about quality control. Finding a fellow One can be like meeting another Atlas carrying the world on his back. Finally! Someone else who shoulders a lot of responsibility. Ones also say it's a lot of fun to compare notes with discriminating people. Half the fun of meetings is the debrief, when you get to pick apart the presentations. The liability of double One lies in the tendency to create a liaison of superiority: a small, exclusive club that keeps itself up by putting other people down. The positive aspect of double One is a mutuality of purpose—hard work, earned advancement, and a devotion to professionalism. Good workmanship is a mark of character for Perfectionists.

Ones expect to rise in a hierarchy that they trust, but control issues are common in a double One partnership. The manager does "what's right" for the business, and the employee wants "what's right" for staff. One managers, for example, can make less than generous decisions that favor the company at the employee's expense. A raise may have contingencies that depend on "continued good performance," with the manager making those evaluations. One managers will be confident of their correctness, and One employees will feel equally right. Sensing the possibility of being used for someone else's gain, Perfectionists withdraw into stony, nonproductive silence. They fall back on the letter of the law and will not expend a drop of extra energy or put in an extra second of time. The standoff is a One-style power struggle. Each waits for the other to "break" by showing anger. Each monitors the other, hoping to find a mistake. It helps if the system can be loosened so that each saves face and both receive a benefit. It helps if respect can be given to those on the losing side.

Detail control can be a mutual blind spot for the double One partnership. They may collude to magnify small matters into obstacles. An adequate job won't do; it has to be absolutely right. Decisions are hard because both Ones see all the relevant points but have difficulty initiating a solution. Broad solutions have too much room for error, which makes Ones very cautious. One managers are likely to repeat something that has worked in the past rather than to try an experimental route. Outside counsel is often effective: Ones respond to expert advice. One managers relate to valid, reliable information; they need a roster of consultants, credible people to call on for help. One employees can blank-out when a decision has contingencies. They are susceptible to performance anxiety. They need a rule for red alerts. One employees appreciate procedures: they want to memorize who, what, when, and how in case of an emergency.

One with Two: A Perfectionist-Giver Couple

This is an attraction based on differences. Ones deal with practicalities and Twos relate through feelings and style. Perfectionists are flattered by the attentions of the more emotionally flamboyant Givers. Twos carry the social ball. They initiate, whether they are male or female, which cuts through Perfectionistic criticality and social anxiety. Ones' needs shine like a beacon to Twos. Ones need pleasure; Ones need help, so Givers think, "I could be of help." Ones are guilty about having needs, but Twos aren't guilty about meeting them.

Twos are attracted to steady, dependable mates who express love through responsible action. Perfectionists can be anchors during emotional turbulence, and Twos will seek that safety when the world starts to shake.

As the relationship progresses, Ones work overtime and Twos push for juice. Long days and no hugs make Perfectionists feel pure and drive Twos crazy. Twos need a lot of attention. From a Two perspective, the Perfectionist agenda of pleasure in a job well done seems grim and punitive. The trick is to blend a well-ordered, stable life with enough social and emotional outlets to keep both partners happy.

The couple meets at Four and may therefore have a mutual understanding of disappointment and depression. Ones get depressed when work efforts fail. Oddly, Twos can be saddened when they are secure, because then they feel their own needs. This couple often expresses a wish to shield each other from shame and disappointment. Four can become a point of solidarity for the couple. Ones respect people who struggle, and Twos are helpful when they see pain.

Over time, the shoulds that govern a One's life can feel repressive. Shoulds produce a stable life, but they also deaden spontaneity. If romance dries up, the Giver will wonder, "Where do I stand?" "Don't I come first?" Dependent on positive approval, a threatened Two fights to get some attention. Two's pride happily inflates when a partner cares enough to react. At an all-time low, the Giver looks unstable and the One looks rigid. Ones impose structure to fend off chaos, and Twos fight the rules as a way of getting back.

Ones under pressure can bury themselves in work rather than deal with their feelings. The lack of contact can drive Givers wild. A stiff "Good morning" over faultlessly buttered toast, no telephone call during the day, and lots of overtime. Rather than feeling rejected, Twos need to know that work suppresses Ones' anger. Twos can meet a need by taking some responsibility for the difficulty, accepting whatever blame is deserved, and agreeing to reasonable guidelines for behavior.

Ones can help by understanding Twos' need for attention. Is a need for approval really frivolous or wrong? Rather than being judgmental, Ones can remember to make a gesture of affection. They can also try to accept help in return. Ones commonly feel criticized when help is offered. Perfect people don't have needs. "I should take care of myself." Ones tend to see offers of help as either pure generosity or attention-seeking manipulation. The truth is it's not either/or. It may be a little of both.

One-Two Partnership at Work

Givers are often professionally successful, but they work for love. Work should elicit approval from loved ones, and if it doesn't, Twos change jobs. This partnership may collude to put One in charge and Two as helper, even if it's not logical on the basis of experience. Ones need to be right and Twos need to be liked, which can make Givers uneasy about challenging Ones' authority. Twos can be happy as the power behind the throne. It's a good combination if the One is likable, because Twos can be meticulous and highly productive when their emotional needs are met.

One managers focus on skills and procedures. They offer concise long-range planning and precise details. Ones may emphasize technical skills without much attention to the way staff feels. Giver employees are going to notice, but may not confront. Why make trouble? Why risk anger when you're paid to provide support? It helps if Twos risk making needed suggestions. The manager may indeed feel criticized and may be temporarily upset, but if Twos can support the task rather than seek approval, the manager may take more risks. The best use of this partnership shows Twos feeling confident enough to challenge the manager's thinking rather than trying to be pleasing and safe.

Two managers emphasize image, appearances, and often an inner-circle connection with workplace favorites. One employees are going to be uncomfortable with social posturing or with an evaluation or promotional possibility that depends on favoritism. Ones earn their way with hard work and dislike having to garner attention. They want a fair authority who acknowledges merit without being asked.

One employees may be threatened by the manager's moods. Givers are prone to bursts of temper that blow over quickly.

Givers forget, but Ones believe words spoken in anger. Weeks later Ones will still be worried about an offhand criticism. Timing is important for this pair. Ones should realize that the manager has emotional highs and lows, that it's not manipulative to appreciate the highs and avoid the lows. It is enormously beneficial when the Two manager remembers to repair the damage. Simply saying "I may have overreacted" spares One employees a lot of unnecessary worry.

One with Three: A Perfectionist-Performer Couple

This pair is energetically well matched. They are both active, they both focus on status and social image, and both find their identity through work. Activity is a natural meeting place. They both tend to like sports and exercise, family events, projects for the house. Valuing productivity, each can take pride in the other's efforts and success, particularly professional interests. This couple really profits from a weekend away, because relating through activities easily slides into the kind of compulsive doing that blocks out intimacy and feelings. Ones relate by reviewing the day: "Listen to what happened to me today" or "I had this great conversation at lunch." Threes, however, relate to results. Once the job's over, they would rather move on than keep a topic going for its contact value.

Both types are very concerned about what other people think, but they act out that preoccupation in different ways. Ones compare themselves with other people and are scrupulous about the difference between an actual accomplishment and an impressive image. They judge themselves against the highest standards of success and pride themselves in not being taken in by a shallow pose. Ones rarely puff out their image, whereas Threes project an exciting public facade. Threes' public self-presentation can be a source of irritation. Ones will ask, "Is this honest or deliberate deception?" Threes want to look good to people, while Ones want to look right.

Playing to the crowd can look like falsification to Ones and brings up fears about possible dishonesty in other areas of the relationship. Ones are purists. They want absolute honesty, which grates against Threes' deceptive public persona. Meanwhile Performers, convinced that image is a way to earn love, may keep looking for the right way to impress their Perfectionist mates.

Threes retreat when image is attacked, and Ones pursue when they're angry. Anger is liberating to Ones, and they will put the focus of their anger on the table, whether Threes like it or not. If Performers retreat, Perfectionists will bring them back to the table. If Threes can't deal with the image issue, Ones will pick a fight about chores. The peril for this couple shows Three unable to engage in self-reflection and One in angry pursuit. Threes can avert this peril by seeing themselves as 50 percent of the problem and acknowledging that some anger may be appropriate.

Conflicts are best resolved when Ones stay focused on a single area of difficulty. An argument need not become the spark for other resentments. Threes dislike "negative" emotions and generally don't engage in self-reflection unless they can see the point of it all. What matters to Threes is a workable solution that allows them to move on. Threes will come to the table to resolve a problem, but they dislike having the discussion spread, especially to sins of the past.

In a fight Ones have total grievance recall. They think, "You did it once and you might do it again. Have you really changed?" But past grievances are anathema to Threes. "OK, I admitted I was wrong. I paid my dues. Now why can't you forgive and forget?" It helps when Threes can deal with the early signals of Ones' anger while it's still attached to a specific issue. It is not productive for Threes to evade a confrontation by pleading work commitments. Discussions have to be put on the schedule. It also helps if Ones can remember that Threes slip easily into image and that social facades may be just a different way of meeting the world rather than telling a lie.

One-Three Partnership at Work

Threes get the job done, but Ones do it right. It's a question of quantity versus quality. Performers do volume production, and Perfectionists want a perfect result. Both types can be workaholic, but Threes take the most efficient route. They set goals, aim, and energize, taking every possible shortcut. Spotty directions are fine for Threes; they can learn on their feet. They improvise. Details can wait until later. Meanwhile this kind of procedural inconsistency can drive Ones up the wall.

QUANTITY VERSUS QUALITY

[A One nurse in a Three-like work environment] I've worked with a lot of Three doctors in my hospital. They come on shift at sixty miles an hour, do a spot check, give orders, and exit at high speed. I, on the other hand, have been there for twelve hours, observed the patient closely, and accumulated an immense amount of data. I know that what the physicians want is logical but impossible. I also know that they're not going to listen to me. I used to bloody myself a lot, worrying about not following orders, until I figured out I should just do it my way, requesting as little input as possible. I finally got it that they just want it done and don't care about the way it's done.

Three managers have several projects afloat at the same time. New ventures are begun before the current ones are finished, so there's never time to catch up. Threes want to initiate, delegate, and move on, which places the responsibility for followthrough on the staff. Meanwhile the equally hardworking One employees backtrack in search of a plan. No plan equals full stop. What look like minor details to Threes are fundamental necessities to Ones. Perfectionists hesitate in the face of uncertainty. There are too many balls in the air. Ones think: "We need to schedule a meeting. This could result in costly mistakes."

Ones stop to plan while Threes speed up. The distance between the two increases if the goal-oriented Three manager takes the employee's follow-through for granted. Focused on goals, and personally identified with success, Threes are infuriated when tasks are blocked. Three managers think: "Employees are responsible for small matters. It takes only a minute or two to order and organize. I'm on the front line, I represent the business, I'm visible. Everything else is secondary."

Underappreciated Ones are trouble. Perfectionists invest enormous time and effort in researching, comparing, considering, and refining. They know where the pennies go and where the files are kept, and they will slow down if they're unhappy. A standoff occurs when a Perfectionist, grounded in principle and backed by carefully assembled data, faces a Performer who wants something that works. Neither will admit error, because error questions competency, and both types are heavily identified with their professional profiles. Conflicts can develop if the Three gets angry, speeds up, and won't listen. Now there are two angry people who are both right.

Conflict resolution should focus on the fact that both are committed to job excellence. Threes may have to be bluntly informed, "This isn't working," which usually brings them up short. It helps if Threes are mature enough to see that success depends on cooperation rather than solo performance. Three managers should schedule "Employee input day" and "Employee recognition week," with a star next to the One employees' names. Ones offer great input and go all out when they're identified with a project, yet they do not put themselves forward for the recognition they need. In addition, it helps if Ones can learn to couch their suggestions in a Three-like language of efficiency, profitability, and competitive edge.

One managers can be highly controlling. They want to be sure of details, which is guaranteed to make a Three employee bend the rules. Threes are focused on the goal, and Ones have to account for all the steps that lead to the goal. Ones are focused on character, honest effort, and fair return. Threes want instant personal success. Three employees are working for security, prestige, and image. They respond to competition, bonuses, and titles, which may run counter the One managers' more conservative traits. Perfectionists may impose bulletproof guidelines for job success, which Threes will either ignore or finesse. It takes too much time to count the pennies and correct the files. Small mistakes don't matter to Threes, but they matter a lot to One managers. This pair is often successful with Three positioned as the point person who deals with events in the field. A Performer employee can handle rapid turnovers of information and will make on-the-spot decisions. The Three's input can be invaluable to a One manager, who will modify the plan accordingly.

One with Four: A Perfectionist-Romantic Couple

This is usually a volatile relationship that embodies the potential for deep self-understanding. The couple shares the One–Four line of the diagram, which means that each sees a version of himself or herself in the other. Romantics often act out "improper" emotions that frighten Perfectionists. Romantics move through shame, depression, envy, competition, and despair on the way to joy and creativity. Perfectionists often recoil from seeing their own shadows in action, but it cannot be avoided in this pairing, because Romantics dramatize the emotional needs that Ones have suppressed. This relationship can introduce Ones to a life of feelings rather than a life determined by right-or-wrong thinking.

Fours' dramatic moods can become repellent to serious and practical Ones. It looks like self-indulgence. Ones think: "Pull yourself together. There's work to be done." Ones see emotional exhibitionism and Fours' need to be special as traits that should be brought under discipline. A cycle can develop in which Ones' criticism reinforces Fours' lack of worth. In retaliation Fours point out what's missing in Ones: "You're unfeeling," "You're cold," "You can't be touched." The implication is that Fours are better people because they feel so deeply. The cycle can be interrupted if Fours see why Ones are driven to control a "bad" emotion. From the One side, it helps to see the integrity of deep emotional connection, that rules cannot govern matters of the heart.

On the high side, Fours' emotionality can loosen the shoulds that inhibit Ones' happiness and creativity. Ones often say that they "found" their life direction or "found" their creativity at their risk point of Four. They also say that Romantics can be true companions during times of emotional pain. Fours are riveted when any issue becomes charged with emotional energy. It's not that Ones' right-or-wrong thinking becomes palatable, it's that those same ideas of right and wrong become meaningful to Fours when they are deeply felt.

Romantics can be attracted to Perfectionists' emotional steadiness and practicality. Afraid of abandonment, Fours can sabotage their relationships when they realize the depth of their own commitment. They bail out by disappearing, pushing the partner away with a fight, or becoming immobilized by depression. All of this tumult reads as "wrong" to Ones, who tend to hold their ground when they feel unfairly treated. Ones get actively angry when they're wronged, and they remember fights for a long time. Oddly, Romantics respect people who don't respond to attempted sabotage. It's "proof" that their partners want to stay and will not abandon them. Someone who won't be bullied by push-pull tactics can be trusted. Fours can lean on someone who deals with the practical mechanics of job and family regardless of their own emotional state.

The disadvantage of the One-Four connection can be a shared dissatisfaction with life. Romantics suffer because something is missing, and Perfectionists see the flaws. The relationship can be animated by focusing on the good things in the present moment and by taking pleasure in the satisfactions of here and now.

One-Four Partnership at Work

Ones have perfect standards, and Fours have unique standards, which can bond the pair in excellence. The partners are mutually respectful of special achievement and jointly critical of substandard performance. The emotional overlap indicated by the One–Four line is less obvious in the workplace, where the focus of attention is on projects rather than feelings. Romantics are certainly less volatile at work than in more intimate and private settings. Likewise at work Ones' perfectionistic streak is largely focused on tasks.

One managers' attention to structure and order will make Fours feel secure. Structure is a container for feelings, and a well-run, orderly setting can be appealing. There may be difficulty if One managers are personally distant and relate to staff through rules and social convention. Fours will dismiss this posture as emotionally dishonest—a way of making rules more important than people. Fours need special treatment, and if they don't get it, they will simply dismiss the rules rather than feel shamed by submitting themselves to petty authority. Fours have a reckless, delinquent side that comes out when they feel caught by the ordinary. Guidelines that govern others simply don't apply to them. To stay involved, Fours need personal recognition from an acknowledged authority, particularly if they have to compete publicly. Any genuine interest that can be taken in their project area goes a long way toward making Four employees feel worthwhile.

Fours in the security of their own One position can act with a clarity of purpose that may otherwise be obscured by emotion. This is the time when creative strivings can be perfected and made practical. The meeting at One can be a high point of the partnership. A practical One manager supports production and could therefore help a unique Four-like creation become operational.

The meeting at One can also be a disaster if the Four, finally feeling secure enough to express dissatisfaction, moves into low-functioning, picky judgment. Wham. Suddenly whatever the One manager proposes isn't good enough. One-Four work teams report some of their worst moments during a so-called secure period, when the Four employee becomes bitter about what's missing. The employee feels used and tells everyone about it. There's usually a public scene. The Four is insulted by the pay scale, the projects, and the decor. Already saddled with an inner critic of their own, One managers may retaliate in force. Paradoxically these fights can be healing, especially if they're mediated. Ones get to be angry without feeling guilty, and Fours experience having their fatal flaws exposed without being abandoned. Mediation can help Ones to see that there's more to work relationships than following orders, and Fours can learn to tell the difference between a bona fide grievance and bruised feelings.

As managers, Fours can either run the office with Three-like precision or schedule events to revolve around their own emotional needs. Competitive Four managers often look and act like Threes, keeping their feelings to themselves and flying into high-risk performance. Competitive Fours can become captivated by an extraordinary maneuver and throw caution to the winds. The more emotionally based Fours become the office centerpiece. They may be highly effective, but moods will affect the style and pacing of projects. A fast, bright clip at work can be followed by disinterest. A priority decision can be upstaged by psychological drama. Staff members may be devoted to Four managers, who become a part of their lives, but over time, One employees become anxious and irritated about erratic supervision. Perfectionists want to keep the office calendar in order, because long-range planning reduces the fear of chaos. Four managers may thus be blessedly relieved of supervisory details. Romantics are drawn to creative ventures and are likely to bring new enthusiasm to the workplace when they can be spared more routine matters.

One-Five: A Perfectionist-Observer Couple

This can be a look-alike pair. Both are highly independent, both like to work alone, and both place value on emotional control. The relationship may be played out pragmatically rather than romantically, emphasizing livelihood, practical projects, and a well-organized family life. Tension can develop from lack of information when Fives' blank affect affects Ones' worry scheme. Observers can be emotionally detached for days, while Ones clench, waiting for the critical shoe to drop. In truth, Fives may not care.

Perfectionists tend to interpret silence as judgment. Neither partner wants to get angry, so important topics are neglected. The tension eases when Fives can speak; the tension dissolves if Fives will fight. To Ones anger shows that Fives are invested; emotional distance vanishes when something matters enough. Fives see an intensity of emotion in Ones that is attractive—it's a wake-up call to life. As long as Fives are not forced to show their feelings, they can position themselves as counselors and advisers, a posture they prefer to being the center of another's emotional life.

Ones find a steady, knowing presence in Fives, with the lack of judgment that detachment often brings. Valuing emotional control, the couple tends to be somewhat dry by nature. Long-term couples say that it has helped immensely to move into their anger and sexuality rather than following their tendencies to suppress feelings or detach from negativity.

One-Five Partnership at Work

When they separate from their feelings, Fives seem remote and aloof; but when they connect with their intellectual curiosity,

Fives come alive and can be actively critical. Rather than being a point of difficulty, the pair's shared criticality can be a bond at work.

A One manager will be relieved to find that Five employees are meticulous with information. Here's someone who cares! Joined in their powers of criticism, and practical to the point of thriftiness, One-Five partners do well in clearing systems of inefficiency and waste. A tug-of-war may develop over information. When Perfectionists want more, Observer employees give less. It helps when the Five knows exactly how much is required, and it helps if the manager does not call for further improvement once those standards have been met.

Their work styles are remarkably similar. Five managers set clear objectives and are methodical, which is pleasing to Ones. Both are highly independent workers. They like an assignment that they can shape by themselves. The emphasis will be on formal job contact rather than feelings. If difficulty arises, the first line of defense will be for each to withdraw. Five managers will need to initiate the conversation, because silence reads as criticism to Ones.

When a work rhythm is set, One-Five partnerships are capable of well-researched and well-documented products. Both want to gather voluminous data for a fully informed decision. Fives value knowledge for the sake of knowing, and Ones enjoy building an impeccable case.

One with Six: A Perfectionist-Trooper Couple

Initial attractions often involve a shared vision that requires hard work in order to become a reality. The couple bonds through effort and a kinship of ideals. Sixes are identified with underdog causes, which coincides with Ones' dedication to perfection. Joined by a similar worldview, and prepared for adversity, the One-Six couple is often dedicated to a dream.

Both types can be perceived as negative thinkers. Ones are preoccupied with error, and Sixes are focused on doubt. But precisely because they anticipate difficulty, they also see the beauty of the human dilemma and the creativity that springs from pain. They understand the importance of asking hard questions and the courage of daring to try. Both types have an appealing willingness to hang in during troubled times. The attendant effort produces unusual levels of trust. Each sees the other's high intentions and each sees the other's fear of success.

One-Six couples report both a deep affinity and periodic standoffs caused by mutual projection. Both feel guilty if they can't perform well, and both procrastinate. One is afraid to make a mistake, and Six doubts success. The climate is ripe for mutual projection. "Why don't things move faster?" "Look how he keeps stalling." "Is this deliberate?" "Why can't she decide?" The partners are afraid to argue. Anger frightens Sixes, and Ones think anger is wrong.

Without a reality check, either partner can become paralyzed by inner worry and doubt. A complicated web of unacknowledged feelings can develop. One sees Six as holding out, and Six feels blamed because what gets done is never good enough. One is likely to take the superior stance: "I'm right; and it's true, you aren't good enough." Secure in their own moral superiority, Ones can alienate Sixes by acting "better than." The Six may be quite willing to look bad as a repulsion technique. The Trooper hopes that the Perfectionist will leave in disgust, thereby providing a guilt-free way to end the relationship.

It helps to nip projection in the bud, before losing sight of a partner's good intentions. A good talk reduces projection. It's such a simple strategy, but very difficult to implement. From time to time each will see the other as "causing" the problem. Sixes fear their own aggression, and Ones deny anger because they think it's wrong; consequently irritation can boil over without warning.

The answer for this couple lies in disclosure so that projection never takes hold.

One-Six Partnership at Work

Ones are dedicated workers who expect to rise through their own efforts. Sixes bring a creative flavor to their work and are ambivalent about hierarchy. One is the most rule-bound of the types, and Sixes have their doubts about rules. Under perfectionistic managers, Six employees will eventually bend the rules and encourage others to do the same. Sixes roam in packs for mutual support. It's best to be a benevolent authority, as long as Troopers can meet standards.

Successful One managers will remember to reassure employees even when it doesn't seem logical or necessary. Ones are sparing in praise because they focus on the flaws. Six employees are likely to interpret lack of praise in the worst possible light and feel targeted. If the manager is angry about morning traffic, Six employees will register that anger and refer it to their own worst-case scenario. Hungry for certainty, Troopers can build a case and are likely to spread the alarm to others. They are threatened and want support. "Can this manager be trusted?" "How do we know for sure?" The conflict will not be resolved if One managers entrench in right-or-wrong solutions. Reframing the problem or offering a face-saving solution is fundamental. For example: "That was an experimental phase. We have learned from that, and now we can move on."

Faced with uncertain consequences, a Six employee will either fall at authority's feet or go for authority's throat. Be careful to dispel rumors, possibilities, and potential loopholes. Both types are alert to hidden intentions. Sixes, particularly, assume that authority is untrustworthy.

Troopers manage well in the short term but often waver on long-term projects. There will be deadlining, last-minute saves, and a stop-start managerial style. They are strong leaders during the groundbreaking stage but have trouble expanding, even with the certainty of success. Six managers need to focus on task, which brings the meticulous Ones into support positions. Ones are dedicated to good leadership and are willing to rally around a deadline when they are inspired by example.

Informal, roundtable sessions really pay off. Checking in for a few minutes each week to see how everyone is doing does a lot to clear the air. Both types feel targeted if hostility is circulating in the workplace. Ones feel worried about what people are thinking, and Sixes expect attack. Both pull back when they feel threatened, and both think it's "negative" to broach their concerns. Informal meetings serve the purpose of simple reality testing. The Ones and Sixes of the world are always surprised to discover that their project is still safe.

This partnership can produce well-documented, airtight analysis. Both types like to ask hard questions. They are excellent troubleshooters, and inclined to foresee problem areas and to propose solutions.

One with Seven: A Perfectionist-Epicure Couple

The couple shares an Enneagram line, which means that each sees a major aspect of himself or herself in the other. From the Seven side, the clarity of One is attractive. Sevens admire the fact that Ones are disciplined, dedicated to matters of principle, and follow through on what they believe. Ones are practical people who work toward tangible products, and their focused concentration can ground a Seven's planning monkey mind.

From the other side of the relationship, Ones are attracted to Epicurean spontaneity. Sevens can be a lot of fun to live with. They enliven the household in such a way that an evening by the fire takes on theatrical proportions. Holidays can be expanded into heroic events. Ones particularly welcome their Seven security point as a place of happiness and freedom, yet Perfectionists can also see their Epicures as flakes.

SEVEN HEAVEN

[Perfectionist mother, Epicure son] My son had been trekking for months in the Himalayas and wrote glowing descriptions. He got situated in a hill town at about eleven thousand feet and asked me to come visit. He was wildly enthusiastic. He wrote that it was the adventure of his life, and would I come for the summer? So I, the accommodating parent, get myself to India and follow his route. I also enjoy myself, until it's time to settle into his place for two weeks. There's no running water, it's really hot, and we have to eat out because there's no stove. One day I'm sitting opposite him at lunch. We're cramped, I'm sweating, and I hate the flies, but he is in a kind of ecstasy. His face is so enrapt that he actually looks drunk. I ask him what he is thinking and he says: "This is the best restaurant in town. I can eat at the best place in town every night."

As the relationship progresses, Ones push for product, and Sevens want fun. A successful relationship unites those agendas. Perfectionists can be spontaneous if the lifestyle says that spontaneity is the right thing. If we're supposed to hang out and follow the flow, or the rules say that there are no rules, then Ones learn to act with flexibility. Because Ones want precision and Sevens want options, a successful pair can make their adventures functional. Together they look for ways to make fun produce results. However, it is far more common to see the couple in parallel play. Each partner does his or her own thing while honoring a basic agreement about money, time, and family commitments. Sevens have changing interests, and Ones may go deeply into a study that Sevens find repetitious and boring.

If Ones try to pin Sevens into practicalities, Sevens will fight back. Stressed-out Sevens who have moved into One act out Perfectionism in a Seven-like way by fighting limits and rules. Sevens think: "Limits are for lesser beings," "Rules are for inferior minds." Unfortunately Ones value boundaries and self-control, and if their black-or-white thinking takes over, Epicures look selfish and therefore bad. In a fight, Ones get rigid and Sevens evade. Sevens try to demean the problem, and Ones move in to control.

Faced with anger or "negative" feelings, Sevens become highly defensive. They take a superior stance and think: "One is being difficult. One has a problem." Sevens can use Ones' fury to obscure the facts. Perfectionists can be baited into taking the offensive, giving Sevens an excuse to disappear. It helps if Epicures come halfway in negotiations, face Ones' anger, and try to deal with the problem.

Ones embody precision and follow-through, while Sevens show joy and spontaneity in life. Ones on vacation will naturally look and act like Sevens. The trick is for Ones to bring some vacation back home to family life.

One-Seven Partnership at Work

Sevens like to network; they like to take their show on the road. This partnership shows Seven as inventor, planner, meeter, and greeter. The Perfectionist provides structure, follow-through, and control.

Their business skills are underscored by different styles of thinking. Ones are right-wrong thinkers who rely on logic to implement a plan, while Sevens think in terms of interlocking concepts. Sevens require a flexible structure that can absorb new technology and ideas. Perfectionists can't easily follow Sevens' multioptional thought, and Epicures feel limited by a logical, linear approach.

One managers can enforce right-wrong thinking by pointing out small mistakes. Caught off guard, Sevens retreat behind a barricade of excuses: "I meant it to look that way." "The timing wasn't right." Evasive tactics are deadly to Ones, who see lies instead of "process thought." Rather than assuming that the employee is dangerously irresponsible, Ones might lend themselves to nonlinear thinking. Ones should manage Sevens with a light supervisory touch. Don't focus on procedures, set reasonable deadlines, and evaluate results only.

Seven managers can literally go on vacation leaving a swath of unanswered questions. Unexpected decisions and sudden shifts of direction are particularly threatening to Ones. The manager may have produced a "clear memo" or "airtight instructions" that are in fact sketchy and incomplete. Ones will think: "This is mismanagement. This is abusive to staff." Angry Ones exercise the letter of the law. They will do exactly as directed, rather than assist the floundering boss. Epicures would do well to spend a day producing exact instructions. That day may seem endless and frightening as the One employee exposes loopholes in the manager's plans; yet Ones are the perfect employees to shape the details of a project, freeing the manager to take a real vacation.

One with Eight: A Perfectionist-Boss Couple

If there's such a thing as Enneagram opposites, this is it. The relationship is going to produce fireworks: Both are anger types, prone to black-or-white thinking, and convinced they're right. Initially Ones are mesmerized by the force and sexuality of the Eight persona. It looks wonderful to be so free. Eights are often attracted to the discipline and good intentions of Ones. Their moral stance looks truthful to the somewhat lawless Boss.

As the relationship matures anger will surface. Eights insist on direct expression of anger; and Ones, once goaded into a fight, retaliate in force. Direct expression of anger can be a real blessing to Ones. At last they're engaged with someone who won't judge anger as wrong.

Both partners are good at neutral decisions, like who to vote for in an election or where the family should go on vacation. Personal decisions are more difficult. Eight and One are wing points of the self-forgetting Nine. Eights "wake up" by going against other people; Ones, by knowing the right thing to do. Both Eight and One are therefore reactive rather than proactive. If they begin to prod each other, they become polarized. Neither will budge.

WHY ONES AND EIGHTS FIGHT

Ones are right because they're good, and if they're not right, they feel guilty. Eights are right because they're bad. It's good to be bad. Bad is lawless and free and exciting. Bad is more interesting than good and is not wrong. It's bad to be wrong, but being bad doesn't make you wrong. If you're not wrong, you're right; and if you're right, you shouldn't feel guilty.

If Ones begin to look supervisory, Eights become lawless and out of control. The inevitable clash of wills can be healing. Ones teach Eights about limits and boundaries. Eights teach Ones to go for what they want. Anger gets Ones off their prissiness; it gives them permission to be irreverent and to find their humor. Anger can bond this couple. It looks a lot worse from the outside than it does from the perspective of people who sometimes need to fight.

This couple gives something helpful to each other. Ones are disciplined. Eights have juice. The two in combination have the potential for focused power, or they can fall into a cycle of conflict that drives them apart.

One-Eight Partnership at Work

Eight is the partnership's id and One is the superego. They can either unify or struggle for control. Anger can be accentuated at work, where the intimate outlets of a good fight or good sex are missing.

The control struggle will center on different styles of supervision. Ones control with "one right way." Eights insist on "my way or the highway." One managers would do well to base evaluations on performance only. Eight employees may perform well but refuse to account for themselves. Even rules that are logical and fair will shriek supervision. If the Eight employee produces well, leave her or him alone.

Eight managers control by sheer physical presence. This can be difficult for Ones who are out of touch with their own aggression. When hit with open anger, Ones' inner critics go wild. The boss is angry, so the boss is bad. Eights get angry and blurt whatever they think at the moment. Ones control themselves until they're in the right.

When id and superego agree, this is a unified pair. Both are obsessive workers, both are committed to practical results. Eights can use Ones as guides for behavior: "Is this appropriate? Are we pushing too hard? Am I overdoing it?" Eights can take a load of worry from One: "Come on. I'll take charge. We'll take a chance. It'll be fun."

One with Nine: A Perfectionist-Mediator Couple

These two can look remarkably alike. Ones and Nines have so many traits in common that they are bracketed in the same category in some psychological systems. They are both anger types that repress their anger, and they are both obsessive, which means that they ruminate about decisions for a long time before making a move. Nines tend to see a decision from many points of view, and Ones worry about error. Needless to say, unless the couple stays on a structured track, important decisions will be slow in coming. There may be a conspiracy to postpone difficulty until later. It's just easier to wait. Ones become preoccupied with details, and Nines wait for someone else to initiate. This couple wants life to be peaceful and comfortable. Both like the security of a household and become fused in a family routine. Mediators are usually agreeable and accepting, which reduces Ones' anxiety about being right. In return, Nines find structure in a Perfectionist's "correct" worldview.

The difference between the pair is evident when action is called for. Ones go into fast forward when they're committed, while Nines can sit on the fence even when they agree. Ones can jump-start the couple into action. Ones' conviction creates a spearhead that forces Nines to take a position, but if Ones make "what ought to be done" the priority, Nines will be thinking: "This is someone else's idea." Nines in retreat can look scattered and stubborn. Ones push hard for what "we should be doing," while Nines are still waiting for a priority to appear. Nines in distress go to field focus, where choosing is hard. No single choice stands out as significant, all the options seem the same. Pursuing Ones want answers: "Be explicit. What do you want? Explain yourself." Under fire, Nines vague-out and go numb. There may be bitter fights about very small matters, because small fights are vents for distress. Any show of anger is healthy for this couple; with anger a position comes forth. People know exactly what they don't want when they're angry. "Not that" eliminates an option and puts Nines and Ones closer to a final decision.

It helps when Mediators can see the good intentions in One-like anger, and it helps when Perfectionists see that anger won't work. You can't push Nines into commitment, but they will merge and join with a loved one's needs.

One-Nine Partnership at Work

The obsessive quality of mind is ideal for setting up and consolidating systems. Endurance is a key factor. Both types like to take known procedures and make them stronger. Disliking rapid change and the constant pressure of decision making, Ones and Nines can commit themselves to refining an organization that will last. Both types flourish with structure. Rather than feeling stifled by procedures, they like to become masters of specific areas of expertise. Both are detailmongers. Both procrastinate about decisions, and neither is attracted to risk.

One managers create structure, and Nines rely on structure to be effective. Mediators can be focused by goal-oriented Ones.

It's important for One managers to remember positive reinforcement. Nine employees respond to encouragement, but Ones are focused on flaws. Underappreciated Nines control by silence and slowing down. A disaffected employee knows what the manager wants but won't do it. Nines feel in control if they don't show anger, so they'll make the manager dance. It helps to keep positive and negative feedback balanced. Nines like a clear set of rewards for effort, but most of all they respond to unconditional positive support.

Nine managers can set up systems and coast. If their attention spreads to details, a One employee's critical faculties can be useful in roping the project back in. Nines should try to delegate when they become overwhelmed, and a One is the ideal person to narrow a task.

Double Two: A Double Giver Couple

Double Two couples are a rare sighting. After all, if you're in the giving business you look for someone to help. With two Givers there is no one to receive, and each is embarrassed about being the center of attention. When Twos help partners reach their potential, they feel like they have succeeded as well. When someone they help is successful, they are also spared the risk of losing face. Twos share in the glory from behind the scenes. They pulled the strings. They made it happen, they succeeded, without having to risk a public failure.

But double Two is a setup. Each is thinking: "I'm being forced to go first." It's embarrassing to find that you fear public humiliation. Having their dependency on others exposed makes Twos angry. A stalemate can develop. Each wants the other to be the mover and shaker. Each prefers to fall in and provide the support. Each is waiting to be inspired, and both are bored because there's nothing to do. Each is impatient with the other because neither knows who to be without the catalyst of someone else's need.

Tempers explode as repressed needs surface. It feels embarrassing to ask for help. This couple can unify around a common venture. They can run a business or solve family problems together. Hard-pressed to find identity in each other, the couple turns their attention elsewhere.

Both partners lose themselves in others; if they can't stand together against the world or help each other, they'll seek inspiration outside the home.

They need to bring attention back to themselves, however painful that might be. To honor their own emotions. To see their own potentials, although Twos have to brave a lot of terror to accomplish this. "Having needs equals being rejected" is the formula from the past. Each will have to learn to be alone rather than looking outside for someone to help.

Double Twos need to redefine their idea of relating. Relating doesn't mean denying your needs. It doesn't mean refusing to be separate. It doesn't mean moving outside yourself. Only half a relationship can be built on serving a partner's potentials; the other half is developing yourself. Double Twos are often friends, less frequently mates and lovers. As friends they can encourage each other to receive.

Double Two Partnership at Work

Although double Twos are an uncommon intimate couple, they often do well at work. Both can serve a task as if it were a third party. A task has needs, a task provides an identity, and a task has emotional juice. The partners may compete to be indispensable, and it works if each has an equally important role. This can be a graceful and productive partnership. Two good promoters focused on a common effort.

Two managers are personable. They want to be liked. They lead aggressively for a popular decision, but if the focal point of hostility, they can be manipulative and vengeful. Manipulation involves the power structure, going over someone's head. Two managers can seduce the power elite. Two employees can put down peers in order to impress management. A clear set of boundaries makes manipulation unnecessary. A clear structure allows Twos to be direct. Those in power will have to be aware that Giver employees are ingratiating. As managers, they help favorites by private agreement and indirect support. It helps to make the conditions of advancement public and objective, which eliminates the indirect approach. Twos need a lot of initial support to enter public competition. Once they have successfully qualified, they hold their new position with pride.

All Twos are sensitive to criticism. You can't be indispensable if you make mistakes. When their pride is injured, Twos try to defend themselves. They will sidestep the issue: "It wasn't my fault." Reassure Twos about the future. "We have a problem, but we can get through it. Our relationship is not at risk." It helps to separate Givers' personal worth from their professional merit. Givers need to be respected as people rather than as performers.

Two employees can feel as important as the manager, so the job description has to be clear. If Twos feel socially accepted, it can shock them to be left out. "That was a major decision. Why wasn't I called? They should have asked for my opinion. I should have been asked to help." Twos can feel like they're running the show from a corner of the room. Pride inflates, and they feel indispensable. Pride deflates when they haven't been asked. It helps to involve Twos in specific work so they know they have a place. Reassure them about their future. If they don't see a niche for themselves, they may become manipulative. These employees respond to consideration. If they are excluded or taken for granted, expect a move to the low side of Eight.

Twos may play favorites whether or not they are in managerial posts. Important and beautiful people are worthy of attention. Approval is not extended to proletariats. Twos want approval and are afraid they won't get it. They monitor who's popular. They know who's moving up the ladder. Getting close to power is their way to control. A Two rarely marries another Giver, and Twos may compete with peers, but when they cooperate, they can serve each other well.

Two with Three: A Giver-Performer Couple

Twos give attention and Threes expect it, as the couple unites to support the Performer's needs. Even Twos with worldly recognition will adapt in order to be appealing to their partners. Twos work to achieve the approval of loved ones, while Threes are driven to get personal success. These types can look very similar, but their motives are entirely different. Givers work to be loved, and Threes love to work. This couple often bonds in a relationship of "successful love." Each supports the other professionally, while the Giver interprets family feelings and becomes the emotional center of the home.

The most common complaint is the Three's work status—late hours, then coming home to fall asleep. Even a Two with an outstanding profession in his or her own right waits by the phone. "Where's the attention? I'm not needed here." It helps if Performers put time for romance on the schedule. It helps if Twos can state their needs. If Givers need time and attention, Performers will have to focus there. Threes are not deliberately neglectful. They do to others what they do to themselves. Givers bring feelings to the couple, and Threes are primarily focused on task. In a fight, Twos feel superior because they're more emotional, while Threes feel superior "because of all that I've done." It helps if Twos can read effort as affection. Feelings are not a tangible product, so Threes can miss the point of romance.

Reassured of their importance, Twos are less demanding of time. This couple has a great deal in common: high-profile image and a desire for success. It's an easy relationship if the Three focuses on feelings and the Two doesn't have to compete with a job for the mate's attention.

Two-Three Partnership at Work

This is a high-powered work team. Both know how to produce and promote. The natural position puts Three as manager. Performers expect to lead, and Givers are happy to back them if the need for attention is met. If a Three manager recognizes Two's contribution, things work well. If the manager becomes self-centered or self-promoting, the Two will find another candidate to back. Performers get angry when tasks are interrupted, and in their haste to get to a goal, they step on people's backs.

Giver employees can soften a manager's image. Twos do not see using image as deceptive; they are sensitive to human connections and can help Threes promote an image that works.

Two employees must be attended to and recognized for what they do. If they are taken for granted, Twos may initiate an exposé. Suddenly people will see the Three as a loser. The office pipeline will be alerted to the Three's falsifications. "They only look good because you don't know them." The "real" story will come out. The Three will feel undermined in the vulnerable area of image. It helps if Three managers remember to show interest and to have private talks with Twos. Givers won't ask and Performers don't remember, so the pair falls into a communication impasse. Three managers should keep constant contact with Two employees. Twos don't work well in a vacuum. They work for the person, not for the task.

Two managers want to be liked and may have difficulty with competitive Threes. Threes go around authority. They want to be the authority. They want the manager's job and may be insensitive about how they go about getting it. Performer employees may be confrontational and directly competitive, which makes the manager feel unliked. The important thing is for Twos to set limits. Threes need to know the scope of the task, or they will crash through boundaries, usurp other people's territory, and redefine the goals. Threes can be overpowering if their drive for success is not adequately contained. Giver managers will do well to apportion a small domain of influence to Three employees, remembering to set limits and to cap the goals. Given a healthy chance for advancement, Three employees will probably adopt a Giver's people skills. Three employees are in touch with what serves the product. Given an example of Two's management style, Threes will learn the value of meeting people's needs.

Two with Four: A Giver-Romantic Couple

This relationship is like a dance. Both partners have a push-pull pattern in relationships. Each pulls back when a partner is available. Each pursues when the partner disappears. The similarity makes an interesting romantic tango. You come forward, I go backward. You go backward, I want you again. Each appreciates the other's capacity for feeling. At last there is the possibility of being met emotionally. This couple can bring romantic love into being without embarrassment. They are partnered in a dance of emotional distance, because each is afraid to commit.

The couple shares the Two–Four line in the diagram. Each will see a part of himself or herself dramatized in the other's style. Twos moving to the security point feel free to seek authentic commitment. It's OK to be dramatic. It's all right to be selfish, to be yourself instead of giving yourself away. Twos see an exaggeration of their own emotional story in the Romantic temperament. Fours are people who can make emotion public, who put their feelings first.

Fours are stressed when they have to reach out to people and they can feel deprived by having to meet others' needs. They appreciate Twos' capacity to win others over, but they also see Twos' flirtation and flattery as lacking emotional depth. If Four rejects, Two pursues, enjoying the challenge of obstacles to the relationship. A Two's power is in pursuit. But if Four turns around and becomes available, Two is frightened away.

The dance is completed when the partners agree to commit. With commitment, the push-pull pattern stops. It helps if the Two can find real feelings instead of changing persona in order to please. What comes up for Givers is the fear of being ordinary. "Will my Four abandon me if I am myself?" The Four needs to question the urge to criticize. "Why do I see the flaws when my Giver is with me?"

Two-Four Partnership at Work

The emotional tone of the workplace will be important. Fours like to feel special, and Twos cultivate relationships of all kinds. There is likely to be an unusual ambience and attention to people. Even in the anonymity of a factory, attention will be paid to personal life. These people are likely to know about each other's personal life. It's not a way of hanging out and wasting time; it's a motivation. It's a plus to feel included in someone else's family; the workplace can be a place of belonging. You listen to each other's story at lunchtime; you know each other here.

Two managers use their persona in conducting business. This may turn Fours off. It looks like sucking up to people or selling out for a pat on the back. Seen from a Four perspective, the stress point of Two looks exposed. "How can she be so obvious about trying to draw attention?" "How tasteless to be so needy." "Why does he have to be liked?"

Feeling criticized, Two managers may try to find a need to fill. The Four employee needs support, attention, help. Four employees may see this as focusing on flaws or being unfavorably compared with peers. If Fours become competitive, it's better to give them their own territory, delegate, and fall back. It helps to single Romantics out for special responsibility, an area of their own, something unique that they're called on to do. A Two needing to be indispensable and a Four needing to feel unique will become competitive. That inequality can be diffused if Four is respected in a special area of work.

Four managers enjoy their status. This arrangement allows Twos to help. Two employees like to be indispensable and to meet the needs of a manager who leads with distinctive flair and style.

Fours reward people who are "understanding." Twos will realize that the manager is moody and learn to act accordingly. If the manager is self-absorbed with work or private life, Two employees will feel ignored; but it's unsafe to ignore people who are indispensable in the workplace. Givers retaliate by pulling out—they may not be obviously angry, but suddenly nothing seems to be on schedule. A typical revenge is to support someone else's work. Romantic managers see employees as working for them, but Twos don't work *for*, they only work *with*. It helps to make the Giver feel absolutely essential. Twos need to know they're not being ignored; they need to know the manager's moodiness is purely personal and not directed at them.

Two with Five: A Giver-Observer Couple

This is definitely an attraction of opposites. Five is the most contracted Enneagram type, and Two is the most extended toward others. Twos are attracted to the self-possession and quiet of Fives. Emotional detachment is the antithesis of the big feelings that are characteristic of Givers.

Fives exude a sense of quiet and interiority that feels restful and steady. It's as if they grant others permission to take interior solitude seriously. Givers sense that there is "someone at home" who considers and decides for themselves rather than finding identity by altering in order to placate the needs of others. Observers are free to go their own way, independently of the wishes of others. Most precious of all to the relationship-bound Two, emotional detachment produces relative immunity from what other people think.

The attraction from the Five side will be to the open-hearted generosity that Twos often display. Twos' willingness to engage with life and activity is compelling to aversive people. The common configuration shows Two as the couple's socialite. It may seem that the Two speaks for the couple at parties and gatherings, while the more contained and cerebral Five waits for the conversation to turn to a topic of intellectual interest. It is definitely easier to spend a casual afternoon with the couple than alone with the Five, unless you happen to share a similar interest. If your interests coincide with the Five's, the afternoon may be full of information, but the conversation will rarely stray from the common interest that you share.

Twos and Fives can look like they're from different species. The Two is one of those people who "go out" and "try things" and who enjoy parties filled with new faces. Someone who, strangely, seems to enjoy small talk and who claims that feelings are a useful source of information. The couple operates from startlingly different perspectives. Twos go toward people to interact and socialize, while Fives move away to analyze and think. This dynamic can either produce a balanced life in which each demonstrates the integrity of his or her own worldview or it can turn into a tug-of-war in which Two pulls for emotional contact and Five contracts and withdraws.

If the separation solidifies, each will see the other as "the case." The Two will see withdrawal and a minimalist lifestyle as demonstrations of emotional deprivation and need. Fueled by the need to find identity by meeting others' needs, Twos are attracted to the challenge of overcoming obstacles to a relationship. The challenge with Fives is obvious—to open someone's feelings who is set against the importance of emotion. Twos win big if they can get Fives to respond. The Five may not agree that detachment equals deprivation. The counterargument to the notion that big feelings are the criteria of caring is to see the Two's emotional oscillations as signs of instability.

The couple joins at Eight, which will ensure a powerful aggressive meeting when Five feels secure enough to fight and to find those very feelings that Two has been pushing for. It helps for Two to pull back, so there is enough emotional space for Five to come forward.

Observers in long-term relationships say that they have had to learn to come forward, to stay in the room when it feels emotionally uncomfortable, and to deal with feelings rather than withdrawing to think. It helps if Fives don't summarily dismiss spontaneous feelings as trivial. Observers might initiate a system for handling questions of the heart. It's all right to consider an emotional position if a time is set for future discussion. Givers feel reassured when they know that the matter will come to the table rather than be buried and forgotten.

Two-Five Partnership at Work

The difference in type can make for an effective work relationship: Two's orientation to people and their needs in combination with Five's ability to work abstractly and in isolation. Each is likely to find an appropriate place without having to say much about it. The setup works best when the focus is on task, and each draws on the skills of the other to serve a common purpose. Their talents are so different that the relationship works well with either type as boss.

Two managers will want to know how their employees feel about them personally. This may read as intrusion to Fives, particularly if Two managers try to draw Five employees into the social scene. Two managers may be concerned that Five employees are unhappy off by themselves, especially in the absence of any information about their private lives. In their need to be helpful, Two managers can violate the boundaries of personal space that allow Fives to function comfortably in a work environment.

The Two needs to focus on the projects at hand, rather than becoming curious about the Five's emotional life. It helps to give Observers specific tasks and, if possible, separate offices, and let them be. The manager will be pleased with Five's ability to self-direct and make decisions. A Two manager's attention is often directed to the more influential people in the organization. Fives are the perfect employees to mind the shop while the manager extends the base of operations.

It's a good interaction when an Observer employee is left to produce useful information for the outgoing Two manager who, in exchange, can provide the inestimably valuable service of protecting the Five from dealing directly with people. If the Five is manager, the door to the inner sanctum may stand politely ajar, but an aura of unavailability will permeate the office. The Two will feel cut off from a source of presence and advice. If the Five is wise, she or he will place the Giver as a special representative. Givers are natural links between the public and power. A good arrangement would show Five setting up what could be semiformal meetings with each staffer, even when these are not strictly necessary to the work. The meetings are to solicit opinions from employees. Just a chance to be heard will be vital because the Five manager does not personally model interaction or cooperation. Fives should also learn to tolerate group meetings at which employees speak directly to each other.

Lack of availability on the part of the Five manager can create employee discontent. "Where is leadership when you need it?" The idea behind the semiformal meetings is to establish a place where conflict can be handled. If the Five disappears under fire, the Two may be able to run interference for the nonconfrontational manager. If the Five disappears from the Two, however, the abandoned Giver may protest loudly.

Two with Six: A Giver-Trooper Couple

A typical interaction shows Two moving toward Six to disarm the fear of intimacy. Six doubt may become a catalyst to the Giver, who likes to overcome obstacles to a relationship. The message will be: "Believe in me. Believe in us." Initial attractions show Two moving in to help the doubtful partner, and Six learning to feel safe with that degree of regard. It helps when Givers support the underdog goals that seem important to the Six partner. In this way, the Six can trust the Two's intentions because efforts are going toward a worthwhile cause.

It may be more difficult to make the Trooper personally successful. Afraid of being recognized authorities, Sixes may see Twos' help as self-serving. The skeptical Six may wonder whether the Two in fact stands to benefit. The Six may feel set up to be the vehicle for the Two's ambition. Already stressed by public exposure and success, a Six may sabotage the effort by failing Two's expectations. The Six may be in a bind: on the one hand, feeling soothed by the Giver's care and concern; on the other hand, frustrated by doubting the genuineness of flattery. The Six will feel expected to perform and may rebel instead. Frustrated when expected returns fail to materialize, the Two will become actively critical of the Trooper's stop-start progress toward goals.

Mutual mistrust can be reduced if the Six is able to separate personal goals from those that the Two favors, and can set those personal goals as a priority. It helps if Six can remember to be physically demonstrative and to learn to accept honestly intended affection instead of dismissing Two's natural warmth as flattery.

It's important for Twos to discern whether the help they offer is altruistic or self-serving. Six doubt will center on the Two's unconscious agenda of giving to get. It helps for Twos to find their own professions and activities. Sixes can be unusually loyal supporters for the family's efforts.

Two-Six Partnership at Work

This is another partnership based on differences. Twos are attracted to power, and Sixes are ambivalent about becoming an authority. This is a natural alliance in an underdog context, such as a business turnaround or a popular cause that is under fire. Both types lead well when they are aligned with a cause they believe in. Twos want worthwhile potentials to flourish, and Sixes are identified with struggle.

Conflict is likely in a "regular" work setting that brings out self-interest and competition rather than dedicated altruism. The reason for this is that both types are vulnerable to faltering as long-term leaders. Sixes because of their stress in the performance aspects of point Three, and Twos because they want to be liked. Six managers will want to ensure loyalty from the employees and will be disturbed if the Two alters to please a powerful rival. The socially aware Two is going to try to become attractive to whoever is worth cultivating, which will raise a Trooper's suspicions. The Six manager will think: "Just where does this employee's loyalty lie?" "Can they be trusted with sensitive information?" Both types can believe themselves to be the targets of any free-floating animosity in the office. A Six manager will try to discover the source of difficulty in order to eliminate it, and the Two will try to make friends.

A Two employee can interpret the manager's hesitancy as lack of commitment to the task. Givers are confused by Doubting Mind, because Twos generally trust people on impulse; but for Six trust is a very slow build. The Two may also be aware of the manager's potential, and if those talents do not materialize, the Two employee will feel threatened and find a primary work alliance elsewhere.

Troopers want to be egalitarian. They may not think it's fair to encourage any single employee or to "manipulate" people into being more productive. The Six misses an important opportunity by not cultivating Givers with personal attention. Twos must feel that they wield private influence in order to feel safe.

Loyal Six employees can see trouble coming from a great distance. In this partnership, Two managers can then go into action with their political and people skills to ward off danger. If Sixes see the manager as self-serving and therefore dangerous, Twos will face the possibility of a behind-the-scenes coalition aimed at exposing the authority.

Two with Seven: A Giver-Epicure Couple

This can be a classic fun couple. Givers want to help Epicures realize their plans and will share the enthusiasm that Sevens bring to a relationship. The Seven's vision is often the focal point of the couple's emotional life. Both will share the hope of a bright future together.

Both types have broad interests—Twos, because of their many selves, and Sevens, as a result of multioptional thinking. The pair is drawn to the very best in entertainment and current events. The Giver will focus on the Seven's potential talents but will also see the Seven's hidden pain. Givers are fascinated by Sevens' sunny exterior and are doubly attracted to the fact that Sevens are dissatisfied. Givers often interpret Sevens' gluttony for experience as revealing a search for emotional depth.

Twos see that Sevens need to focus. They also see through some of Sevens' plans. Givers may feel called to make Sevens fully productive people and to heal their underlying fears. In return Givers receive adventure and attention. Sevens can be charming as playmates and romantic ideals.

Both types are optimistic. The charm of Seven and seduction of Two produce an attractive pair. Sevens are self-directed and will follow their interests whether or not the mate is around. Wise Twos will pursue the interests of the many selves, rather than wait at home. Both can enjoy a spread of activities, so there will always be something new to enjoy. Given freedom, Sevens can face the *C* word. Commitment is possible if Sevens don't feel limited.

These are naturally seductive people. Each likes to consider the potential availability of other partners. It helps to ground the relationship in commitment and to determine how much outside attention each of the partners will need.

Both types are wary of prolonged contact, which Sevens feel might limit them, and Twos feel might expose them. The Seven escapes into pleasant activity. The Two then feels challenged and pursues the Seven. The Two may want more attention than the Seven can easily give. The Two thinks: "Plans seem to shift and change so easily. Is my partner going to stick?" An attention crisis may develop: The Two sees a superficial lightweight, and the Seven sees an emotional drag. If the Two presses for attention, the Seven will rationalize: "This was never meant to be."

This couple colludes in optimism; both want to hear that life will be OK. It helps when they can focus on real feelings rather than intimate ideas. It helps when the couple joins in the adventure of moving from fascination to emotional depth.

Two-Seven Partnership at Work

This is a popular work combination. When the Seven has ideas, the Two makes them happen. On the high side, the future visioning of Seven falls into the capable stewardship of Two. The danger is that neither will be able to lead a project to a successful conclusion. Epicures are at their best in the initial stages of a project, and their energy winds down from there. Givers are at their best supporting a strong leader, one who produces tangible results.

A Two employee with a Seven boss may attempt to manifest all of the options, hoping to fill a need. The Seven may just be thinking out loud, which sets the Two up for a lot of hard work and rejection. Sevens are not often strong leaders. If the Two perceives this and also feels neglected, the Two may try to manipulate a better deal somewhere else. Twos do not waste time on unappreciative people.

If the Seven is narcissistically preoccupied and the Two is unhappy, none of the Seven's grand schemes will turn out. If plans change quickly and goals fail to materialize, the Two will feel ineffective. If there is no personal bond between them, the Two employee will find another niche in the organization. Unhappy Twos will work the system in order to find a graceful exit.

Two managers should put Seven employees in positions where they are protected from boredom. Sevens are hard workers as long as they're still learning or being challenged. Two managers may realize the slippery nature of Seven and be concerned about performance and deadlines. They may also feel that their authority is threatened. "How will it look to superiors if this employee gets away with something?" "How can I control my employee and still be liked?"

When in doubt, Twos either make friends and allies of their employees or withdraw and cut them off. It helps both types if the manager makes consequences clear. Seven-like charm, rationalization, and reframing all disappear in the face of a deadline.

Two with Eight: A Giver-Boss Couple

This couple aligns around the seduction of Two and the power of Eight. The Giver moves toward others by trying to please, and the Boss moves against them to uncover the truth. The desire to be central in a partner's life is familiar to both types because they meet at Two. Both want attention, but their manner of earning that attention is radically different. Twos adjust their feelings to meet the need of others, and Eights insist that their own needs be met. Physical attention is significant in the relationship, as Eights are sexually expressive and Twos often equate sexuality with love. The focus will be on the Eight's agenda. The lust platform demands goal satisfaction, and Twos take pride in making wishes happen.

The most common interaction shows Two trying to soften the Eight, and Eight holding out. This creates a certain attraction that can remain in force for years. The self-referencing Eight gets a lot of attention, and the Giver is focused on the other, which neatly prevents their own needs from emerging. In return for the indispensable help that Givers are able to offer, Bosses can provide energetic protection and forceful leadership.

Following the lines of the Enneagram diagram, a secure Eight can shift to the more empathic Two position. It's not that Eights "turn into" Twos when they feel secure; rather they act out the Two-like need for attention in Eight-like ways, either by controlling the Giver's life or by offering solid support of those goals.

Less commonly Eights surrender control and allow Twos to direct the course of the relationship.

Eights "in Two" can be extremely generous. They show affection by trying to make things happen for the others. This puts a Giver in the uncomfortable position of having to receive. It may feel like the Eight is dominating even when the support offered is entirely legitimate. If Twos are able to look within themselves, discover their private agendas, and go for what they want, Eights can exercise power as the second in command. But if the Two is afraid to have personal needs exposed, or if an Eight does indeed dominate, Twos will explode, fight for freedom, and shoot across the diagram to their own stress point of Eight. Many Two-Eight pairs report that open hostilities can serve the constructive purpose of drawing the couple closer together. Eights feel more secure when all the cards are on the table, and Twos are pressured into knowing what they want.

Another outcome of open hostilities shows Two, cut off from emotional contact, quickly disappearing into the arms of friends or another relationship. Twos who feel indispensable will see themselves as having been used in the relationship. They gave their all and weren't appreciated. Now they want revenge. A conflict between an enraged Two and an Eight ex-partner can escalate into a full-scale war. A meeting at Eight can engage the couple in intense, lustful, and often intriguing animosity.

Twos in Eight can be deadly manipulators. Unaccustomed to direct confrontation, they may resort to the more indirect routes of personal influence and social pressure. Twos want to keep their own images intact, so they will present the Eight as "the case." If Twos' pride is injured or they are openly rejected, they can be public and loud about their difficulties.

Customarily a crisis shows Eight feeling betrayed by manipulation, clamping down on soft emotions, and becoming increasingly belligerent. The message is: "You're dishonest. Don't mess with me."

Two-Eight Partnership at Work

The key word is *trust*. This pair is capable of almost synchronous action when they trust each other's intentions. Their shared line on the diagram is commonly acted out in the workplace by Eight as the heavy and Two as the liaison with staff members. The pair can fall into good cop–bad cop patterns, with the Boss as enforcer and the Giver offering concessions. It's a good alliance when Two receives enough attention and when Eight feels safe enough to relinquish some of the control.

A Two manager will have to win an Eight's support. Insisting on strong leadership, an Eight employee is likely to focus on the Two's image of popularity. "Is leadership genuinely honest, or is this manager self-serving?" A Giver's proclivity to favor people who are "worth it" looks dishonest to the justice-minded Eight. Once alarmed by the possibility of workplace injustice, an Eight will simply try to eliminate as many controls as possible. A Two manager can be at a disadvantage in an escalating rebellion. Eights are not focused on face-saving solutions and, having little in the way of a public persona to defend, can be particularly irritating to image-oriented types. It helps to set clear limits and consequences for both management and staff and to document agreements. Without documentation an Eight employee may feel too threatened to cooperate fully. "Why give your all for management's benefit?" Eights will think: "Maybe there's a hidden agenda here. Let's test it out."

Eight managers will be either loved or hated by their Two employees. If they are loved, then the Two's natural tendency to want approval from authority can provide Eight with loyal support. It helps if Two employees learn to give full reports. When information is not immediately forthcoming, Eights may imagine an escalating conspiracy. The employees should provide what may seem to be overkill reportage. It also helps if the Eight manager can place the employee on a search-and-discovery mission. In that way, a Giver is made somewhat indispensable and the

Eight is still in control. If the pair does not get along, a Two tends to deprive the manager of useful contact and information, taking comfort in the shelter of a small, personally chosen clique.

Two with Nine: A Giver-Mediator Couple

This couple can look alike. Both say that they merge with other people's agendas, both say that they take on their partner's emotions, and both are focused on fulfilling needs. Although both types merge emotionally, they do so with different motives. Nines want a reason for living, which can be found through a mate, while Twos try to find identity through others. Because both partners merge, each can be deeply affected by the other at a nonverbal level.

Givers want to help Nines find purpose. The Giver will be especially helpful if the Nine has the potential to excel in an area in which the Two can take pride. Twos may also be attracted to the gentleness and caring quality that Nines frequently emanate. Nines enjoy affection, which allows Twos to be as affectionate as they wish. Either type can use sex as a way to wake up to real contact, and Twos often feel that sexual attention is equal to love.

Sexuality could stand as a metaphor for the best that a Two-Nine couple can offer each other. The Two is asking, "What do you want?" and the Nine is responding, "I want you as you really are." The Nine is suited to helping the Two tell the difference between the adjusted self and an authentic emotional self, and the Two is able to energize the Nine erotically.

A crisis will emerge if the Two becomes indispensable and the Nine feels controlled. The Nine will suspect that he or she is filling Two's unrecognized needs and will stubbornly refuse to cooperate. Nines hold back their own potential as a way of getting even, and they spread attention to other things. Twos get bored if Nines fail to achieve their potential and furious if attention is withdrawn. Twos will resent feeling forced to take the rudder in the relationship when they prefer to be inspired and led. Feeling abandoned by the Nine's lack of initiative, the Two may become complaining. A painful cycle can ensue: Nine withdraws in the face of Two's demands, causing Two to pursue more forcefully, causing Nine to entrench in stubborn silence.

If the Nine becomes stubborn, or fails to realize her or his potential, the Two will demand freedom. Fearing separation, Nines wake up but may also become possessive. If the Nine moves forward, the Two falls back with loud demands for freedom, but the Nine can choose to withdraw attention, which makes the Two frantic to reignite the connection. This severe standoff can be eased when Givers support their mates' real needs.

It helps when Nines turn attention to themselves rather than fighting someone else's agenda. It helps for Twos to know that Nines take time to decide. The most important decisions are last. Twos should initiate a question, negotiate a deadline, and leave Nines alone for the duration.

Two-Nine Partnership at Work

This partnership can be like introducing a jump start to a source of potential energy. Givers go into action for other people's needs, and Mediators need to be activated. This is a common partnership in both marriage and business life. It works very well when agendas coincide.

The Nine holds the agenda but has managed to bury it under secondary commitments. It matters too much. It's too much to hope for. It's too important to complete. A Two's magic lies in meeting needs, in making hopes happen, in drawing people out. If the work agendas match, an energetic jump start activates Nine's agenda. The Two focuses on structuring the Nine's potential, and the Nine rides the current of energy and regard.

The partners' rhythms are very different. The Two will be impatient with the time taken over simple decisions. Twos can prioritize more easily than Nines, and once merged with the Nine's workplace rhythm, a Two boss will be impatient with the steady pace of a Mediator. Two employees may feel infuriated by the repetitious discussion and meetings often favored by Nines.

Because both types merge, they will have a certain nonverbal understanding. Both are concerned about the feeling tone of the workplace. Nines absorb the emotional distress of others and will be interested in hearing all points of view, with an eye to defusing potential conflict. Twos are good at spotting potential winners and placing them at strategic points in the organization.

As managers, Twos rely on developing key people rather than on meticulous structure. They strive for a well-knit community that prospers with good care. They will appreciate Nines' awareness of other people's positions. They will also appreciate the fact that as employees, Nines rarely compete with the boss. Nines can be very loyal to benign authority, and in return Twos give public credit and recognition, something that motivates Nines to go beyond the call of duty.

Two managers generally have favorites. Nines relate to authority through structure and may resent the inequality. If the manager chooses the Nine as one of the inner circle, this employee will tune the problem out rather than take action. If they are not one of the specially chosen, their unexpressed anger can lead to problems with supervision. A manager can get Nines back on track with apologies and a productive routine. Nines generally settle in and become cooperative after a struggle.

Nine managers are effective when there is a clear course of action, and when leadership is efficient, Twos offer support. Two employees can help the manager with key information. They can funnel opinions through the office pipeline, they can point out the politically expedient course of action, and they can help Nines cut through the conflict of decision making by charting a course for Nines' self-advancement.

Double Three: A Double Performer Couple

This relationship may be an endangered species. There are relatively few Threes in our Enneagram classes, and double Three is a rarity. Performers are far more common in business circles, and they do appear in force at Enneagram business trainings; but even in that setting there are few sightings of long-standing couples.

Threes have attractions all around the diagram. Some are drawn to "similar" high-energy, high-profile types like Twos, Sevens, and Three-like Fours. Other Threes say that they're drawn to highly emotional partners because of the dissimilarity to themselves. The most frequently reported Performer partnering in my corner of the world is Three with Five, the stated reason being a balance of opposites. The very few double Threes I have recorded say that they enjoy each other's attitude. Everything seems possible, and they usually have a number of projects going on at the same time. They find that they become impatient with each other and tend to compete when they're involved in domestic projects, and for this reason they characteristically maintain elaborate professional connections, each in his or her own field. The couple's social life revolves around people who share similar work interests or those who are raising children and like to do things together. Their social orientation is definitely activity related. This is a couple who does things together, and they relate through shared activity rather than hanging out and "being" with family and friends.

The trick is to support each other's accomplishments without falling into a pattern of parallel play in which each leads a separate life while living under the same roof. This can be a situation in which everything looks great on the surface. A picture-postcard life with all the appearances of happiness and prosperity but without the inner intensity of strong emotional connection. Threes say that relationships can look great and feel empty. They may find interest and excitement for projects but a growing indifference toward building for the future. "Yet another challenge? Do we have to mobilize again?"

These couples speak of having had to deal with a certain emotional deadening that takes the edge off enjoying the fruit of their own efforts. There's a need to hurry on, to finish quickly and proceed smoothly to fulfill the next task, the next expectation, the next phase of life. It's all supposed to look normal and be well-organized and produce useful results, but over time it becomes apparent that something is missing. It's the same feeling that Sevens often report when they reach midlife. "Haven't we been here before? What can we do if we don't do the same things over again?"

The need to turn inward and to deepen emotionally usually presents itself as a weariness with external life. Projects and fast-paced, work-related connection seem superficial. There is a gathering awareness that something vital is missing, that we are being deprived unless our efforts are accompanied by a range of feelings about what we do and a willingness to absorb, to be affected, to be with the feelings that are stirred by activity.

A double Three relationship can either compound the Performer worldview in which feelings are incompatible with getting the job done or provide an educated source of help for the turn inward.

Double Three Partnership at Work

Threes are highly valued in the go-ahead phase of a business cycle. They customarily enjoy selling and promoting products and often embody the personal enthusiasm that can be a company's best advertisement. They have a natural affinity for the fast-paced, rapid-turnover business style that characterizes the steep upward climb of a rising enterprise. A new, potentially profitable project is Three territory.

Difficulties may arise when Threes have to outperform each other. They thrive in a competitive environment, but if the merit system pits them against each other, they can become adversarial. Threes work hard for a bonus and promotions because, more important than material benefits, their psychological well-being depends on winning. They are more vulnerable to professional loss than other types of people and will defend themselves from the subjective pain of losing status. New job opportunities will be covertly cultivated. Threes are likely to jump ship. Contacts and potential clients can be hoarded, secreted, and traded. It may not show on the surface, but the competitive edge will take on a self-serving, win-at-all-costs attitude that can be confused with increasing one's personal marketability. It helps to give Threes their own domain to shape and direct and to encourage them to exchange information by modeling the efficiency of cooperation and by attaching status to a group win or a team effort.

Double Three can also develop into an invincible partnership when goals are aligned. This is definitely a can-do pair that ensures progress if it's humanly possible to move ahead. They think alike, which is both a blessing and a bane. On the high side they can move systems forward, and on the low side they can move forward compulsively. Polarized against doubt and failure, Threes can be quick to reframe signs of imminent difficulty. They may want to shift to ensure short-term gains without fully considering the consequences. Threes are high-profile contenders and may find themselves straining at the leash during a consolidation phase of the business cycle. Like people, businesses move through phases. There are also likely to be useful periods of contraction and down-sizing, all of which can read as failure and loss to

Threes. Performers are at a disadvantage during a business turn-around, when controversial or unpopular decisions are called for, or when meticulous long-term planning is needed.

Three managers will have to model the image that they expect a Three employee to follow. Performers take on the look of the environment in which they find themselves and will imitate the workplace ideal. If cooperation is called for, then Threes can be successful at cooperating. If personal achievement is rewarded, then the same Three may become highly competitive.

Performer employees look for openings through which to rise professionally. It helps if these are clearly demarcated so that Threes have no reason to manipulate people or the structure for self-advantage. The guiding idea in personal work with Threes is to ensure public recognition while downplaying competition with other employees. It helps if the system reflects participation over competition. It helps to build systems that reflect the effectiveness of cooperation rather than hierarchy and personal power.

Three with Four: A Performer-Romantic Couple

Both are focused on image and the degree of regard that they receive from other people. Performers want respect for achievement, and Romantics need to be seen as distinctive and unique. The couple usually presents itself well in public, often adopting a lifestyle that emanates successful elegance. Initial attractions show Three drawn to the inner drama of Four as a counterpart to their own desire for public recognition. From the Four side, a Three's preoccupation with worldly events can be equally challenging. Performers seem perpetually focused on their work, even during private moments. This displacement of attention can be irritating to Romantics, who crave intimate connection, but a Performer's task orientation also creates a psychological distancing mechanism that can be attractive. Four partners never seem to get enough of their Three's attention, which makes them focus on the best features of what seems to be missing. Here's an example of the difference in the couple's point of view.

DREAMS

[Three with Four] My wife and I are driving into a Santa Fe sunset. We're sailing into heaven. Three hundred sixty degrees of moving color, including little shades of green. We park on a ridge above town, and it's just dazzling. We hold hands with the light blazing through the windshield, and then I start to hear her sob. "There'll never be another like this, and soon it will be gone." At the same moment, I'm aware that I'm thinking of an elaborate scheme concerning second jobs for both of us, which will buy us a piece of the ridge.

The couple's major difficulty will concern Four's moods and Three's suspended feelings. It's a recurrent theme in this relationship. Four longs, while Three promises more time and then reneges. It will be difficult for Fours to let the image of promised intimacy assume a reasonable shape. Three's unavailability can be magnetizing because the couple never has quite enough time together to make the relationship ordinary. Deprived of intimacy, Fours often go into high drama, recriminations, or deep depression, which is just the kind of emotional demand that Threes detest. Fours overvalue emotional life, and Threes undervalue it. A crisis can develop if Four competes for attention and Three goes into evasive action by overscheduling other commitments. It helps if each can enter the other's worldview. Threes, for example, typically demonstrate their commitment by working "for us." Wise Fours might lend themselves to this "unemotional" way of loving and learn to see the difference between using work to numb emotion and working as a demonstration of commitment.

Threes want to be successful in the eyes of their significants, and Four's dissatisfaction can feel like a blow to self-esteem. Rather than retaliating by trivializing Four's yearning spirit or feeling underappreciated for "all the work that I've done for us," it helps when Threes can lend themselves to the Romantic's fascination with things that are missing in life. Learning to experience the full range of emotions that Fours exemplify could be the task of a lifetime, and one that could make this relationship deeply satisfying instead of merely successful.

Three-Four Partnership at Work

This is another juxtaposition of differences that can be either mutually supportive or a workplace disaster. The pair can accomplish a great deal because task focus requires a bypass of tender feelings. Three's go-ahead attitude ensures consistent production, while Fours make products that look elegantly successful rather than successfully slick. The combination does well when Four can be valued for an unusual and slightly controversial contribution, which becomes successful through Three's support. The partnership comes to grief when the two compete. Both want recognition, and they can compete to the point of ruin rather than give in.

Three managers can "do for show." Their Four employees are going to see the difference between doing something because it's significant and doing what looks good to the crowd. It won't be OK if an awards dinner turns into a photo opportunity for the manager, and it won't sit well, for example, if difficult meetings are efficiently scheduled so no time is left for emotional fallout. Three managers who assume that employees are equally committed to task over feelings should remember to pencil key words into their daily schedules like "Don't yell" and "Ask permission."

Threes love creative productivity and can be captivated by people who insist on authentic, meaningful work. It seems daring to insist that work reflect oneself rather than molding yourself to fit a job description. Fours often prefer to hold out for years rather than compromise themselves with a safe relationship or uninspired days at the office. This insistence on self-expression is noticeably different from Three's willingness to submit to periods of numbing drudgery in order to rise professionally. Any employee who has a viable idea that improves efficiency or product development is going to be encouraged by a Three manager.

Romantic managers may be disconcerted by Three's overt competition. The partnership works smoothly when the Three is well occupied but can fall apart when the Three moves in to impress the hierarchy and staff. Fours in authority tend to see Threes as gauche. They may be smart, but they don't have style. The image of a high-fashion model looking down at a trendy college kid conveys the sense of social distance. How ridiculous. How tacky to be so pushy. Any manager trying to block an up-and-coming Three should expect an end run. This employee will simply grab the ball, dodge the manager, and try to score with the power elite.

Fruitful Three-Four partnerships are greatly assisted by third-party input. The Three needs to see that it's important to respect social boundaries with a Four in authority. Mediation should reaffirm interest in the task, to dispel the impression that Three is a heartless social climber, and to reaffirm the Four's seniority. Three employees will be encouraged to respect their own lesser place in the organization when managers have the backing of a hierarchy. Threes are impressed by successful models and will cooperate more fully with a clear chain of command.

Three with Five: A Performer-Observer Couple

Threes usually describe themselves as extroverted, and the vast majority of Fives fit the classic introversion profile. An introvert's privacy needs pose a challenge to Performers, whose self-image rests on recognition for tasks. The pair's natural differences invite Threes to move toward the more emotionally retracted partner and to commandeer the mechanics of a relationship. When a trip is planned, for example, Threes are likely to send for brochures, suggest the itinerary, and book the reservations. All the Five has to do is pack and go.

This is a very common coupling in both love and business life, and it initially shows an almost unopposed movement toward the emotionally distant Five. Performers show their affection by giving time and energy to a relationship, which fits the needs of a reclusive partner.

Saying yes to a committed relationship is fraught with difficulty for Observers. It's so easy to detach and let go that a Five's continued presence is de facto commitment. They often "initiate" a relationship by positioning themselves to be emotionally drawn out by other people. Threes may have to hold back so that Five's boundaries are respected, rather than barreling in and inadvertently causing the Five to withdraw.

Observers show their availability in nonverbal ways, by sharing information about themselves, by investing energy in household maintenance, and by their personal presence. Nonverbal understandings seem to work for this couple. Given a mutual attraction, Threes move ahead unless they are opposed, and Fives commit themselves by presence. These obvious differences in psychological style form the hub of the relationship. Three's need for social contact has to be balanced with Five's desires for privacy and predictability.

The most typical arrangement shows Three as the pair's social secretary. The Performer filters the couple's phone messages and engagements, consults with the Five in private, and then conveys their decisions to the world at large. Home life can develop into a pattern of mutually acceptable parallel play, in which each partner conducts a separate life and meets at designated times for meals and family time.

Unexpectedly it's often the Five partner who objects to Three's frequent absence from home. Once attached, Observers can get territorial within the security of the castle walls and, Eight-like, may want to limit a partner's outside interests. Threes usually reduce their schedule to keep the peace and then gradually increase their workload again. It can become a cyclical crisis in which Fives sulk and withhold comfort, presence, and sex while Threes bury themselves in work, hoping that the difficulty will pass. When Threes feel threatened, they commonly work harder to numb their feelings. This has the adverse effect of increasing the distance between themselves and others.

This is a relationship that profits from sitting down and negotiating mutual commitments. Neither partner is particularly fascinated by the language of feelings and sentiment, and both types have intimacy issues; Threes are afraid to be seen separately from their achievements, and Fives are afraid of being drained by other people's needs. Both do, however, relate to shared activities and agreements that take a predetermined amount of time and energy. Fives can be forthcoming if they know what is expected, and Threes express themselves through action.

The couple may find it easier to talk when attention is deflected to a golf game or hiking a trail together. Each demonstrates affection by doing things for loved ones—Threes in the literal sense of producing tangible success "for us," and Fives in the more subtle sense of giving up private time and space. It helps these naturally independent people to formulate a system of negotiation that allows them to adjust to each other's style of relating. Fives, for example, can learn to enjoy the pleasures of social life, and Threes can open themselves to be touched by silence and quiet contact.

Three-Five Partnership at Work

This is one of the most frequently reported business partnerships. The Observer is typically positioned as the analyst, leaving the Performer to handle public matters. Fives often produce the basic concept and theory, which is then amplified and sold by the energetic Three. The Performer will initiate contacts and handle adversarial matters, which protects the Observer from conflict and unannounced intrusion. Threes want control of the visible, image-oriented sector of a partnership, which provides a natural counterpoint for Fives, who may develop significant conclusions in their private reveries and then find it impossible to carry that work to the public. A Performer can be the conduit through which an Observer's solutions become marketable.

The partners may be poor at problem solving. Both suspend feelings, and both avoid conflict, which makes it easy to turn away from negative truths. Threes reframe negative feedback to preserve their public image, and Fives may simply let a troubling matter drop. Both types have a delayed reaction time for feelings. Threes suspend their emotions by working, and Fives need a long time to figure out what they feel. It helps when a difficult issue can be broken down into stages and dates set for a sequence of meetings. This seemingly mechanical device is effective for people who like to resolve their differences methodically rather than emotionally. Fives like to detach and prepare at each stage of negotiations, and Threes can buffer negative feelings with activity.

Three managers may want more input from the internalized and avoidant Five. "Why doesn't this employee come forward? Where's the spark of enthusiasm? Why does she or he disappear?" Needing personal recognition, Performers can feel devalued by an employee who wants to work alone and who withholds vocal support. From the employee side, there may indeed be partial commitment. A Three's work style can drain Fives to the point of exhaustion. The more you do, the more the manager wants. There's no downtime, and the pace is driving. A Three manager's need to be recognized may go over a Five's head, leaving the manager feeling disrespected and the employee feeling coerced into showing a pretense of interest. Fives hate being used for other people's purposes and will withdraw to conserve their own energy. It helps if managers can schedule so that employees know exactly what is going to be expected of them. Fives are willing to carry a large load when they know exactly how much it weighs and how far they have to carry it.

Five managers do not fit a Three employee's interactive style. The obvious solution of positioning Performers in people-related jobs, like advertising or sales, may work to a certain extent, but it will not quench Three's desire to be personally validated by authority. Threes are pushy, and Fives hate intrusion. The manager operates from behind closed doors, and the employee finds reasons to knock on the door, which becomes a source of mutual frustration. By withdrawing, Fives can become attractive to employees who want personal contact.

Fives frequently wear the business mask of Three-like behavior. An extroverted pose permits them to operate within a well-rehearsed professional role. They direct with confidence when they are protected by the boundaries of a predetermined agenda, and they are often generous with their time and energy when attention is focused on task rather than on themselves. Five managers will have to be explicit in their relationship to Threes. Innuendo and subtle signs simply will not work. A precise definition of roles and expectations helps to relax Three's need to compete for favored status. With a clear goal to shoot for, Threes can implement the manager's agendas in a wonderful way, bringing the best of this partnership together with Five as analyst and Three as frontline performer.

Three with Six: A Performer-Trooper Couple

This is not a frequently found couple, and its success depends on resolving the tension between performance and performance anxiety. Threes are go-getters whose key concept in relationship is stop. Having to stop and talk about the relationship will activate a Three's anxiety about self-worth. Terrified of powerful feelings, they will speed up exactly when the more internalized Sixes want to stop and discuss their doubts.

A wise Six will time discussions about emotional matters to coincide with a period of shared activities. A Three partner relates through the filter of activity and will need to be reassured that feelings do not signal a dead halt to all the pleasure and rewards of work. From the Six side, the key concept is go. Go toward success, toward pleasure, and toward trusting your partner. In relationship the couple slides to and fro along a line in the diagram's central triangle. That line shows that Threes doubt their own emotions and that Sixes are stressed by performance.

The pair is in a position to help each other in an essential way. Threes feel frightened by relating to someone whose worldview hinges on doubt. Sixes challenge image and doubt success, those very features of a relationship that Threes count on to feel good about themselves. Threes can be saddened when they see their Six caught in a cyclical return to the underdog position. Paradoxically, by trying to encourage a Trooper to do his or her best, Performers can become the object of paranoid attention. Sixes are stressed by the Three position. Public image feels like a setup. You can be attacked and ridiculed when you're publicly visible, so the Three partner's well-intended efforts often feel like a trap or like being tested, which adds to Six's performance anxiety.

It helps when Threes can drop success as the measure of personal worth and focus on the feelings that underlie a Trooper's self-doubt. If dealing with success is conceptualized as a life task that is bound to uncover many interesting facets of a loved one's personality, then Threes are the perfect partner to make that venture successful. If, however, Performers disown their Six's recurrent doubt as silly or untrue, it often indicates an inability to look within and acknowledge one's own anxiety.

From their side, Sixes are chronically disillusioned by what they see as high-profile Performer boasting. The couple definitely views success through different sets of eyes. Threes feel accomplished if they can perform a task, whereas Sixes have amnesia about success and need to be repeatedly reassured. Threes feel like pros when they're successful, while Sixes have to go back to the beginning. It helps when Sixes learn to focus on the task without deflecting into mental doubt. By disowning Three's performance skills as superficial, Sixes announce their own inability to maintain concentration on goals.

Three-Six Partnership at Work

The most natural alignment of talents sees Six as the creator of original ideas and Three as the creative promoter. Troopers can stay with a controversial or difficult idea long enough to refine the theory and break ground for a product or service. Typically a Six's creative powers are sharpened by adversity, and the Six can forgo immediate recognition.

Performers' talents shine in the arena of packaging and promoting a well-formulated concept. They are good at sensing the market and tailoring materials to suit current public interests. In a partnership of equals, Six is often placed as the idea person and troubleshooter, who formulates a sound product for Threes to promote and sell.

Three managers will have to respect their Six employee's input. Performers are famous for jumping on good ideas without paying due attention to other people's contributions. If the Six is invested in having his or her part of a project recognized, and if that recognition is not forthcoming, then the manager looks like an oppressive authority who cannot be trusted. The manager's skills of positive visioning and long-term leadership will then appear to be acts of self-advantage that do not serve the employee's interests.

Six's suspicions about the Three's intentions should be put into their proper perspective before the alarmed Six employee projects a worst-case-scenario concerning the project's future. It's imperative that the manager remember to apportion credit, particularly for the conceptualization of ideas. Sixes can be territorial about their mental contributions and may want these valued above any other form of public recognition. The manager will be welcome to the limelight when Troopers are assured of credit and their rightful place in the project's future.

If the Three suspends feelings, and fails to notice the gathering perception of opportunism, then Six is likely to take an underdog stance and broadcast a workplace call to arms. It helps when managers can treat the call with respect, knowing that it probably emanates from a more widespread base in the organization than a single dissatisfied Trooper. Threes are especially likely to discount negative feedback, which will only fan the fires of employee opposition. To take advantage of the insight that their shared line on the diagram can offer, Threes would do well to begin to doubt their perception of themselves as popular leaders and to entertain the Six mode of self-questioning.

A Six manager may be too cautionary and rule-bound for an ambitious Three employee. Fearing loss of control, Sixes can be quick to point out negative intentions, which discounts the positive aspects of competition and personal initiative. Threes are especially sensitive about being passed over and will quickly seek other job opportunities when a project fails to offer room for advancement. Performers flourish in an atmosphere of rapid turnover and expansion, which is countered by a Six manager's ambivalence about visibility. If they are to learn from their shared line in the diagram, Sixes need to risk in ways that are exemplified by Threes. Rather than controlling employee loyalty with regulations Six managers can model the image and efficiency that Threes admire.

Three with Seven: A Performer-Epicure Couple

This is a great energy match that can produce a lifestyle of successful adventure. To the extent that the couple shares the same interests, Three's goal orientation is well matched by Seven's multioptional mind. There won't be any complaints of depression or boredom as long as projects multiply, but the couple may not spend much time together. Unless care is taken to narrow their interests to a common purpose, this pair may wind up giving each other a weekly news update.

Both can overrate the fun parts of their relationship while glossing over the defects. It's just not interesting to dwell on financial matters or disciplining the kids when your mind wants to move on to tomorrow or to plans for next year. Grand ideas in concert with marginal resources can collude to make life happy regardless of cost. The couple may not inform each other of, or in fact may not realize, the full extent of their own difficulties. Limitation signals fast-forward to both partners. Threes deceive themselves that everything's OK and work harder to outspeed failure. Sevens avoid pain and rationalize failure by envisioning the future. The potential for accumulated neglect makes this couple vulnerable to "surprising and unforeseen" external problems such as financial crises or a child who's acting out.

A standing Enneagram diagnosis joke is that you can spot Threes and Sevens because they like themselves. The upside of liking yourself is a positive outlook. You expect that others will be impressed because you're impressed with yourself. The downside of a positive self-image is a certain superficiality. It's hard to look long enough to find out when you've gone wrong. Both types disappear when their public image is questioned: Threes by changing image and telling partial truths, Sevens by switching options and rationalizing the change. There's a conspiracy to let each other do his or her own thing rather than using each other as allies in personal growth.

Either partner can become overtly anxious when emotions deepen. Threes are anxious when they love more and work less because suspended feelings surface, while Sevens are afraid to lose their options and be stuck with a single commitment.

A mature couple will face these anxieties rather than bury them in activity; and when they do, Threes will find that they can be just as tenacious about the goal of overcoming relationship anxieties as they are about overcoming work obstacles. A good first step in releasing the paranoia raised by an emotional commitment is to set concrete short-term goals, like taking a weekly sauna together or setting aside two hours a week to photograph each other.

From their side, Sevens can bring pleasure to a relationship. Concepts like pleasure and choice can be liberating to Threes who think about looking right rather than feeling right. Feelings don't enter the picture when Performers work for other people's approval, so an Epicure's insistence on satisfaction and freedom of choice can be a real godsend. Long-term couples describe themselves as having "productive fun" together. The Seven partner has developed steadiness of purpose, and in the process some of Three's product orientation has become a pleasure.

Three-Seven Partnership at Work

This partnership often flourishes at the beginning of a project and founders before completion. Performers and Epicures are Enneagram lookalikes—they both bring a go-ahead attitude to the workplace, and they both stay interested by increasing the scope of operations. Focused on the future, Sevens fit multiple options into an interesting synthesis, and Threes parlay their current assets toward a future success. Each will keep several projects, or multiple dimensions of the same project, in motion. You have to have a lot of balls in the air when your attention is geared to the next event, the next attraction, and the next project on the list.

Threes are focused on a personal win and will take on breathtakingly boring work to achieve that success. The task itself is important, but a prestigious title and financial benefits are crucial. Sevens take a gourmet's approach to livelihood. They can compete well, present an appealing image, and are often found alongside Threes as front-runner competitors. Epicures look and act like Threes, except that the work agenda is adventure over achievement. They like jobs that are new and exciting, preferring to step back from leadership that limits their personal freedom. Sevens focus on work that feels good, and Threes focus on what looks good to the crowd.

A Three manager is likely to mistake a Seven employee's enthusiasm as willingness to drudge. Both types are good producers, but both cut corners, which may jeopardize quality control. Three managers want goals and results, which can sacrifice step-by-step quality in the interests of efficiency. As employees, Sevens also cut corners simply to avoid boredom. Sevens are commonly interested in the work process and will save time to talk, to experiment, and to introduce their own options.

Threes take command, and Sevens try to equalize authority. Wanting to expand the base of operations, Threes increasingly delegate responsibility, which lends support to the Seven's co-management style. A common mediation dilemma involves a Three who forged ahead under the illusion that commitments were being kept while in fact a Seven became derailed during the boring phases of a project. Uncowed by the hierarchy, Sevens can take off in new directions without realizing that they are acting on their own orders. It helps when a manager directly supervises the final phase of a Seven employee's project. It is especially important that this pair specify the lines of command. Seven employees are generally happy to have a designated leader to focus public attention, but they will tend to work around that leader's authority in the interest of their own freedom.

Seven managers are invariably inspired and popular during the early stages of a project. Successful Sevens like to delegate power once the project is in place and position themselves as networkers and promoters, returning to lead the demanding, short-term bottlenecks. A Three employee can be the perfect person to bring this manager's project to fruition. Threes want goal satisfaction, and if the Seven can become practical and specific, the employee will carry out those directives.

The partnership's most frequently reported misperception involves fuzziness of purpose. Sevens who can't delegate commonly leave holes in the implementation of their projects. Plans change, and new directions emerge, which may be difficult for employees to follow. An Epicure manager may not notice that the frustrated Performer has had to take on a management role to make Seven's theories more coherent. If leadership is erratic or operating at cross-purposes, Threes step in to fill the power vacuum. When Threes are respected in their own vocabulary of salary and public recognition, the pair works well. Seven should give Three a specific title and role rather than abdicating leadership, which invites the employees to make a role for themselves.

Three with Eight: A Performer-Boss Couple

This is another candidate for the Enneagram endangered species list. Both types are used to being the active partner in relationships: Eights want to protect and Threes want to provide. Eights take control and deny their softer feelings, while Threes work hard to numb out what they feel. Personal power is accentuated in both profiles, but neither partner is experienced with the power of emotional surrender. Consequently, a breakthrough in the relationship commonly occurs when either partner faces a failure. Three-Eight couples say that adversity has caused them to lean on each other. Performers find that Eights are loyal to them as people even when scandal occurs or a public image is shattered, and a Boss will be disarmed by Threes who save the day during an out-of-control emergency.

A good position shows this pair as confidants. Secure in their own and each other's capabilities, they are likely to be successful. Threes must, however, learn to be appreciative. Threes tend to think they do it all by themselves, but Eights in love show marked Giver-like tendencies. A Boss needs reassurance and attention when the tough outer persona first melts. This couple joins in activity and action, but the areas of feeling and being are new territory to be explored. A doing bond is entirely different from emerging bonds of being and feeling. An Eight's feelings open when control of the relationship can be safely surrendered. Threes' emotions flourish in a relationship where they feel loved for who they are and not for what they achieve and produce.

Three-Eight Partnership at Work

Three and Eight have prominent American leadership styles. Both types are aggressive and territorial. Both types value product over process, and both are enraged when tasks are interrupted. It's an unbeatable action team when they're on the same side, and a guaranteed power struggle if they're not.

The Eight style is direct and confrontational. What you see is what you get. Threes can act like chameleons. They change hats to be liked and duck and weave in the field. Eights build a strong basic platform, set a goal, and launch. Threes are more artful: They get into motion, patch a strategy out of whatever is available, and learn on their feet. As adversaries they struggle for power. Threes see Eights as bullies, and Eights see Threes as liars.

The more usual arrangement shows Eight as the manager, with Three as top producer in the field. If Three feels valued, the partnership will grow. Threes want tangible rewards for effort, and a wise manager will respect that inclination rather than try to control. Eight managers are wary of a challenge to their power, and Performers are exactly that. It helps to establish guidelines for salary and status. Threes respond to the opportunities within a system. They want a ladder to climb, and their ambitions can be channeled through that structure.

Three managers have to demonstrate fairness. Eights think, "Can a chameleon be trusted? Is the manager loyal to the staff?" Eight employees are a challenge to authority. "Will I be sold out when it's convenient? Is the manager honest? Let's find out!" The Eight may foment unrest in the workplace, and the manager will have a rebellion to quell. The question is really about the integrity of management. Eights can't invest unless they feel secure. A Three manager can help by reaffirming the Eight employee's place in the future. Eights need to know their position in long-range business plans.

Three with Nine: A Performer-Mediator Couple

Performers want to impress their intimates, and Nines tend to merge with other people's ideas. This pattern of attraction encourages Threes to project an image that captures a Nine's heart. Pleased by the attention, a Mediator will feel drawn to support the Three's course of action, making it easy for the couple to agree in placing performance goals as a centerpiece of their relationship.

Hungry for a personal life goal, Mediators are often animated by a mate's agenda. Another's views seem far more invigorating than having to face the confusion surrounding their own priorities; as a consequence, Nines are caught up in other people's interests, sometimes for years. Impressionable Nines can try out Three's appealing public persona and think, "I have found myself. At last I have discovered what I'm supposed to do in life." The couple shares a line in the diagram, and that line predicts that Mediators gain security by merging with the image and identity that a work role provides. To the extent that Three's goals are an actual reflection of Nine's discounted inner needs, a productive lifestyle, spearheaded by Three and shared by Nine, can emerge.

The diagram's Three-Nine line also suggests that Performers feel ill at ease without an activity. Threes in stress fall into Nine-like uncertainty about goals, which makes them feel aimless and unproductive. Both partners dislike the lethargy that develops from difficulty with choice. Mediators dread the grinding down of energy that occurs when they lose focus, and Performers prioritize quickly so there's always something to do.

Without the rudder of someone else's priority to direct their choices, Nines can fall into a day-to-day routine that feels akin to sleepwalking. They act out their unhappiness by lowering their energy and reducing participation to mechanical duties. They may not say no out loud, but presence and enthusiasm have been numbed. A relationship crisis can emerge without much being said. Family life goes on with Three being drawn to outside activities and Nine going to sleep. Three works hard, and Nine, often with an equally busy schedule, has sectioned off just enough attention to fulfill the routine. Neither recognizes the dilemma. Threes are working "for us," and Nines are working to numb their disappointment and anger.

Eventually Nines who feel dragged along by a partner's agenda will begin to think, "How did we get to this impasse?" "Did I choose this course of action?" "Do I belong here or not?" The questioning can become obsessive if Three's priorities do in fact dominate the couple's life. Tied up by inner questioning, Nines move into their own stress of Six and doubt the validity of the relationship but find it difficult to propose solutions. It will drive a Performer wild if Nine's mental questioning produces a halt in family expectations. By default it's usually Threes who take action, either by burying themselves in work, veering away to another relationship, or initiating a change.

Threes are often eager to support "constructive change," particularly if "productive support" enhances the couple's possibilities for success. It helps when the couple grasps the fact that Nine's search for personal direction really applies to both partners. It can be all too easy to trivialize searching for an inner position as self-indulgent; and Threes can be especially impatient about spending time on questions of commitment and being rather than filling the day with doing. "Why dredge so deeply when short-term projects beckon? Why probe for deeper motives when they seem to unearth pain?" The focus on identity that emerges from one's own being can be alarming to Threes, who, chameleonlike, can win approval by projecting an appropriate persona. Both parties want the Nine to flower, but why does it take so long?

An interesting feature of the search for identity is that Nines who find themselves may not ever change careers or consider leaving their relationship. Instead they can feel vitally recommitted to the life they've already built, "a life that became my own, when I could see that I wanted it."

Three-Nine Partnership at Work

Performers' activity rate can automatically set the workplace standard. Their high-energy profile is suited to business life, and Nines particularly admire people who can "find themselves" through a career. Molding themselves to the positive aspects of Three's work persona, Nines can develop a go-getter's habits, mainly by pacing themselves with deadlines to steady their energy level.

Nines generally like the characteristics of their own security point. They can look and act like Threes, with certain key differences: Nines will continue to see all sides of a question, they will be likely to merge with other people's agendas, and they will avoid conflict. From the Three position, these attributes slow the pace and may be seen as workplace liabilities, while Nines think that attending to other views means conducting a business with heart.

Three managers tend to expand their own sphere of influence. Once an agreement is finalized, there's an urgency to move on to the next event. It may be difficult to get the manager's attention unless the topic is task related, which places other considerations, like office morale, off-limits for discussion. Nines themselves may agree that it's unbusinesslike to be internally caught in the cross fire of office politics, but the fact remains that Mediators can be pounded by unarticulated employee resentments that a Three manager doesn't notice.

Performers tend to get conveniently called away from quarrels and will get belligerent if the schedule is interrupted. The prime directive is "Keep going" and if task tunnel vision takes over, the Three may treat employees as objects that do or do not serve the work. It will seem logical to drop people who have no value and to drive those who do. Unskilled Three managers treat people in terms of what they can contribute to the enterprise. Mediators may be the first to feel threatened; and because they are committed to keeping the peace, they may be among the last to voice a position. Merged with employee opposition, Nines will see all sides of the question and demonstrate their dissatisfaction indirectly. It just won't go the manager's way.

A Nine manager's indecisiveness can threaten goal-oriented employees. Threes find extended search and discovery especially unsettling. It seems that data collection can become an end in itself rather than facilitating decisions. Too much information overloads a Three's system; it's frustrating to think that important results could be diffused by contradictory thinking. Three employees see concise, short-term goals, and Nine managers see how goals can change under fluctuating conditions. Their different ways of paying attention can find a Three employee frantically pushing for closure while the manager is still examining evidence.

Third-party input is extremely helpful in bridging the partnership's key differences. Nines can declare themselves to a safe listener far more easily than they can deal with face-to-face confrontation, and Threes like to put their problems on a schedule that ensures results. It helps when each can see the constructive aspects of the other's problem-solving strategy. Nines need to prioritize, confront, and see the value in assertive leadership. Threes need to wait, to value other people's insight, and to see the relationship between performance and people's needs.

Double Four: A Double Romantic Couple

This pair may be a candidate for the Enneagram's endangered species list. I've seen only a few double Four intimate relationships, although Romantics love to hang out together and frequently become best friends. The best-friend status is often supported by a mutual avocation. Fours go to the opera together, they circulate petitions for children's rights, they go jogging and talk about their relationships, they cry, they dress well, they make up after a fight. Best friends affirm each other's value as people sharing a unique vision, which helps to neutralize the underlying shame of not being good enough to merit love. Best friends can also afford to be more open with each other than intimates, since Fours believe that revealing a fatal flaw to an intimate will lead to abandonment.

Double Fours are bound by an attraction to intensity that is evoked through aesthetic sensitivity, tenderness, and equally powerful moods of depression. A good relationship is permeated with the whole spectrum of feeling. How can joy be authentic without repercussions about the loss of joy? Doesn't emotional union have its counterpart in separation and pain?

Double Fours may elevate the search for a fulfilling relationship to extraordinary importance. By comparison, simple affection seems like a superficial sham. "A real relationship" should become an artistic achievement. "Why are other couples willing to settle for so little? Where's the magic? We can't let that happen to us!" Sometimes Fours can't help each other because each overvalues his or her own sensitivity. They may realize the pitfalls of expecting too much, but questioning the quest for love seems to cheapen its worth.

Romantic needs are highly idealized; an intimate relationship cannot produce permanent bliss. Ecstatic moments are transient, and insisting on too much guarantees a missing piece. The missing ingredient for happiness leads Romantics astray. The house is never big enough, the mate is not quite ardent enough, the salary isn't generous enough, the coffee doesn't have enough cream. The relationship can be a primary source of dissatisfaction, with years spent in a litany of insistence that a partner needs to change. "I can't bear to leave you, and I can't send you away; but if you were enough, then I'd feel different, so you're the source of my pain."

Needless to say, the blame factor is compounded in a double Four relationship. At a low point each suffers and sees the other as the source of suffering, each wants a perfect lover, and each feels flawed. Each criticizes the other for being imperfect, and each wants to bail out as his or her own flaws are unearthed. These two share a move to One, the Enneagram's Perfectionist type, and if their intimate relationship bottoms out, both are likely to fall to the low side of their security position. Perfectionistic Fours can be biting. Both think, "I've been hurt and you're to blame," but the subtext is a fear of abandonment. "I fear rejection because I am flawed, and to save myself I'll dump on you first."

On the high side, this couple can keep the spark alive for a lifetime. We need not be Fours to experience the swell of nostalgia arising when we are separated from our beloved, but the Romantics among us have plumbed that longing. Once entwined, Fours are forever connected to another through their feelings. It takes years to process the nuances of a relationship, and Fours are likely to do so with loving acceptance of both kisses and tears.

Double Four Partnership at Work

Fours can be high-profile achievers, which doesn't fit the stereotype of a tragic figure, but in fact their drive to succeed is often motivated by the assumption that a high-performance schedule kicks depression. Furthermore Fours need tangible evidence of their value, and success in the eyes of others is balm for low self-esteem. Those who favor their Three wing, and especially the competition subtype, mobilize against a rival, a trait that is greatly valued in the American marketplace. All Fours tend to put a spin of specialness and uniqueness on their achievements, and even a shame subtype will be activated by the thought, "If they can do it, I can do it! What do they have that I haven't got?"

We expect to set our feelings aside in most professional settings, and consequently Romantics can remain undetected in the workplace. In a team-building session, it's not uncommon for Fours to identify themselves and then be met with round-eyed surprise. "*You?* You're what's called a Romantic? I would never have guessed!"

The majority of Fours swing between a drive to succeed and fatal disinterest. There's a rising euphoria connected to challenge, which turns to disappointment when a job becomes routine. Suddenly the enterprise seems fruitless, the days are only ordinary. It's just not worth the effort when so much seems to be missing. Romantics can sabotage their gains just at the point of success. Fours who favor their Five-ish wing, and those who have shame as their subtype feature, are particularly shy about public exposure; being seen just isn't worth the risk of public humiliation.

Success signals boredom and the fear of becoming ordinary. The situation becomes charged if creative stagnation sets in, for Romantics need a hit of magic to be effective, the kind of magic that emerges by throwing caution to the wind. As managers, Fours learn to intervene before their Romantic employees sabotage promising careers, and astute Four employees will attend to details so that agreements are kept. Double Four combinations produce an unsettled work environment: untried theories, long shots, unlikely personnel, and emotional rescue missions. Double Fours produce well when there's no competition, but unless each receives special attention, cooperation can shift to envy and spiteful covert attacks.

Four managers develop their personal signature. They like to innovate rather than follow the crowd. They may confuse emotional impulse with genuine creative insight. Fours can forget to verify their intuition with research. There's also the likelihood of forming an in-group circle—some of the staff are interesting and others are not. Double Fours are prone to becoming entangled when they're drawn together through crisis and then lose interest once the crisis has passed. An in group sets the stage for unhealthy competition; staff members feel set against one another when personal attention is highly valued. As employees Fours will suffer if they're out of favor and may encourage office chaos as an attention-getting device.

Mediation should focus on structural guarantees that eliminate in-group favoritism. Binding agreements cannot be compromised by shifting affiliations or emotional cronyism.

Four with Five: A Romantic-Observer Couple

This is another pair that may begin to resemble each other over time. Both Fives and Fours are prone to enclosing themselves in an interior world, but that interiority has a vastly different focus. Fives can live in a world of intellectual abstraction and mental imagery that seems curiously devoid of emotional content, whereas Fours are exquisitely attentive to the fluctuations of mood. Heart and mind are such different organs of perception that both can feel misrepresented or misunderstood when they are expressed to each other. The Romantic partner may think, "My lover has no heart," and the Observer may feel, "My mind is filled with my beloved." The partners' modes of expression are so vastly unalike that they can sometimes feel like ships that pass in the night, invisible to each other's presence.

Despite their obvious differences, these two share a worldview that is imbued with meaning and often overshadowed by symbolism. Both concur that there are principles and keys of hidden meaning that operate beneath the surface of ordinary events, and sharing that conviction can draw them together. The sense that real life is lived behind the scenes of superficial appearances doesn't mean that either is a magical thinker, simply that they can inhabit a private world of perception that differs from mainstream beliefs.

Their years together can attune them to each other's tastes, blending Four's aesthetic self-presentation with Five's observational powers to create a kind of aesthetic distance. They express themselves to each other through a lifestyle imbued with symbolic meaning. Deciding on the colors for a fall garden may be a way of saying, "We will sit together in that garden when it flowers." Tenderness can be carefully acknowledged by pouring each other's morning tea. Another distinct possibility is that the partners become isolated in separate, self-preoccupied interior worlds, finding little need to communicate.

Boundary issues are common. Fives are preoccupied with conserving energy and will protect themselves by controlling time spent with others. Romantics, on the other hand, require a great deal of attention; their moods shatter Five's protective mental concepts. Romantics rail about scheduled intimacy, with a worst-case scenario showing Five closeted in the study while Four lies abandoned in the bedroom pining for recognition. Observers can easily find excuses to cut communication and refuse to be touched. The more a Four laments, the more a Five withdraws to think, "That's your idea of our relationship—not mine."

It helps when either can find the proper degree of contact, which partially explains why long-term couples begin to look alike. Each will have to adjust his or her style of relating to accommodate the other: Observers have to stay with their feelings, and Romantics have to throttle back. The saving grace of balancing the most contracted and the most emotionally dramatic Enneagram types is that they really have something admirable to teach each other. These are partners who can learn to meet in the middle, if each modifies in the direction of the partner's emotional needs.

Commonly Fours fall into a half-distant relationship—not far enough away to feel abandoned and not close enough for flaws to be seen. The Observer may find that emotional distance can be attractive to a Romantic partner, giving each an incentive to meet in the middle.

Fives, who are abstract thinkers, should appreciate the knowing of the heart. An actual key to secret knowledge can be discovered in the nuances of feeling that connect people to one another. In relationship that treasure-house of information can be opened if the key to the heart is recognized. From their own side of the equation, Fours need to modify their greediness for love by identifying with Five's emotional detachment.

Four-Five Partnership at Work

Observers can be far more expressive in professional relationships than in intimate settings. They can be caught up by a cause or a business venture that captures their imagination, and they become highly emotional when the focus is on task rather than being purely personal. Both types are free to move forward when an Observer's increased availability gains a Romantic's confidence.

As managers Fives operate within the boundaries of a set agenda, timed meetings, and prearranged telephone calls. Their employees are expected to run interference and act as a protective filter. It's hard for Fives to disengage attention once they've begun to concentrate, so privacy becomes a prime directive. To the extent that Fours are privy to the inner circle of management, they may be happy to run the office in a personal, stylish way that conforms to the individual Four's taste. A Five manager is likely to let the Romantic shape the look and feel of public appearances.

Fours overreact to lack of attention, especially if the Five resorts to intermediaries and memos. A severe situation can develop if a Romantic employee feels ignored and turns to attention-getting tactics such as moodiness or negligence to force a confrontation. The manager may want to fire the Four rather than deal with the situation, which provides a Romantic with fuel to fight and force the manager into a face-to-face meeting.

A standoff can be averted by a show of interest from either side. Fours want personal recognition, and Fives want organizational efficiency without the burden of personal presence. The employee has to move from an emotional stance and the manager from a primarily logical position. It helps when Fives encourage discussion and when Fours can offer objective solutions that rely on structure.

Four managers can find that they are well supported by their Five employees. Both want a private relationship, which may simply be a special project. Observers shine in a circumscribed area of expertise, and Fours need the stabilizing effect of well-documented support. If difficulty arises, a Five employee is likely to withdraw behind a wall of intellectual formality rather than become embroiled in confrontation. Distressed Fives can control a whole department by giving nothing. You don't get an answer unless you ask exactly the right question in precisely the right vocabulary. The entire burden falls on the manager when a Five employee has to be cornered to disclose information. When Observers withhold, there will be periods of no communication, and single-page reports. As employees Fives typically hide by adopting an appropriate office pose, so the infuriated Four manager will be unable to pinpoint the problem.

When finally cornered, Fives can say exactly what they think in a blunt manner without realizing the humiliation created for others. The situation becomes deadlocked if the shame-based Four evens the score by demeaning Five's intellectual expertise. Romantics are shamed by having their flaws exposed, and Observers can be just as hurt when their intellectual contributions are questioned. Mediation should take advantage of the fact that both types are capable of dropping old grievances and starting over again without regrets, especially when Fives are intellectually recognized and Fours are rescued from anonymity by a guarantee of special mention.

Four with Six: A Romantic-Trooper Couple

This couple frequently discovers similar characteristics in each other. Romantics, for example, can be as fearful as any Six, and Troopers can feel plugged in to the same sense of universal suffering that is so characteristic of Fours. Rather than being divisive, their shared perceptions strengthen the relationship. Because they stand together in sorrow, they may also share equally compelling emotional victories. Both are privy to the depth of purpose and meaning produced by voluntary suffering.

This couple reveals two very different motivations that energize a similar worldview. Both types identify with fear and sadness, but for different reasons. Troopers see themselves as outcasts and underdogs who fear persecution, whereas Romantics describe fears of being misunderstood and abandoned. They are bonded to each other by a similar destiny and by sharing the surge of creativity that can drive oppressed people to undertake an act of significance.

Both expect a great deal of themselves. Each may feel the need to produce a conceptual or creative breakthrough in some sense motivated by that early conviction of self as set apart from others. They are likely to protect each other in that careful way that develops between people who have endured together; Fours are attracted to those with emotional depth, and Sixes are faithful to an underdog cause.

On the high side these two can support each other's vulnerability, particularly when they see the beauty of the human condition. But on the low side that same vulnerability can become mired in inaction. In a down phase each blames the other for feelings of low self-esteem. The Romantic will think, "I would feel better if I had a better partner," and the Trooper will periodically lose faith by asking, "How can this be love when I both love my partner and entertain my doubts?" In a stagnant period each partner is preoccupied with proving himself or herself to the other, and neither can move forward.

This couple reports breakups and reunions because mutual blame causes mistrust. Fours writhe under criticism when their flaws are exposed, and Sixes want unwavering support even when they fail. A crisis develops if both collude in worst-case thinking about their future; it just seems easier to go it alone than to go on together. Romantics become contrary in crisis, refusing to see their own flaws and determined to vindicate themselves by making the partner wrong. The equally contrary Six is also adept at pushing people away by arguing against whatever position a partner thinks is important.

It helps when either can back down long enough to reaffirm their commitment. A good reminder would be: "This is a difficult phase; but remember, we're committed to changing and staying together." Fair-fight guidelines are useful because either type is likely to quit under fire. In the event of a breakup, Romantics will idealize the disappearing relationship, see its better aspects, and want the Trooper back; Sixes, because they deeply mistrust broken commitments, will be far less eager to reconcile.

It helps when both partners can see through their own ambivalence about intimacy. Fours oscillate between being loving and wanting to reject another, whereas Sixes shift between belief and doubt. It's a breakthrough when either can see the similarity between Four's push-pull habit of relating and Six's alternating pattern of belief and mistrust. That insight can open mutual compassion, because all these changes of heart are merely self-protective. It may be too frightening to surrender to love; it may feel safer to reject first rather than face the fear of not being enough.

Four-Six Partnership at Work

Either type can entertain catastrophic thinking, which paradoxically spurs this pair to action. Risk can be mesmerizing to competitive and reckless (dauntless) subtype Fours and to counterphobic Sixes. These are people who feel creatively alive in risk-taking ventures.

On the other end of the Four-Six behavioral continuum, the shame subtype Four and phobic Sixes of any subtype are cautionary at work. These people tend to think dutifully about hierarchy. They entrench in a professionally safe niche that shields them from visibility and open competition.

Four managers need to have their public image validated. Accolades for competence won't be enough; there has to be recognition for a personal statement that declares, "I am different." A Six employee is generally willing to back any trustworthy authority, however idiosyncratic. Troopers are obedient as long as management can be made accountable for its actions, but when an authority gives the impression that she or he is above the rules, Sixes become wary. Four managers should present a consistent image and avoid apparently high-handed policy changes. Their suspicious Six employees will read meaning and hidden intention into every gesture. All of this maneuvering and divisiveness can be avoided if the manager becomes ordinary and unthreatening, usually by simply informing, explaining, and asking for feedback.

This partnership can either rally through mutual trust or disintegrate into the kind of personality struggle that wrecks a business. Six employees distrust managers who hold themselves above the ordinary working crowd. It helps when Fours become visible to their employees rather than holding themselves apart.

A struggling Six employee can be appealing to a Romantic, especially if a rescue mission is involved, where the Four can nurture a budding talent. Romantic managers are often willing to encourage people in difficulty, which produces exactly the kind of people-oriented environment that inspires fearful people to succeed.

As managers Troopers have to contain their doubt. A Six manager is likely to see himself as having caused employee dissatisfaction or, worse, may begin to feel attacked personally. Troopers attribute too much importance to minor disagreements. The manager needs to pinpoint any source of irritation, and Romantic employees can help by being as disclosing as possible.

Mediation should expose the differences between each type's perception of crisis. Fours can feel at home in a struggle and can honor the authentic feelings that emerge when ordinary events are disturbed. Sixes, on the other hand, overreact to conflict and can therefore see Fours as erratic and dangerous to business interests. The partners face a widening gulf of misunderstanding when Four's boredom creates an outburst that Six desperately tries to contain. Romantics discover an answer in the midst of crisis, but Troopers suppress crisis while desperately seeking an analytic solution. Mediation needs to focus on the positive results of conflict while noting both Four's eagerness to point out what's missing and Six's fear of crisis.

Four with Seven: A Romantic-Epicure Couple

This is one of the Enneagram's attraction of opposites, a commonly found pair that strives for a balance between Seven's many options and Four's commitment to emotional depth. Fours experience the world through their feelings, and Sevens are primarily mental. Each has a joy to share—of the heart and of the mind—that can either produce a true union of opposites or an atmosphere of alienation.

This couple sees the extraordinary in each other. Fours feel special, and Sevens feel entitled; they can therefore support each other's unique talents or can unconsciously expect their union to produce too much. Oddly an Epicure's emotional unavailability fits well with a Romantic's longing for missing things. Fours yearn for a better relationship even when the present one is doing extremely well. There's juice in the challenge of pursuing whatever is missing; both types seek intensity, often with Seven focused on the event and Four focused on the Seven.

The natural optimism that Epicures bring to relationships is a deterrent to Four's possessive melancholia. But more than that, Sevens are not easily affected by the push-pull Romantic pattern in relationship. Fours actually respect a partner who is not drawn into the drama of seduction and rejection, although they may pine to be emotionally matched.

The pitfall that this couple faces involves Seven's intolerance of negative emotions. Epicures have a hard time concentrating when a difficult topic arises; other plans and possibilities beckon and carry attention away. Positive feelings are infinitely more acceptable, and the couple will enjoy the high side of stimulating ideas and activities. Sevens crave experience, and a Four who wants the relationship will have to participate. Romantics rarely complain about the pace and range of interests as long as the Seven doesn't go too far away. Activity automatically displaces depression, which stabilizes Four's moods without much being said, but Romantics are universally impatient about Seven's inability to tolerate pain: "Why do you leave just because I'm sad? Where do you go when we need to talk?"

The partners argue about how to deal with loaded issues. Fours think it's important to discuss negative feelings, and Sevens see negativity as a waste of time. Each can feel controlled by the other. Fours are unhappy about holding their feelings back, and Sevens are afraid to wallow in emotion. Romantics will spend considerable time convincing Epicures to feel rather than think, but the Epicure is likely to say in the most charming manner, "I do feel deeply and fully, but only briefly." Sevens have to be convinced that feelings are going to be worth it. They love the optimistic rush that heralds a new venture, but deep experience feels like getting mired, and the fear of limitation sets in.

An all-time low shows Fours complaining that the Epicure is emotionally shallow, while Sevens feel strangled by Four's emotional needs. With time and maturity, Four's depth engages Seven's attention, and in return Seven lifts a Romantic out of depression. When emotions become "interesting," a Seven will consider it worthwhile to stay with negative feelings.

Outsiders may feel pressured to take sides if the couple argues. Because the partners are so different in their orientation, it may seem that only one of them can be right. Four's plaintive note and Seven's equally convincing positivity tend to invite friends and witnesses to assume the role of counselor and adviser.

Fours are entitled to time for genuine emotional questions, and Sevens are entitled to expect a resolution. Guidelines for dealing with loaded issues are a must. Fours must distinguish between a genuine need that has a potential solution and emotional neediness that creates problems in order to get comfort. From their side, Sevens have to be willing to talk in spite of boredom, frustration, and other resistance. Epicures come up with quick, "brilliant" solutions or excellent reasons to keep the conversation brief. Guidelines should differentiate between reasons and excuses. Seven has to commit time for processing feelings, and Four has to realize that feelings can interfere with communication.

Four-Seven Partnership at Work

When Sevens see the cup of opportunity half full, Fours can see it half empty; but rather than getting stalled, this pair often works effectively together. Each is energized by the other's style and sense of being distinctive and special, while their combined perception of what's possible and what's missing can lead them in novel directions. It's as if they conspire in believing they can develop something that's never been seen before. It is their differences that make them effective in the relative neutrality of an office setting. Seven's refusal to be pinned into a dead-end possibility spurs activity, and Four's emphasis on form and appearances prevents a hyperactive explosion of plans.

A Romantic manager will probably enjoy the far-seeing Epicurean employee as long as real results materialize. Both types are susceptible to charm and may insulate each other from drudgery in a cocoon of special dispensations, a tactic that alienates other staff members. Four managers may also feel bombarded by Seven's brilliant speculations and will dislike having to do the work of distinguishing between mere cleverness and feasible solutions. Both types are mesmerized by unusual possibilities, but the day-to-day execution that good beginnings require feels tedious. Coming to closure is difficult, especially when either has to face the prospect of evaluation, and both are notorious for losing focus during the final phases of a project.

Four managers commonly lose interest when goals start to materialize and may prematurely shift priorities. That shift feeds into their Seven employee's ever-changing matrix of possibilities and inevitably produces confusion. Romantic managers seem poised amid chaos and are noted for last-minute rescue missions, but Epicures will rationalize the fact that they have made a mistake. Seven employees believe their own rationalizations, putting a manager in the position of having to enforce standards.

The most frequently reported Four-Seven office dispute has to do with incompletes. The Four manager eventually feels disrespected and banishes the Epicure from favor. The pair can also develop a prodigal-son relationship in which the Seven employee withdraws without a trace until all evidence of conflict blows over. When the Seven returns, the rest of the staff is again likely to wonder why they seem less interesting to the manager, especially if they've been working hard during the prodigal's absence. It helps when Fours are willing to set absolute professional standards, because both manager and employee bend the rules. Regulations and deadlines have to be unusually clear when a Four manager who feels above the rules colludes with an employee who evades limitations.

Sevens can be unusually fine promoters, but they are erratic as day-to-day managers. Preferring to plan and delegate follow-through to others, Epicures will do well to set the project in motion and let Romantics get the job done. This pair is motivated by Seven's conviction that good ideas are sure to materialize and Four's equally powerful perception of the missing components that will actualize those plans. The key to engaging a Four employee's support is inner-circle rapport. This employee has to feel special, and a Seven manager often tends to take staff for granted. It will be imperative for the manager to remember to establish ongoing personal connections, or Romantic employees will feel slighted and therefore justified in letting office affairs slide. It helps when Sevens set a chain of command that allows them enough freedom to come and go as they please. Romantics are delighted to be designated for in-group responsibility and may be the perfect representative for a manager who wants to get away.

Four with Eight: A Romantic-Boss Couple

This is a partnership of intensity acted out by fight, flight, fascination, and flair. Each feels somewhat awed by the other. Eights feel themselves to be coarse and blunt in comparison with the elegant and socially adept Romantic. From their side Fours can be utterly magnetized by the socially shameless Boss. It can be a real cliff-hanger when a Romantic drama syncs with Eight's lust for life. It's a sex, drugs, and rock-and-roll relationship, acted out either literally or metaphorically, because intensity can be achieved through any number of lifestyles. One couple described their twenty-year relationship as "a continuous lightning storm. You're out there swung around by the power of it. We've moved all over the country, had five children, worked incredibly hard, and had thousands of great fights."

Fours demand a huge range of feelings from a partner, and Eights love to match strong energies. They appreciate each other's inclination to push the limits and will probably unite in ignoring social convention. Both fight boredom by intensifying the emotional climate: Eights by becoming aggressively demanding and Fours through dramatic acts and suffering.

Because they appreciate a Romantic's personal style, Eights will want to be included in matters of taste and presentation. Fours are notoriously attracted to the Boss's blunt emotional stance as being in touch with "real" or "authentic" feelings. Eights don't waste a lot of time worrying about what people will think, and it's that very lack of pretension that is so appealing. Fours can hide themselves behind a glamorous image, but Eights are re-markably natural. What you see is what you get.

Romantics will also interpret Eights' ability to move into a fight and hold their ground under fire as further proof of emo-tional authenticity. Eight partners are not likely to become enmeshed in Four-like depression and will be able to hold a con-sistent course of action when Fours enter a push-pull cycle in the relationship. Bosses stand firm when someone tries to push them away, and they pride themselves on being able to see through the pull of seduction.

This relationship has several natural congruencies that allow the pair to help each other just by being themselves. For example, an Eight will prefer a Four's company when she or he is emotionally upbeat but may withdraw if the Four becomes depressed. A disgruntled Boss may simply go off to have a good time elsewhere, leaving Four to wail. Misunderstood Romantics get infuriated about being ignored, which may have the positive side effect of breaking a depression. If depression is really anger turned inward, then Eights are the ideal partners to make that anger direct. Eights dislike self-absorbed emotional drama and will provoke a fight to evoke real feelings, which in the long run can serve to bring the couple closer.

An impasse can occur if the Four becomes self-occupied, masochistically drawn to Eight's punitive side, or embroiled in the push-pull pattern of relating. Predictably Eights will blame the mate and walk out, probably without much insight into their own half of the problem. It helps when either can see that anger may be merely a way to intensify the relationship. Both are attracted to a lightning-storm life, and if one partner develops a blazing personal interest, it will ignite the other's support. Severe situations can be mitigated if the Four shifts focus from wanting Eight's attention to a project that Eight assists. A Boss can apply the pressure to make other people's projects happen and in return can profit greatly from witnessing a Romantic's complex interior life. When Eights see the value of engaging their own emotions, this couple is on the way to a true intensity of spirit. Between Four's emotional range and Eight's practical stability, the couple can stay interested in each other for a long time.

Four-Eight Partnership at Work

Both are likely to think of themselves as above the rules. Both types have an amoral streak: The usual rules just don't apply to Fours, who are special enough to be above the law, or to Eights, who feel stronger than the law. This is an unbeatable partnership when both are able to focus on task; but Eights are prone to wasting energy on personal appetites, and Fours lose focus to emotional concerns. Competition is a key issue that can either be constructively handled or create bitter mistrust. Fours demand special status to cover feelings of inner shame, but they are also highly innovative and committed to the emotional needs of others. Eights are a competitive force in any partnership, especially in matters of leadership, but they also embody the will and staying power upon which every successful business depends.

Cooperation will depend on absolute honesty. These are territorial people who both want leadership status. Neither will submit to the other, but trust builds when each is aware of the other's intentions. Eights want predictability rather than blind submission, and they admire a good competitor. Fours want recognition for their special contributions and are dedicated to a partnership that satisfies their own brand of creativity. Fours need not be Romantics in the poetic sense of the word: They are also scientists, cowboys, doctors, and librarians who find themselves drawn to self-expression. Each Four will want to make a unique contribution in her or his own field, to achieve success in ways that have never been seen before. If powerful Eights can support that special vision, they will receive Four's complete cooperation.

A successful configuration shows a Four manager who initiates a creatively daring project in sync with an Eight employee who can shepherd the project to completion. Both are attracted to worthwhile, somewhat controversial ideas, and when they trust each other, each will find his or her own niche without much discussion. As managers Romantics can envision and inspire but may not be interested in the boring work of materializing a concept. A wise Four will orient an Eight employee and then relinquish control. Eights are dedicated workers once they embark on a course of action, but Eights also overreact when their base of operations is threatened. Do not change the rules or frustrate this employee's expectations once everything is in motion. Eights oppose policy shifts on principle unless they understand management's point of view. They can feel justified in stalling a project just to force management to the table, all of which seems personally insulting to Fours. As managers Fours must create an opportunity for feedback from staff, even when they feel abused. It helps when Romantics—who are sensitive to suffering—can see the insecurity that motivates an Eight employee's often offensive behavior.

Eight managers are notorious for making the rules and then breaking them, which is appealing to Fours as long as they have a special connection to the Boss. Rules don't matter, but the emotional connection matters a lot. Four employees who fall out of favor can develop a thirst for vengeance that matches any Eight's. Predictably an irritated Eight manager will either become vindictive or want to dismiss the Four without consideration. This combination can become the stuff of legend for mediation teams. It helps to coach Eight managers concerning their impact on others. What may seem like good leadership to a Boss can seem insulting to the more emotional Romantic.

Four with Nine: A Romantic-Mediator Couple

We have all felt the immeasurable power of emotional bonding, but that extension of self to others is particularly dramatic in this relationship. Fours describe a lifelong yearning to be "awakened through love," while Nines seek vitality and an agenda from a mate. During the best times each can love the other dispassion-ately without either expectation or blame, but at a low point each expects the other to deliver the impossible: The Romantic part-ner craves permanent emotional satisfaction, while the Mediator wants to be handed a life.

Initial attractions are often voiced by Romantics, who are thrilled to feel accepted, flaws and all. A Nine's patient presence inoculates Fours against the fear of abandonment and low self-esteem. Nines try to avoid conflict and can be remarkably toler-ant of others, feeling no need to urge a partner toward change. But in return Nines want unconditional acceptance. Nines will bridle at Four-like conditions such as, "I could love you if only" or "I see what's missing in your character" or "I can't love you fully until you make a change." Both partners hate to be criti-cized, and both tend to blame others for their fate. Fours see what's missing in a lover, and Nines see a partner as the active, aggressive force.

Romantics can become despondent about their Mediator's lack of intensity. It feels like going softly to sleep instead of authentic love. If a Mediator slips into the background, Roman-tics will think, "What's happened to us? We've lost it. Where's the juice?" Craving an awakening through love, Fours want strong signals of recognition. Acute attraction, exquisite pain, and the full cycle of passion. Being ignored ignites a smoldering drama, an agitated twitch that flares into blame.

The Mediator may be quite aware that the couple's "we-ness" has been disrupted. Merged with others, Nines know when they're expected to deliver, and at the best of times they do; but during an impasse Nines wait and do nothing. They space out, busy themselves with secondary activities, or energetically disap-pear. A Romantic will feel neglected and abandoned, but Media-tors can truthfully reply, "I've done nothing. I have not left you. How could I be neglectful when I'm standing right here?"

Abandoned, Fours can go for the jugular. Bitter accusations seem justified: "I've been hurt and you did it." Romantics say the worst to save face. Four's provocative behavior can be a wake-up call to sleepy Nines. Something has to be done when real emotions are forced to surface. You can't fall asleep with your mate acting out.

Nines in intimate relationship with Fours feel alternately rejected and adored without much change in their own behavior. Four's push-pull pattern seems to make Nines think, "Why change if it won't matter anyway? Why try when my efforts are overlooked?" Long-term couples say that Mediators develop special interests as a way to be alone. Going fishing or playing cards creates enough distance for Romantics to find Mediators attractive again. It helps if Nines can see the positive intentions behind their Four's attacking behavior. Yes, being told to wake up feels like criticism, but Four's purpose is to intensify the relationship. This is another couple that profits when either partner discovers personal purpose. Nines can be incredibly patient with other people, and Fours are inspired by a self-directed mate.

Four-Nine Partnership at Work

This is a common partnership that usually places Four as a frontline figure dealing with the public while Nine supervises the mechanics of the product or service. The pair's differences are especially complementary in the workplace, where goals take priority over bonding. Fours like stimulating creative moments rather than attending to predictable long-range ventures, whereas Nines want consistent guidelines to eliminate constant choice. Well used, Four's personal stamp can shape a venture that can then be implemented by the more methodical Nine. A productive interaction shows Four relying on Nine to stabilize fruitful ideas, while Nine's input in making those ideas practical receives equal consideration. A crisis interaction shows Four bored and alienated by a Nine who favors safe, known solutions. Expect trouble when a disappointed Four meets a Nine on autopilot. The Four may sabotage the business before Nine wakes up.

A stereotype of Romantic managers pictures them as unduly preoccupied with appearances, but in actuality Fours may not be at all interested in a fashionable office filled with sensitive people. Romantics can be as ambitious as any Three in a competitive profession, and in fact a Four-Nine duo is likely to meet at Three and produce with high-performance visibility. A Four manager can set an energized pace that draws employees into orbit and encourages Nines to cultivate the Performer in themselves. On the high side Nines merge with the speed and excitement of a lively environment.

Nine employees blend with their surroundings, and a Four manager must seek them out. Merged with their environment, Nines may look steadfast and active while inwardly feeling, "I don't belong here. My efforts are being ignored." The manager feels secure because no grievance has been stated, but the Nine employee feels overlooked. Mediators slow down or spread allegiance to other office factions unless someone pays attention, and a self-involved Four manager may not catch on until Nine's letter of resignation arrives.

Nine managers can seem enigmatic because they give the impression of saying both yes and no. This apparent ambivalence threatens Four's special status and triggers the fear of public humiliation. It helps this partnership enormously if a welcome can be extended that allows Romantics to feel included. It can be as simple as inviting them to observe a meeting or seating them next to an influential figure. Romantic employees are sensitive to who gets what: "Who's close to leadership? Who's getting special attention? What did the manager say?" Covert favoritism rattles Fours' stability and makes them either withdraw in shame or become highly competitive with peers. In this situation both types profit from unambiguous guidelines concerning status and benefits, but it will really please the Romantics on staff if those guidelines are implemented with some sweetening from the person in charge.

Double Five: A Double Observer Couple

Five is the Enneagram's detached type, which produces any number of fascinating relationship stories, like the young American man who met his Five wife in Paris. Since neither could speak the other's language, they communicated through signs and phrases from a guidebook. They cooked together. They drove to the country and rented a rowboat. They visited each other's favorite places in the city, and they married within two weeks. According to the French wife, who later came to America, the silence of that courtship allowed a profound nonverbal commitment to develop. Not having to speak freed her to feel. She was not required to explain herself, she didn't feel drained by expectations, and she could choose to interact or not as she pleased.

Double Fives often live well together because they can respect each other's boundaries. It may not look like much is happening from the outside, because there's so little small talk and hugging, but the unspoken bond can be palpable. Fives say they can relax around people who contain their emotions. They also describe an automatic contraction that takes place when others' expectations invade the silence.

Double Fives sometimes inhabit separate sections of the house, each with its own entrance. They may divide the floor space down the middle and get together at prearranged times when the children are at home or for an evening out. There can be plenty of family activity as long as there's enough time to recover. Five hell is an uncontrolled environment where anyone can barge in on you, so double Fives learn to maintain privacy while living with other people.

A chance to disappear into "my space" makes cohabitation a lot easier, but the option of withdrawal can also frustrate developing intimacy. It's just too tempting to cut communication, yet each in turn will become resentful if the other detaches from feelings. Anger is a likely meeting place as each eventually moves to Eight at home. Fives know that they're committed when they're willing to show up and fight. It's so much easier to think, "I can do without this," and unobtrusively disappear. Double Fives say that the most annoying part of relating to a similar is the distress of being ignored. They say that they had never realized how painful noncommunication could be, until they wanted something and their Five partner silently went away.

Censored information may be the norm. It doesn't seem necessary to reveal what you're thinking to the people you live with. Lack of information may not disturb a double Five relationship because both partners value the freedom of silence. Although they can unhook from many of the emotional struggles that plague other couples, Observers can begin to dread the emotional emptiness that develops with prolonged detachment. Fives often begin a relationship to fill that inner emptiness, but involvement opens them to a barrage of feelings. Even a good time is draining when you have to fight an undertow that pulls you back to solitude. Each will want an invitation to participate, each will position herself or himself to be drawn out, and each will feel threatened when it's her or his turn to initiate.

It's unlikely that sexuality is the issue. Sex is an exciting short-term happening that's strictly confidential. Sex can also seize the senses in a way that may not be emotional. Most of us can separate our physicality from our emotions, but in an unusual twist, Fives sometimes report "feeling used" or "had" when their emotions engage. "Now look what's happened—you've aroused my feelings" is more of an issue than sensual stirrings. "Now look what you've done—I can't detach." A double Five lifestyle is often focused on short, meaningful interactions followed by emotional rest. Time apart allows each to review the feelings that are suspended during face-to-face encounters, and the conclusions that emerge in solitude may be especially poignant because they fill the inner emptiness.

Double Five Partnership at Work

Positioning is going to determine success. Fives do not flourish in frontline interactions that require charm or rapid conceptual shifts. They gravitate to information-driven settings, research, and depth analysis. Both partners need time to digest the facts, and each will insist on boundaries of private space, punctuality, and precisely worded instructions.

An Observer's vision can drop off at the edge of her or his designated area of responsibility, and the ensuing lack of communication leaves important connectives dangling. Each may focus endlessly on a private topic of interest without communicating the information. Five managers can delegate pieces of a project while neglecting to provide a forum for open information exchange, and Five employees can produce a piece that stands alone but does not integrate into the total picture.

The focus is on long-range planning, part-to-whole logic, and predictable results. A Five-like business can compete well in terms of cost efficiency and product excellence. "Economical excellence" is a byword, because Fives find pleasure in what the Scots call canny transactions, a business style that unites quality with thrift. Both will see the control of personal time as an attractive part of their job description. Autonomy in simple matters can be a major perk, like choosing to disappear for a break without having to sign out. Observers think about conserving time, energy, and money and can value their free time in the same bracket as salary.

Two Observers working together collude in avoiding confrontation. Meetings are orderly and likely to be conducted within the formalities of each participant's role. Five managers commonly adopt a wait-and-see attitude; they like to prepare for a long time and can ignore pressing signals for immediate action. It's difficult for an Observer to commit resources in the face of uncertainty, and the fear of acting without sufficient data inhibits spontaneous policy shift. Rather than take either financial or emotional risk, Five managers tend to fall back on protocol and a formal negotiating stance. Letters replace face-to-face interactions, and intermediaries will be appointed to handle meetings.

Five systems are prone to poor in-house communication. Observers just don't volunteer information. Vital connections are lost when good workers apply themselves to separate pieces of a puzzle without respecting each other's information needs. Logical to the extreme, Fives tend to reduce data to core constructs and symbols and in the process may overlook remote associations and an emerging matrix of interactions. It helps when Fives can interface with aggressive, outgoing people who like to promote and sell. Left to their own devices, Fives can find that coming to closure is difficult. When you're fascinated by data, it's hard to finalize a project, because the definitive answer always seems just a few days away.

Five with Six: An Observer-Trooper Couple

This relationship can convey the feeling of drawing inward during winter. We blanket ourselves with companionship when it gets dark early, enveloping ourselves in familiarity and warmth. This couple may not seem publicly demonstrative, because they relate through quiet continuity. Reading in the same room without interrupting each other's concentration, having meals together without feeling pressured to talk.

An Observer's detachment makes even a phobic Six seem like the active agent in a relationship, and Troopers often welcome the opportunity to affect and direct. An active role satisfies Six's preoccupation with strength and beauty while at the same time relieving Five of the burden of leadership. Troopers can be highly motivated when they feel called to duty for others; their tenderness can be safely expressed through loyalty to a mate. The couple's primary bond is usually mental, even when the two are sexually matched and emotionally wedded. Both understand that there's more to love than feelings.

The relationship flourishes as long as Six feels accepted, but if the Observer contracts by withholding sex or information, Six paranoia goes wild. It can be intensely frustrating to be met by a blank screen when you're seeking reassurance. Fives are secretive, which may startle a Trooper into making accusations. Under fire, Fives withdraw further to protect their privacy needs, and if in fact there is a secret compartment in Five's private life, demands for self-disclosure may drive them deeper into the hidden pocket. Observers may not realize how punishing their detachment can be. By saying nothing, they appear to be aloof and uncaring, and that silence broadcasts as an admission of guilt to Six.

Fives respect people who can contain their feelings. It helps immensely if the Six can back off, agree to a time for discussions, and assume an attitude of neutrality. Five's need for space and distance may sound like avoidance when the Six is desperate for reassurance, but in truth Observers do need time for real feelings to emerge. A Trooper can deactivate Five's fears of engulfment by circumscribing a trouble spot. "I want to talk about who does the dishes" is far more appealing than a general need "to talk about us." From their side of the discussion, Observers can help by revealing their own thinking. A Five's honest "I don't know" is infinitely more reassuring than saying nothing. Sixes find themselves imagining the divorce court when lack of information feeds worst-case thinking. An Observer holds enormous power in this relationship because a Six's fears are activated by lack of presence.

Each needs to read the other's signs of affection. Insecure Sixes typically badger their partners for reassurance, which can drive Fives crazy; but seen from a slightly different angle, Six's querulous "Do you still love me?" is a genuine concern. Sixes demand reassurance because they're afraid of losing someone significant, and just showing up to deal with trouble is a Five's testimony of commitment. Both partners will periodically find themselves wanting to let go and step back. It's a lot easier for Fives to think "I can do without this" than to stay with their feelings; and waiting can be torture to a Six who struggles with fight or flight.

This couple has staying power as long as communication stays open. Both types are known for long-term relationships because permanent commitment and the feeling of "forever" cut through detachment and doubt. They are also low-maintenance people, able to pull together against adversity and to endure long periods of worldly frustration. Once committed, they relate through shared ideas as much as through romantic involvement. Observers commonly cerebralize feelings by defining romance as an action. "Are flowers appropriate for birthdays?" "How can I prepare for a 'spontaneous date'?" Sixes are unusually susceptible to affection. Warmth disarms doubt, and once freed of anxiety, Troopers become tender partners. In Five-Six relationships, a single tender moment can become a cornerstone of commitment when it is cemented in the mind forever.

Five-Six Partnership at Work

Both are mental types, which creates the possibility of a partnership gone dry. Ideas easily replace action, and fresh currents of experimentation are dampened by a disinclination to risk. Both partners are positioned as part of the Enneagram's fear triad, which is generally acted out by exaggerated attention to obstacles. The actual power of potential competitors may be overestimated and a great deal of time spent on troubleshooting. The partners are unlikely to be consistently high profile (even counterphobic Sixes find themselves withdrawing after periods of being onstage). These are not self-promotional people, although they, as anyone, can mobilize to go public for short presentations. Their mutual strength lies in strategy, teaching, planning, or in any situation that demands discriminating analysis.

Observers want to know how individual pieces fit into a long-term, whole-picture perspective. They are devoted to factual evidence but may become embedded in data retrieval. Fives find it difficult to come to closure until every factor has been analyzed; they like to be completely prepared before taking action, a style that mirrors Six's procrastination in the face of success. This mutual hesitation is the partnership's most obvious pitfall, and it can be forestalled by having others do the first cut or first draft of a new undertaking. A Five-Six pair can be far more successful if they set the mission, allow others to produce an initial draft, and then reenter to refine the first cut.

As managers, Fives may not recognize that their Six employees need personal contact. Fives tend to be technical in their communications. They relate logically rather than supportively, usually through factual reports. Information is parceled out according to the need to know. Employees don't need to know the whole picture, a managerial tendency that can make Sixes feel disadvantaged or played off against their peers. General information sessions and open forums are a plus, because they are opportunities to question authority gracefully. Closed meetings will bother a Trooper. "Why wasn't I notified? Why are we being separated from each other? Where is all this leading?"

Faced with a manager who models isolation, and feeling controlled by censored information, a Six's quest for reassurance can turn ugly. Ill prepared to deal with conflict, a Five manager will retreat or try to force the recalcitrant out. It takes a lot of self-awareness for Fives to see that initiating communication is a promising strategy. In this case, any move toward visibility will relax employee suspicions.

Six managers are afraid of insubordination that may crest in the future, and Five employees control by silent nonparticipation. Each may read his or her own agenda into the other's actions. Six sees withheld hostility, and Five sees intrusive expectations. This mutual projection can be amplified if Six's management style seems ambivalent. The Trooper may be trying an idea out to see where the employees stand, but imprecision alienates an Observer. A Five employee wants to know exactly how much energy is required and for exactly how long, and rather than improvise the Five will fall into an "I don't get it" stance. It looks like poor management if Six can't specify, and why should Five be required to do someone else's work? It helps when the manager stops speculating and sticks to a plan without backtracking. Five employees feel respected by a fully conceived directive.

What a Five sees as interference may simply be a nervous Six in action, and what the manager sees as insubordination may be an employee who needs time alone. The simple formality of a weekly meeting is the most effective way to handle differences. Six managers need information, and Five employees need time to think before they commit time and energy.

Five with Seven: An Observer-Epicure Couple

Epicures eat experience. They like to travel, take classes, and work on several projects at the same time. Their quest for variety provides a reliable in-house sorting system for Fives, who spend their time and energy cautiously. On Enneagram couples panels, we commonly hear that the Epicure discovered the Enneagram first, checked out our class, and went home to convince the Five that it was a good thing. Pleasant company enhances an evening out, and soon the Epicure had a partner for Enneagram nights. Seven's initial attraction allowed the Observer to participate from a protected background position. Over time, however, it is usually the Five who continues to pursue a study.

Another common scenario places the couple in parallel play. "You do your thing and I'll do mine" is a natural lifestyle for people who relate through ideas. Fives love extended periods of time by themselves, to pursue the quest for knowledge and to sort out their feelings. The outer-directed Epicure could feel severely limited by Five's inner orientation were it not for the fact that both types are highly independent. Sevens find things to do that Fives enjoy vicariously, and neither wants the other to demand a lot of time together. This couple's shared line in the Enneagram diagram seems to generate mutual understanding. Fives admire a Seven's expanded social ease, and Sevens are quieted by the steady reassurance of their Five's more introverted presence. As long as they keep the conversation going, neither is likely to interfere with the other's activities.

Intimacy can be expressed through a common vision or the commitment to children. Sevens need an exterior focus, and Fives have better access to their feelings when they don't have to be the center of attention. Paradoxically the detached Observer often becomes the couple's emotional pillar. Fives in the security of their home can move to Eight, emerging as a powerful force in the family. For their part Sevens find security in Five-like retreat by spending short periods of time alone. In class we routinely hear that Epicures think a day or two in retreat makes them homebodies and very private people, an observation countered by their Fives, who respond, "Yes, dear, but you're rarely at home."

Closely positioned at each other's points of security and risk, the partners share some similarity of outlook. Both are fear types, although they ward off danger in very different ways, and both confuse thinking with feeling. They even look alike under specific life conditions. For example, Fives living in the stress of Seven look like they're coming alive, but self-descriptions reveal a terrible inner tension attached to reaching out. If their search for safety is successful, Fives may indeed discover an unexpected Epicurean pleasure in the company of others, but the commonly reported interaction places Seven as the couple's social wedge.

Fives may not notice when analysis replaces feelings, and most Sevens don't see activity as an avenue of escape. Both types habitually divert attention from their emotions: Sevens distract themselves, and Fives simply detach. It's a bad sign when a Seven moves enthusiastically forward while the Five backs into isolation. Each will secretly look down on the other: Seven is bored—the relationship isn't radiant; and Five sees superficiality—the relationship lacks depth. The resulting move into parallel play can divide this couple into separate orbits of existence: The Observer retreats behind a wall of private interests, and the Epicure's activities draw her or him away from home. It helps when each begins to embody the other's natural orientation. Fives must invest their time, energy, and enthusiasm in the relationship, and Sevens need to develop the single-minded concentration that a full commitment requires.

Five-Seven Partnership at Work

Both are among the Enneagram's mental types—people for whom ideas can replace action. Mental types get seduced by theory and swept off course by interesting plans. Sevens are especially vulnerable—their minds resemble a decision tree. One good concept produces branches of associated ideas, all of which seem viable because they stem from the original scheme. A Five's thinking tends to be more logical, a single idea becomes the focus of extended investigation, and they can work in relative isolation for years. This partnership favors strategy and research, but without equal attention paid to follow-through and closure, good ideas may never be actualized.

The usual arrangement shows Five in the office with Seven in the field. Five managers tend to be orderly; they require full data support and feel secure in limiting their effort to a particular area of study. Five systems can either anchor a Seven employee's efforts or become so narrowly focused that the employee rebels. Sevens favor sweet rebellion, and when they are wise, they see how the manager's central interests can be augmented by an appropriate network. Unwise Seven employees will revolutionize the central concept, do as they please, and rationalize the results. Five managers require accountability and find the Seven-like style of loosely defined connectives highly stressful. On the low side Five managers customarily constrict when faced with options, preferring to repeat a formula that has worked in the past. On the high side a Seven may indeed discover the coordinates that unify a manager's carefully researched sectors of information.

There may be an unspoken agreement to avoid conflict. Epicures rationalize problems out of existence, and Observers entrench behind a barricade of answering machines. Both are prone to seeing through problems rather than dealing with them. Trouble spots can be thought through without much emotion, allowing unrecognized tensions to build. The mind is supposed to find a solution and a way of escape before the point of anger, so it can be startling when feelings finally surface. Mediation should focus on breaking down problem areas into small, manageable chunks. This technique works wonders for people in the Enneagram fear triad, because it softens the belief that anger creates permanent damage.

Seven managers take pleasure in last-minute decisions, but their resistance to closure can make them look scattered. Caught in the cross fire of contradictory information, their Five employees are likely to retreat and wait rather than press for clarification. A wait-and-see attitude doesn't imply agreement, but it protects Fives from having to reach out. Seven managers would do well to hand over a clearly demarcated project that does not depend on networking efforts or shared results. Fives tend to produce precisely what is expected, often without elaboration or attempts to coordinate with other sectors. They may not volunteer information unless asked, particularly in rapidly changing conditions, but when they are committed, Fives can stabilize chaos long enough for Seven to find an angle on the problem.

Five with Eight: An Observer-Boss Couple

The Boss is arguably the Enneagram's most assertive type, and the Observer is the most retracted. Eights want more, and

Fives have minimal needs. Eights are outer-directed, and Fives retreat to privacy. Yet despite their obvious differences this is a frequently paired couple, and the two share an intrinsic affinity. Positioned as each other's point of security and stress, long-term partners begin to resemble each other. After years of living together, the aggressive Boss looks remarkably tame and the Observer seems to have taken assertiveness training.

Fives are far more outspoken in the security of their own home, an attitude that dovetails with Eight's demand for truth. In this relationship an Observer can experience emotional energy, and although they detest every battle, Fives usually concur that their Boss lessons produce beneficial results. The overall effect is enlivening because anger pushes Fives to have their feelings in the moment. It's hard to detach when you're highly energized, and Fives do react spontaneously in a secure relationship. This relationship can initiate Observers into emotional life, and from their side of the interaction Eights learn to wait.

A common interaction involves Five's becoming overwhelmed and Eight's complaining about having to hold back. Fives can drain the force out of an interaction just as efficiently as a partner can pump it in. The couple's emotional currents resemble the cresting and ebbing of tides: Eights press for contact with oceanic force, which is checked by an undertow of withdrawal. The emotional force of expansion and contraction will be entirely familiar to both. Fives' emotions well up when they are safely alone, and Eights' emotions contract forcefully when under stress.

The couple often lives at Eight for long periods, which inevitably involves loud, meaningful late-night debates. Observers are initially overwhelmed and want to flee, but living with a Boss opens feelings. From their side of the relationship Eights are often disarmed when they are met by inner quiet. An Observer's emotional self-control can encourage Eights to look within themselves rather than pick a fight.

Both types place enormous value on personal autonomy. Freedom of action is a must. They know what they like and what they don't like, and neither is likely to get enmeshed in a partner's agenda. On the high side this mutual independence of spirit allows the two to speak bluntly and honestly to each other. On the low side the partners may be unable to compromise and may have very little guilt about their effect on each other. Fives sometimes have the notion that emotional pain stems from poor self-control, which allows them to escape responsibility for other people's feelings. It is also possible that an Eight in pain will seek to even the score. Revenge can play a part in this relationship, with Eight pushing for top-dog position.

When an Observer-Boss couple meets at Five, they often develop great respect for uninterrupted time alone. It's like living by yourself, all the while knowing that someone you love is in close proximity. On the high side the relationship produces both emotional autonomy and a dear companion within calling distance, but on the low side each withholds affection from the other. A Five's withdrawal broadcasts through the house as a loud, petulant pout—an effective way to disappear and still demonstrate disapproval. It's almost impossible to force an unwilling Five to cooperate; the energy will simply drain out of any encounter. In retaliation, Eights hang out their own Do Not Disturb sign, and the resulting battle of wills can escalate into a silence that shouts, "Go away! I don't need you and I don't care."

Because these two share closely connected psychological dynamics within the nine-pointed star, they have an unusual opportunity to witness themselves in each other's behavior. Fives need to see a Boss's assertive manner as an antidote to their own chronic inability to go public. Just knowing that life is worth fighting for can be healing to detached people, and learning to speak impulsively is an exhilarating release. From the other side of the interaction, Eights can trust an Observer who maintains confidentiality and demonstrates emotional control. In the same way that long-term couples seem to become energetically alike, they can also exchange behaviors. In this relationship a successful marriage of qualities begets an Observer who springs into action and a patient Boss who can wait.

Five-Eight Partnership at Work

We often trust Fives in business transactions because they neither seduce nor oppose us with their emotions. They are characteristically low-impact people who deflect attention from themselves by concentrating on tasks. Most of us are more than willing to talk about our private interests, which creates an impression of agreement. We talk and the Five nods, which makes us feel understood.

Observers rarely implement their own creations. It takes tremendous stamina to move their projects from the boardroom to the boiler room where creative ideas are shaped. Implementation always involves heated personal interactions, so Fives commonly conduct business by E-mail or fax. An all-time classic Enneagram story was reported by a Five who enters his own building after everyone has gone home for the day, leaves his instructions on each employee's computer terminal, avoids the team that cleans the office, and disappears before 9:00 A.M. His trusted Eight picks up messages in the morning and goes immediately to work, communicating to the manager by E-mail, often without personal contact for months.

The neutral quality that Fives bring to management can be attractive to employees. Observers can radiate in-control leadership, and they can be resilient negotiators because they do not take negative pressure personally. Observers also bring a dispassionate analysis to decision making that allows Eights the freedom to say what they think without repercussions. A good interaction shows Eight exploding, Five detaching, and both deciding to drop the incident without holding a grudge.

The most frequently reported conflict shows an Eight employee filling the power vacuum created by absentee management.

Upon return, the manager sees the vocal Eight employee as insubordinate, and the staff feels squeezed in a power play. Five managers are famous for minimal presence, which creates the vacuum within which Eights begin to agitate. The situation brightens when an Observer comes into the open. A confident manager can convey certainty to others, and once the facts are out, an Eight employee can surrender control.

Eight managers are self-assured, and it's hard to change their course of action. A "my way or the highway" mentality will frequently polarize staff. Employees tend to love them or hate them, but a wise Five supplies the Boss with data and stands back. Five-Eight is a natural alliance, but strategy differences can be deadly. Fives develop their conclusions slowly and dislike risking a premature analysis; but when Eights want action, they publicly vilify a cautious voice. Observers quickly find a useful niche in developing reports. Those reports are best presented to the Boss in face-to-face meetings, however irrelevant the meeting may seem. The way to an Eight's heart is through personal presence and full information, both of which run counter to Five's privacy stance. Information updates are a neutral way for Fives to show presence, and reworking an analysis reaffirms the commitment that an Eight manager needs.

Mediation will have to focus on style of delivery. Eights are intrusive, and Fives are sensitive to intrusion. Eights want contact, and Fives hold back. Each will claim that the other is controlling—the Eight by stepping forward to take control, and the Five by stepping back to exercise remote control. Regardless of who holds the managerial title, each partner can rely on the other's natural endowments: Fives are shielded from confrontation when a Boss moves into action, and Eights who work with an Observer learn to think before they act.

Five with Nine: An Observer-Mediator Couple

This couple often reports an appreciation for nonverbal communication, because both value being understood without having to ask. Asking creates the possibility of rejection or humiliation, so they will tend to funnel their feelings about each other through an external focus such as planning for the family or the supermarket run. Shared activities create an atmosphere in which the two feel each other's presence. Since both express their love most comfortably in nonverbal ways, they often define emotional well-being as "the way we feel when we travel" or "how it feels when we go on a walk." That intangible quality called presence may be so embedded in their relationship that it seems entirely ordinary. The couple feels each other's presence in their children; or when they travel, they can take it for granted that they sightsee through each other's eyes.

Oddly the Observer, who usually watches from the sidelines, may find herself or himself becoming the object of scrutiny. Nines take on the feelings of people who are significant to them, so Five's nonverbal signals fall on a sensitive receptor. The Observer's needs may become the centerpiece of Nine's life, which will have to be handled carefully. Fives cannot endure emotional dependency and can be unusually cold and aloof if a mate develops "unwarranted" expectations. An affectionate Mediator may simply want to spend the evening hanging out and being together, but open-ended time makes a Five think, "And do what?"

A severe situation can develop if the Observer habitually retracts, leaving Nine to feel angry and abandoned. The situation takes a turn for the better when Nines establish an ongoing goal. The interface of the Mediator's goal gives a positive focus to evenings at home by stationing Five in the protected post of trusted adviser. Both partners are far more effective when attention is deflected from themselves and toward others. Fives like to counsel their loved ones, and Nines can take on another's life as their own.

Both types have delayed emotional reactions. A Mediator's position emerges slowly over time, and Fives commonly suspend their feelings during an interaction. This is a couple that gives each other plenty of space. Both dislike feeling pressured to take action. Nines dig in and go stubborn when they're expected to make a decision, and Fives withdraw from other people's expectations. A no-conflict agreement can develop that allows each to become absorbed in a private world, effectively leaving the other alone. A Mediator's spread of activities probably won't disturb an Observer unless the home routine is affected, and an oblivious Nine will not question the Five's compartmentalized life.

A no-conflict agreement can also deaden a relationship. Fives habitually detach from their feelings, and Nines go on autopilot by numbing out through obsessive routine. On the low side the unwillingness to engage encourages each to develop a preoccupied individual orbit. Both tend to censor information, so if the relationship goes dry, their orbits of interest spin slowly away from each other. A real union requires participation, but the pair may opt for "harmony in the home." If the commitment to harmony is really conflict avoidance, Nine's energy level begins to drop and Five will become increasingly remote. In an apparent paradox, this relationship often profits from a small explosion that breaks the holding pattern. A good fight enlivens people, and a good cry can bring them together. The victories and disasters within an intimate relationship wake us up to the fact that we need each other. Nines can hold a position when they're angry, and Fives need to feel safe with their feelings.

This couple can be physically affectionate and devoted to each other's welfare while still relating through a holding pattern. If there's a confrontation, an Observer will think, "It would be easy to drop this," a sentiment mirrored by a Mediator's obsessive inner question: "Should I be here or not?" Because a relationship ignites the emotional energy that both tend to avoid, it's an ideal arena for Fives to get comfortable with feelings and for Nines to develop an unequivocal, permanent commitment.

Five-Nine Partnership at Work

Neither of the partners is likely to be self-promotional, and both dislike competing for status; however, each requires a particular kind of attention. Fives want to be validated for their thinking, and Nines flourish when they get unsolicited personal respect. It's unlikely that this pair will create an abrasive atmosphere, but the downside of apparent harmony can be lack of initiation. Each waits to be drawn out by the other, and so it is likely that both will look to work roles to define their relationship. Both types build momentum by following a well-built structure, with Nine taking on the foreground role of dealing with the public and Five remaining in the background continuing to refine the task. The most commonly reported division of labor shows an Observer's sparse, well-directed schemes providing the foundation that Nines then shape into a workable system.

The public position consists of calls, meetings, and outreach, while the background position supplies data analysis. Given a viable system, the partners can either expand operations, using the structure to reach demanding goals, or coast with dwindling enthusiasm until the structure finally winds down. Productivity seems to follow the law of inertia, which states that a body in motion tends to stay in motion, while a body at rest stays at rest. At the peak of inertia, new goals follow logically from a completed cycle of work; while at the low point of inertia, Nines follow the rule book and Fives communicate by phone.

Both types need a jump start of vitality. Nines are enlivened by camaraderie and participation, whereas Fives plug in through an exchange of ideas. The pair generally interacts through short, meaningful policy meetings, focused primarily on task. Fives have a lot of input at the meetings, but it's the Nines who are likely to keep the ball rolling.

They may have trouble getting each other's attention, because both find it difficult to shift once they commit to a course of action. Fives are nearly unreachable once they're engaged in an absorbing problem, and Nines cling to a position for fear of getting derailed.

Five managers typically operate by remote control. Meetings are content driven and may be focused on single areas of a project that are isolated from a larger context, giving employees the impression that decisions have been finalized in private without their having had a chance to voice their own views. Sensitive to being overlooked, Nine employees inwardly rebel at being told without being asked. A worst-case standoff shows the Five manager offering brief directives at a short general meeting with no opportunity for feedback. If offended Nines are involved, those directives may never get off the ground. Without speaking an angry word, Nines will defuse the follow-through.

It helps to find a forum of collegiality. Nine employees need to know both who and what they are working for. It helps when a Five manager can see the humanizing value in mottoes like "Shoulder to shoulder, and eye to eye," because in working with Nines that attitude really pays off. Mediators do not flourish in isolation, and with a little thought, Five managers can develop simple ways of interacting with their employees. Fives are always interested in information pipelines and might discover that Nines are often the barometer of group dynamics. Because they recognize other people's agendas, Nines can articulate group aspirations and the fluctuating political currents of a workplace.

The precision of a Five manager's thinking is likely to appeal to Nines. Sound discrimination cuts through a Mediator's tendency to lose focus by spreading attention. When Five managers find a way to interact with employees, they are likely to draw a following among Nines.

Nine managers tend to develop a system, which suits this partnership well. Mediators like to promote and network within the confines of a secure context that does not require renewed decisions. Five employees also appreciate structure, because they focus best when expectations are predictable. They can produce wholeheartedly within a given time frame, exhibiting little of the competitive edge that Nines have difficulty managing.

Both partners will have to adjust their natural styles of communication. Fives prefer highly controlled contact about specific tasks, which counters Nine's determination to hear everyone's position. Fives want a concise conversation, while Nines can prolong discussion indefinitely. It helps when Nines learn to focus on closure and Fives are mature enough to see that meetings serve the purpose of solidarity as well as structuring the work.

Intervention will have to deal with the fact that both types avoid conflict. This collusion creates distance at exactly those times when open communication is needed. A disgruntled Five may reduce performance level and will not volunteer or offer constructive advice. A standoff shows each in a corner where neither is able to draw the other out. To enforce greater participation, a Nine manager will resort to the rules, but the underlying resentment is aimed at Five's unwillingness to speak. Intervention has to establish an arena for negotiations because both types control by nondoing and by hoarding energy. It helps to schedule the discussion of a difficult topic well in advance. Nines need time to discover an independent opinion, and Fives negotiate better when they have a predetermined format through which to handle emotions.

Double Six: A Double Trooper Couple

A Six's habit of mind involves intense internal questioning. This habit often makes the Six seem oppositional: "Yes, but" or "What about the other side?" sounds like negative thinking, but Sixes see a difference between negativity and contrary thought. Negative thinking is a put-down, a denial of what is positive and good, whereas contrary thought can be clarifying because it illuminates the opposite side of a question. Double Six may welcome the fact that a partner is willing to raise hard questions. Cross-examination eliminates doubt and frees the couple to move ahead.

Contrary thinking works like a seesaw in a children's playground. When one partner falls into fear, it naturally elevates the other to envision brighter possibilities. The trick is to pay close attention to Troopers without either confirming or dismissing their ideas as worst-case thinking. Like most people, Sixes simply feel misunderstood and retreat if their anxiety is trivialized.

When both partners feel anxious about the same external event, they unite in an us-against-the-world alliance. This mutual doubt can produce a folie à deux, or shared false belief, that prolongs difficulty as the two reinfect each other with doubt. A small lapse in confidence can magnify to catastrophic proportions. "If it frightens us now, think how bad this could get!"

On the high side double Six couples are a source of strength to each other. They pull together under pressure and often join in civic action groups that support a cause. They can be highly effective in an underdog setting, where doubt is entirely realistic. We all feel somewhat powerless when we're beginners, newcomers, or when we play against the odds. Troopers often find it easier to act for an underdog cause than for overtly promising ventures.

Double Sixes need activities where they can coast on familiar routine without thinking. Either might be half convinced that the relationship is about to end, but the schedule says lunch at noon, and once they both arrive, doubts melt away with a welcoming smile. Scheduled check-ins are a must because lack of contact spurs paranoia. Contrary thinking vanishes with the steady reassurance of routine.

Pleasure is especially healing for types who worry about the future. Like Perfectionists (Ones), Troopers mistrust the promise of a rosy future. This couple needs something to look forward to—a trip to the country, a walk in the park, small pleasures that can deter lingering doubt.

Envisioning the future can also be a source of pleasure. Hope can propel them into action, and a shared dream generates faith. Sixes are highly emotional, but their feelings are often dedicated to a mental vision. They may think about each other constantly, probing their own motivations and carefully analyzing their commitment. From the outside the couple may not look overtly affectionate. Preoccupied with finding meaning in their relationship, they may neglect the physical and emotional attraction that drew them together. From the couple's point of view, sexuality and adventure often seem like wonderful side effects rather than the central focus of relationship. They need the reassurance of a "mentalized" commitment. They want to feel certain. They want to know what's "really happening." The precoccupation with certainty and meaning can crowd out other ways of relating. Sixes are highly emotional, but they put their faith in emotional bonds that depend on dedication of mind.

Double Six Partnership at Work

Troopers can seem vastly different from each other in the workplace. Phobics seek a strong protector and are grateful when someone else will hold the line in confrontation. Counterphobics, who are equally afraid, can come off as office agitators by questioning the people in charge. This type's range of behavior is broad, but the common denominator for every Six is the preoccupation with authority. Troopers are suspicious of the power hierarchy, but they act out that concern in very different ways.

Here's an illustration of the different tactics that Sixes employ in dealing with authority. A phobic Six who is a self-preservation subtype will focus on affection to reduce fear. Getting approval from people in power is paramount, and because these Sixes reach out to others for reassurance, they can easily pass as Twos. Counterphobic Sixes adopt an opposite tactic to deal with the same authority issues. Counterphobics fight against fear in aggressive ways that can resemble an Eight or a One. If the counterphobic is additionally a strength/beauty one-to-one subtype, that aggressive stance will be focused on individuals who hold power at work.

As managers Troopers have to be careful that they don't overreact. Inner doubt creates a climate in which employee concerns can be heard as criticism. A Trooper's loyalty is built on trust, so Six managers will act generously toward employees who have proved to be loyal in the past. Sixes can tolerate a great deal of neurotic or selfish behavior as long as the alliance stays intact. The high side of a double Six alliance is the commitment to seeing each other through difficulty; but the low side is a mutual comfort operation in which the manager is afraid to alienate the employee, and the employee is afraid to confront the boss. Sixes are not always comfortable in management. They want reliable backup from the higher-ups and are likely to test the loyalty of employees. The most frequently reported test involves laying out an ambiguous problem and waiting to see who acts for the benefit of others and who acts out of self-interest.

As managers Troopers can vacillate between being too lax and too strict. A lax Six is uncomfortable about being in authority and seems unwilling to direct. Sixes with a reputation for enforcement are usually afraid of being challenged and are therefore too controlling. It helps to focus on task, because the task determines how people behave toward each other. Laxity and overcontrolling leadership both stem from inner uncertainty. The manager may be magnifying the possibility of opposition and needs to be reassured. Worst-case outcomes should be discussed openly, including the fact that following a safe solution can be dangerous when real risks need to be taken. It helps if a trusted authority can be invited to back the manager's opinions. A friendly voice in the hierarchy combined with a realistic assessment of the obstacles to success can be liberating to Six managers who are afraid to state their fears for fear of looking fearful.

Double Six can compound the problem of procrastination. It's hard to move ahead when attention wanders to reconsider the counterarguments. Ambiguous messages are paralyzing for both employee and boss. Six employees say that an innocent comment, like "We need an evaluation," can bring on major doubt attacks. An evaluation meeting also triggers the manager's fear of antiauthoritarian sentiment at the meeting.

Simply softening the communication will reduce the massive projection generated by ambiguous information. Troopers respond to managers who can be reasonably disclosing and to "soft communication." It helps when a manager says, "This is my thinking about the project" or uses qualifying statements such as "The project's being continued, and we need to evaluate." Management should provide a prior explanation concerning any deviation from employee expectations. Troopers expect the worst until they are properly informed and will notice any discrepancy between what an authority promises and what that person actually delivers. Mediation should focus on clarifying management's intentions, particularly those that affect this employee's future. Forewarning forestalls rebellion in working with Troopers.

Six with Seven: A Trooper-Epicure Couple

Both types are positioned in the fear triad at the left side of the diagram, but they handle anxiety in very different ways. The Six is overtly tentative and often seems cautious in comparison with Seven's breezy approach to relating. Sevens diffuse their fears through a system of backup plans and may unconsciously depend on Sixes to act out their own underlying paranoia. Oddly both types embellish objective events with an imagined outcome, but they arrive at opposite conclusions. Seven's positive future visioning and Six's tendency to envision the worst can both be projections.

An Epicure can dismiss Six's concerns as figments of the imagination, but when Troopers are told to lighten up, they can become more deeply afraid. The two hold opposite assumptions about relationship: Seven sees unlimited possibilities, while Six feels bound by duty and hard work. Reality testing will be a central feature in this relationship. When one partner sees the worst and the other sees the best, they can often meet in the middle. Staying in close contact with each other modifies best-case and worst-case beliefs. Daily calls, shared projects, and family meetings forestall a shift into unreal speculation.

Seven's attraction to pleasure provides an antidote to Six's doubt. Likewise a Six who is loyal during times of trouble can be healing to a mate who is terrified of pain. Difficulties will arise if Seven manipulates the truth in the interest of greater freedom. Inconsistency provokes paranoia, and Six will probably retaliate by threatening to bail out. Sevens become magnetized by a disappearing option, and Six's wavering loyalty can make the relationship look more desirable.

This couple may have commitment issues. Sixes want guarantees before they commit to anything, and Sevens hate to be pinned down. Seven's flights of fancy and time-consuming sidetracks can read as betrayal to an insecure partner. Reassurance is important on both sides. Reassurance for a Trooper that Seven is faithful. Reassurance for an Epicure that Six can relinquish control. It helps if Six can focus on actions rather than possibilities. A Seven's schemes are far more elaborate than what will actually materialize.

A Seven's plans seem hugely self-indulgent to a cautious Six partner. "What's the line between outside interests and hedonism?" It feels disloyal. "Are you committed or not?" If Six becomes meddlesome, a cycle is created in which Six suffers and Seven wants out. Self-absorbed, the Epicure may not see the problem building and may not empathize with Six's pain. It seems that the Trooper is stirring up trouble and complaining unnecessarily. Seven may think, "If I feel pain, then I'm in the wrong relationship." Criticism cuts to the core of Seven's positive outlook. "There could be something wrong with me if I have to ask for help."

The timing of a sensitive discussion will be important in relating to Sevens. An oblique approach is far more effective than a forced discussion. Sixes are notorious for insisting on sit-down panic sessions in which they air their doubts, but Epicures are more likely to hear a buffered complaint administered in short, manageable doses. A frightened Seven will rationalize problems and run, but if there is no immediate threat, complaints eventually come to the table. It helps to frame differences in the perspective of past goodwill and to aim at the light at the end of the tunnel. It does not help if Six becomes fixated on an admission of guilt, expecting Seven to feel remorse about the past.

Sevens get the couple out of the house; a good time washes paranoia away. A sunny afternoon of shared activity can do more toward reassuring Six about commitment than hundreds of hours of talk. Long-term couples say that they've learned to meet in the middle. Six has learned to tell the difference between private doubts and what Seven is actually going to do. Seven has learned to respond by keeping baseline agreements without inserting an escape clause.

Six-Seven Partnership at Work

This pair can either compound the problem of procrastination or learn to move toward mutual goals. Both types are likely to change their minds on short notice. Sixes doubt and Sevens get distracted by ideas. Each will expect the other to stay focused, but follow-through can be an ongoing problem. Ideas are broached and forgotten. Plans can be made, changed, and dropped. Both are likely to fall into endless talk and meetings, but both may find it difficult to identify their own behavior as procrastination. Sevens see their many options as facets of a single plan, and Sixes see their doubts as accurate problem solving.

Both types can also live in the future. Sixes are focused on warding off catastrophe, and Sevens love to envision plans. A good balance can develop if they listen to each other. Epicures can sustain a vision, and Troopers often flourish when they take on demanding work. The pair can support each other to overcome both the dilettante and doubter tendencies, Sevens by staying focused during difficulty and Sixes by daring to believe.

As managers Sixes dislike having to inspire or promote obedience and will resent having to supervise an evasive staff. Troopers can overreact to what feels like deliberate disrespect on the part of Seven employees, who may in fact be oblivious to the problem. Sevens can innovate without realizing that they've redefined their duties, but if the manager senses evasive action, resentments will build. The Epicure may need an explosion to wake up to reality but will not admit to malicious intent. Sixes sometimes harbor the notion that a full admission of guilt can prevent backsliding, but Sevens follow the spirit rather than the letter of the law. What can look like guilty behavior to others seems more like a learning experience. This duo will really profit from staged checkpoints that clarify each other's intentions. Chicanery can be magnified in the mind of a Six manager who expects to be deceived, and Sevens are unusually slippery in supervision.

Seven managers like to delegate and to parcel out their projects. A series of short-range goals that turn over quickly is far more attractive than the tedium of long-range plans. This manager depends on delegating long-term follow-through to staff but may change the course of action without notice. Inconsistency of purpose raises a Six employee's hackles. Troopers who have developed a routine do not like to arrive at work and find out that the goalposts were repositioned during the night. Small items can quickly escalate to threatening significance. "The goals changed, and I wasn't consulted. Why? Am I being dumped?" Sixes are actually quite flexible as long as they're given an adequate explanation. Once reassured about job security, Six employees are very loyal. The trick in mediation will be for each to enter the other's point of view. Sixes can learn to take action more easily, and Sevens can learn to do one thing at a time without becoming afraid.

Six with Eight: A Trooper-Boss Couple

Eights, whether male or female, are active in the courtship phase, which goes a long way toward eliminating Sixes' doubt. Eights find security in taking charge and offering protection, which fits perfectly with the insecurities of Sixes. Freed of the full task of initiating relationships, Troopers are placed in the safer stance of feeling sought after and needed. Eights are refreshingly confident about their sexuality and about moving into success. This confidence can be liberating to types like Six, who contract and feel guilty about pleasure.

This is a meeting of body and mind rather than romantic sentiment. The partners share an aversion to "gushy sentimentality." Sweet support, which may be entirely well intended, can sound faked to types who see the world as dangerous. Devotion is expressed through physicality and ideas rather than intimate innuendo. Actions and inspiration count more than nurturing tender feelings. Trust emerges largely through observation—by seeing that the partner acts for the benefit of others.

Both types expect adversity and stand together during difficulty. Phobic Sixes stand behind Eight partners, giving loyal support. Counterphobic Sixes, pushing against fear, stand alongside. An excellent interaction shows the bigger-than-life Eight relying on the advice of the more mental and strategic Six. Sixes can wait rather than rushing in to take charge, they can observe complicated motivations, and they are far more political about potential repercussions. Equipped with good counsel, Eights can move mountains. Eights value loyalty, and Sixes are unusually loyal in adversity. Sixes value strength, and Eights are most determined when they are challenged.

The typical position shows Eight in control with Six in support. Eights want action, and Sixes are happier in the more protected role. The situation changes dramatically when they find themselves without a barricade to storm. For all their bravado, Eights find it easier to challenge life, or to support someone else's forward thrust, than to search within themselves for a personal agenda. Without a clear and present call to action, Eights begin to coast, to make trouble, or to support the Six's agenda. Eights are very helpful when they are willing to take an appropriate support position; but they can be a royal pain when they take charge of someone else's life instead of improving their own.

Sixes will find themselves trying to move ahead against massive self-doubt, sometimes encouraged, and sometimes insulted and goaded into action, by the Boss. Eights are protectors, and Troopers want protection, but Sixes can quickly shift from seeing Eights as protectors to seeing them as bullies. From Eights' perspective, there is also a thin line between perceiving Sixes as worthy of protection and as wimps who can't stand up for themselves. Sixes need constant reassurance, which makes them seem weak to Eights, who deny their own weakness. Eights are particularly impatient with doubt and vacillation, which looks both weak and untruthful: "Why can't you make up your mind?" "Are you committed to this, or are you lying?"

The Eight partner, when pushing for the truth, or when seeking to revitalize the relationship, may become punitive and say the worst. Dealing with what now looks like an overbearing and possibly dangerous mate, Six's imagination ignites and moves to the divorce court. Finally the Trooper is up against the wall and, whether phobic or counterphobic, will fight when cornered. The subtext of this struggle is power. The Eight can't surrender control until a mate looks strong and trustworthy, and the Six can't commit fully until the Eight looks less dangerous.

Paradoxically some horrendous battles can have positive repercussions in this relationship. The Six has been goaded into terrifying displays of anger, has said the worst, and has survived. Now it's out. The frightened Six has been bullied into setting the necessary boundaries. The Eight sees the limits and doesn't have to push further for the truth.

Six-Eight Partnership at Work

Under pressure Eights tend to charge ahead, to throw energy at the situation, to take over as fast as possible. The Six inclination is to fall back and consider the consequences. This widens the gap between the partners' business styles. Eights minimize opposition and push against the limits. It looks like nothing significant is in the way, and besides, inaction feels dangerously weak. Sixes do just the opposite. Imagination magnifies the power of the opposition and in turn magnifies the negative consequences of Eights' rash actions. Suddenly Eights look like the problem rather than a source of help.

Six managers must take command from the start. Sixes are impressed by Eights' strength of will and tenacity in difficulty. Those same qualities are intimidating if Eight employees show an inclination to bend the rules and to shift priorities to suit themselves; particularly so if the Eights like to argue and self-justify, often under the guise of improving the system.

The Six, caught between feeling intimidated and wanting to be liked, will either want to fire the Eight or to pacify the situation by overcompensating. Worn down by a power struggle, it's easier to get rid of an employee than to watch your back. The Trooper's ambivalence about authority is projected onto the Eight, who now looks capable of the worst. The dirty tricks that disgruntled employees can play spring to mind. The Six worries that complaints may be lodged with superiors or shareholders, that there may be litigation or misrepresentation of fact. Disliking altercation, the Six prefers either to cave in or to get rid of the potential troublemaker. The most likely behavior is a wavering between nonenforcement and nailing the Eight for infractions. Clear boundaries and confrontation are comforting to Eight employees. They see enforcement as competent leadership.

Secure Eight managers see themselves in a top-dog position. They often spread the mantle of power and protection over "their" people, which alleviates Sixes' doubt. Eight managers can also become workplace tyrants, which drives fear types into fight or flight. Six employees may try to doctor bad news or devise ways to avoid the manager's attention. Why put yourself in the line of fire when it's easier to duck? Crises can develop if Sixes hide and Eights pursue. Troopers see Eights as controlling, and the Boss sees Sixes as out of control.

Eight managers should realize how their forceful personas affect others. If possible, set up face-to-face meetings, where employees can talk. Sixes have excellent ideas that are often coupled with doubt. Eights can see through doubt to make ideas happen.

Six with Nine: A Trooper-Mediator Couple

Nines frequently emanate a calm, reassuring presence. It's like coming home to genial surroundings after a hard day; you can unwind because you feel accepted. A typical interaction shows Nine as the comforter, because the couple's fears are carried and voiced by Six. The Trooper's skittish movement between commitment and doubt is entirely familiar to Mediators, who also have trouble choosing a course of action. The couple shares a significant line in the diagram, making it easy for them to exchange places with each other. Nines in stress take on a startled Six-like persona: It looks like cold panic and usually elicits sympathy from Troopers.

Both partners have trouble taking action, and both find it easier to act in the name of another than for themselves. Consequently this can be either a partnership of mutual support or a continuing battle about "who should go first." It's going to be important for each to define personal goals rather than expect the other to lead. Nines merge with a partner's point of view, and Sixes can be unusually loyal supporters, but the flip side of that loyalty and merger produces lack of initiative.

Following the diagram, this couple meets at Three, which means that either can suppress emotions when moving into action. Nines who forget their feelings are numb enough to conduct a love affair on automatic pilot, and doing without feeling is typical of a Six in stress. When Troopers doubt their relationships, they suspend their feelings and fall back on conditional commitment. Now they're in the relationship "just until we see how it works out."

On the high side of meeting at Three this is often a lively couple. Nines can be unstoppable once they gear up, and they love finding the Performer in themselves. For Troopers, action eliminates doubt and makes success feel safe. A meeting at Three can produce full participation from both partners, especially if they don't pack the schedule simply to block out feelings.

Each will try to avoid anger, although Sixes find the passive anger of Nine far less threatening than the critical anger of One or the periodic rage of Eight. An angry Mediator looks stubborn rather than dangerous, which reduces the Trooper's fear of attack. A no-conflict agreement can emerge that either reduces tension between the two or allows energy to sink into safe routine. It's important that this couple learn to risk being angry rather than dimming their energy with unessentials. Mediators find a position when they're angry, and anger is often buried at the root of a Trooper's fears.

It unsettles a Six when the Nine becomes inactive. Inaction feeds doubt, and Six will worry about the relationship getting mired. A common interaction involves a doubtful Six prodding Nine for greater effort. The message is "Get moving and quit spacing out," but Nines entrench in passivity when they feel pushed. An all-time low pictures Nine indecision in collusion with Six doubt. The partners cannot move toward goals, and each sees the other as the cause of their mutual procrastination. "You go first" and "Why should I change when you aren't trying?" are signals of their distress. Either can fall into conditional love during an uncommitted period. Six may commit on conditions—"This is to please our parents" or "Until we're launched in our careers." Nines can sit on the fence forever and wonder, "Should I be here or not?" "Is this what I really want?" Strangely, these two can overlook the depth of their feelings about each other for many years before they finally make up their minds that they're actually in love.

If either partner initiates action, it breaks the stalemate over who should go first. Activity is immensely healing to both types, especially when each can pursue a personal agenda without insisting that the other join in. Action breaks inertia for a Mediator, and realistic progress softens a Trooper's fears.

Six-Nine Partnership at Work

Professionally this partnership usually meets at Three, the position of our American corporate ideal. Nines naturally shift to Performer mode when they feel secure and are often attracted to a Three-like image of success. Sixes doubt their achievements but, like any competent person, will rise to meet professional demands. Both are likely to overbook themselves. Nines have trouble saying no and are distracted by details; Sixes have difficulty keeping up with continuous production and may fall behind schedule.

Six managers should never become isolated; the best medicine for doubt is continuous interaction with staff. Sixes go through periods in which they lose faith in the product, the project, and the whole hierarchy, but they can still direct well if they get reliable feedback. Consistent feedback absorbs anxiety, particularly if the manager gets periodic time off to regroup and think. Time to debrief doubts, coupled with staff members who keep abreast of the timetable, will bring out a Trooper's leadership.

Nine employees measure their energy against the requirements of a task, but when the energy drops, they often lapse into perfunctory routine. Unusually sensitive to insubordination, Six managers may see Nine's lack of initiative as deliberate sabotage.

Explanations such as "It wasn't my responsibility" or "I didn't have time" will enrage Six managers. Troopers build a case when their suspicions are triggered, and Nine's passive evasion creates a perception of hidden agendas. Both types commonly mobilize at the deadline for a last-ditch save. Nine inertia and Six doubt can produce a deadly combination, especially if each holds the other responsible for the resulting slowdown. Conflict resolution should focus on the high points of past projects. Nines are productive when they feel accepted, and a positive framework softens Sixes' doubt.

The usual work incentives such as a bonus or role recognition may need to be framed specifically. Both dislike a win-lose situation that requires competing with people in the same office. While it is true that Mediators want tangible rewards for effort, they do not thrive in a competitive atmosphere, and a Trooper's performance may actually plummet after a public win. A good Six incentive would focus on long-term benefits. Since many of their fears are focused on future events, they are particularly grateful for job security. A good incentive for Nines concerns unsolicited recognition, which saves them from having to put themselves forward.

As managers Mediators try to avoid conflict, and that strategy can make a Trooper afraid. Already wary of authority, Six employees may interpret the manager's ambiguous loyalty as a breach of trust. Nines like to reconcile differences, which often involves hearing every position and apportioning a bit of the action to each, a style that triggers Six's fight or flight. A fighting Six sees inconsistency and wants to know "Who's side are you on?" A Six who flees thinks the future is in doubt, "So why stick around?" An obvious intervention lies in Nine's structured management style. Nines develop procedure-oriented systems that seem to run by themselves. Nine organizations are neutral, methodical, and safe—just the kind of employment haven that can cushion Six's anxieties about the future. Once committed to a goal, Nine managers implement in a predictable, noncompetitive manner, which provides an atmosphere of certainty. Longstanding Six-Nine partnerships are common. The most frequently reported interaction finds Six generating ideas that the more practical Nine then shapes into a product or service.

Double Seven: A Double Epicure Couple

When Epicures write a wish list of what they want in an ideal mate, they pick the same features that they see in themselves. They want a relationship with someone who is "energetic, independent, optimistic, successful, and adventurous"—qualities they also attribute to themselves. It seems that Sevens want a mirror-image companion. Someone who will hike the trails that Sevens like, who will go along to movies that a Seven wants to see, and who will sign on to organize the Seven's pet projects. It's probably for this reason that double Sevens commonly bond as playmates and confidants but rarely commit to a lasting relationship.

It seems that relating to an idealized version of yourself may not produce the depth or substance or worthy opposition that leads to enduring commitment. Sevens form relationships all around the Enneagram and are typically found with dramatically different mates rather than someone who's a mirror image. Fascination and a gluttony for adventure apparently make it tempting for Sevens to play the field once the peak of initial attraction passes.

Epicurean highs are spectacular. What could be better than a good companion in a life filled with opportunity? The feeling is, "We can have it all. It's like owning an imaginary jet. You could wind up anywhere on the planet and keep on flying forever." One California Seven, nicknamed Blondie by her husband, carries the license plate All Now on her BMW. Sevens are thought of as the most spontaneous of the types. They want it all, and they want to share it all with an interesting companion right this minute. The high side of this relationship is apparent when two upbeat, attractive people agree that they've met their match.

The lows may not be obvious to the couple. It may not seem dysfunctional to gloss over difficulty. What's so bad about parallel play? The two collude in the idea that spontaneity and freedom of action are the mainstays of healthy relating. In describing their commitments, Sevens use words like *predictable* and *permanent* as if they meant "boring" and "stuck." The fear of being stuck can lead to ingenious ways of reinventing the usual concept of commitment. One of the most recent that I've heard involves a monogamous double Seven couple who saw each other daily but lived in separate apartments for more than fifteen years. They finally bought a house together and laughingly report, "This place is made for us. It's been renovated into condos with separate doorbells and exits for when it gets boring."

Boredom can really be a code word for terror. A fear of "losing the whole world for just one person." Sevens recoil from limitation. "Just one relationship? That's all I'll ever have?" Binding yourself to one sacrifices the many. You're locked in when you've made a commitment. You can't walk out when trouble comes. Unused to the sobering effects of deep emotion, Sevens conspire to keep things light. It helps when either partner sees the built-in limitation of trying to avoid limits and begins to entertain the full cycle of pleasure, sorrow, joy, and pain.

Double Seven Partnership at Work

This pair's success will depend on correct positioning. Short-term, fast-paced projects are safer than risking a veer-off during long-range plans. Beginnings are easy, but follow-through is difficult. It's wise to look at goals as a series of independent tasks that do not require continuous management. Sevens learn quickly and on their feet. They're most efficient in a new situation or when they can plan and then delegate. It can be a disaster if they find themselves responsible for follow-through. Every good idea will generate instant thought trees blooming with mental associations: "Look at all the ramifications!" "Think where this could lead!" Those tantalizing associated ideas can look just as appealing as the original concept. When double Seven agrees to try a new approach, the possibilities will either draw the two together toward an inventive collaboration or separate them as each pursues a personal vision.

Most doubles stay balanced by accessing features of their wing points and their different security and risk reactions. It would be unlikely, for example, to find a double Seven that could remain professionally viable by bouncing from option to option. Sevens can be goal oriented and aggressively Eight-like in competition, especially when their sense of entitlement is questioned. They can also look like frightened Sixes when their options close down. Sevens who lean toward the security point of Five may well retire into a self-maintaining solitude that gives the other Seven an opportunity to run the business alone. But among all the unique Seven personas, the most difficult interaction occurs when either partner leans toward the perfectionism of One. Criticism is a real Achilles' heel for Sevens because it calls their positive self-image into question. When your future is assured by filling in reality's rough spots with planning, criticism disturbs the mix of fantasy and fact.

Each can feel entitled to more than is actually deserved. A Seven employee is entitled to better benefits, and a Seven boss is entitled to time off. "I want more" can easily shift to "I deserve more." "I deserve more than I'm getting, and I don't deserve to worry about how much it costs." Sevens don't like to postpone gratification, and the atmosphere of anticipated abundance can justify the taking of their share right now. It would be very difficult for this team to streamline an operation or to consolidate resources. When more is just around the corner, why do with less? The inclination is to plan a new approach or to a initiate another system instead of down-sizing. Plans can speed up and become more elaborate during troubled times.

Seven managers like to create and delegate. When they're wise, they find a good detail person to follow through on plans; but when they're unwise, they dismiss priorities as details, and details can wait. Once attention is captivated by an idea, the problems of actualizing that idea become blurred. Delegating the crucial matter of follow-through to a Seven employee compounds the confusion, especially when the manager delegates and disappears, leaving follow-through to staff.

As employees Sevens like to equalize authority. They please their peers and make friends with management through personal charm and by discovering similar interests to share. Sevens emanate a sunny-morning feeling. We're off to a perpetual good start, regardless of the weather. If either Seven stays focused and pleased with the work, the other is likely to remain enthusiastic. Work is fine as long as it's interesting, but if the manager veers off, the employee will follow suit.

The most commonly reported double Seven dispute has to do with magnified expectations. They expected more than they got, usually because of faulty communication. Mediation should focus on discriminating between ideas and actualities. It helps to be explicit, lest direct orders be heard as suggestions and thinking out loud mistaken for fact. There will be problems in delivering negative feedback to two Sevens who won't face pain. It helps to structure negotiations in the spirit of better communication rather than to emphasize poor judgment. Most Sevens become enraged when their positive self-image is questioned and will try to deflect criticism with prolific excuses. It helps when error can be set in the context of a fresh start. Then both can see what's needed now and move ahead without dwelling on the past.

Seven with Eight: An Epicure-Boss Couple

There's usually plenty of juice in this relationship. The Enneagram positions the pair as wing points of each other, which can produce the blend of lust plus gluttony known as "fun hunger." It's a promising energy match for creative entertainment, good sex, and adventure. Both types like to play hard and are relatively guilt free. They account to themselves rather than to other people, and both dislike the word *should*.

Independence is a mutual must. A Boss likes to make and break the rules, and an Epicure sees dogma as death. Both view themselves as free agents and will often collude in preferring self-expression to self-improvement. An unspoken agreement will typically emerge, in which each has the time and space to follow personal interests without offending the other. Both look to themselves for support rather than turning to someone else, and both typically withdraw for self-repair when feelings are hurt. Eights often say they'd rather die than admit, "You hurt my feelings," and Sevens switch to other options as a defense against pain.

A power struggle can develop in which Eight tries to limit Seven's activities. This pattern shows the Boss trying to control the schedule and the Epicure making excuses. "Maybe we can meet for lunch" can be heard as either a possibility or a definite commitment, but if lunch doesn't happen, a disappointed Eight wants someone to blame. A crisis surrounds the fine lines of distinction between a good excuse and lying. Rationales sound like lies to the truth-minded Boss. Frustrated by the lack of contact, Eights are likely to pursue and try to wrench a full confession. Eights take control when they feel threatened, but Sevens are hard to pin down.

A growing commitment can create stress for the Seven, who will fall into critical One-like behavior. Rather than being destructive, a good fight often enlivens relationships for Eights, and for Sevens anger can be a gauge of increasing commitment.

Sevens find it easier to walk away than to stay and try to compromise. Why endure pain unless it matters? Why stand and fight unless you care?

When Eights are stressed, they contract into Five to think, to reconsider, and to heal their wounds. At those times a loud Do Not Disturb emanates from behind closed doors. But Eights also say that they love the privacy of their own space even when they're not stressed.

The diagram shows the pair meeting at Five because an Eight's retreat into privacy coincides with Seven's relaxation into Five during times of security. Secure Sevens are not frenetically active; their less important options have fallen away, and they often turn to the home. These periods of mutual quiet restore the couple's peace of mind, but often at the expense of emotional insight. The couple's shared Five tendency tempts them to detach rather than to deal with difficulty. Each can "forget" and happily forgo the tedium of sitting down to discuss and forgive. The resulting accommodation creates a cycle of denial in which the same problem periodically recurs. It shows a good level of development when either can see through the denial of difficulty by initiating a safe way to talk and resolve rather than deny and forget. In Enneagram terms, Seven and Eight are most likely to resolve their differences when they are compatibly seated in the familiar behaviors of each other's wing points. The basic compatibility of "fun hunger" goes a long way toward cushioning the high-decibel clashes that occur when Seven narcissism meets a punishing Eight.

Seven-Eight Partnership at Work

Both types are self-motivated. There's very little lag time between an initial impulse and a quick move into action. Each assumes the accuracy of his or her own perceptions, and both are more aware of what they want than of their impact on other people. Guided by self-certainty, both types are unlikely to question themselves or to realize when they've veered off track.

Sevens veer off to explore options that are not goal related. They are visionaries who like to pursue several projects at the same time. The projects are related to one another in the mind of a Seven, but it won't look that way to the literal-minded Boss. Eights' projects veer off course because of an all-or-nothing production pattern. The energy is either at full throttle or shut down tight. When the energy is dead, going to work becomes deadly boring; but when the deadline rolls around, Eights can galvanize into fast-forward and work around the clock. The pair's differences are magnified under pressure. The Boss is steaming toward the goal while the Epicure's attention is still divided.

Seven managers have to prove themselves to Eights. The Epicure's multidirectional leadership looks ill advised and full of loopholes that could be used to management's advantage. Eights want a clear set of regulations and a fair-minded supervisor. Without a secure platform of rules, there's no way to predict where everybody stands. Eight employees are unusually sensitive to the possibility of manipulation and are likely to see negative intentions in a Seven's managerial approach. If an Eight falls into black-or-white thinking, management looks either fair or not fair, and the manager is therefore either honest or a liar.

Attracted to power, and eager to protect their own interests, Eights often rise within organizations. An astute manager can rely on Eights to beg, borrow, bully, and bless their way through adversity. Given reciprocal loyalty and a logical game plan, an Eight employee can provide the practical day-to-day support that allows an Epicure to network and to broaden a project's scope. Seven's visionary capability can produce an inventive technology or an ingenious process that enrolls an Eight's support. Seven's optimism and inventive spirit keep the enterprise rolling, and an Eight's protective presence ensures solid support.

Eight managers are famous for selectively enforcing the rules, which may be taken by Seven employees as permission to selectively obey them. The fact is that neither sees bending a few rules as necessarily dishonest. Rules are more like suggested guidelines, something to fall back on when you get confused. Eight managers are also famous for denying difficult information. They can literally forget what they don't want to hear. A Seven employee reinforces the tendency to deny painful possibilities; so when trouble hits, the Eight manager will blame the employee for oversights. It helps when a Seven is mature enough to be methodical about keeping track of documentation and an Eight learns the communications skill of good listening.

Partly in response to feeling bullied, a Seven employee will begin to improvise. The Seven will initiate small changes "when it feels right." Eight managers will go ballistic when these discrepancies are discovered; threatened by a potential loss of control, Eights think, "This is only the tip of the iceberg. What else have they been up to?"

The most often reported dispute involves an Eight who was "just trying to assess the damage" squared off with a Seven who was "just trying to help." Sevens stand and fight when persuasion fails or when their integrity is publicly questioned. It's a standoff between two self-referencing people who are so entrenched in their own positions that they cannot see the value in another point of view. This is a situation in which unconscious agendas come quickly to the fore. Eight's fear of losing control is evenly matched by Seven's fear of domination. It helps immensely when a third party can discriminate between the actual breach of trust and the exaggerated ideas that each has developed about the other.

The Seven-Eight combination will stand or fall on the question of trust. It's a formidable combination when Sevens are committed enough to follow a single course of action and Eights feel safe enough to stop testing Seven's word. Constant updates of information help Eights to feel in control. This relationship improves immediately when Seven employees discipline themselves to report in and account for their actions in detail. The news doesn't have to be good. Eights can deal with bad news, but no news makes them very angry.

Seven with Nine: An Epicure-Mediator Couple

Epicures can be highly experimental. They take classes, they keep abreast of events, and they are often attracted to cutting-edge ideas. They can infuse vitality into family life and are often the wick that draws a predictable Nine out of familiar habits. I've often heard the Mediators who speak on Enneagram panels say that they fell into interests ranging from competition Ping-Pong to mysticism when years ago they were dragged along to a first experience by insatiable Seven curiosity.

The partners share a gigantic worldview. Sevens organize their lives to encompass multiple options, and a great deal of their optimism stems from looking forward to tomorrow's plans. Nines are also big-picture thinkers, living in a worldview that's comprehensive enough to incorporate most points of view—and their opposites. The couple's breadth of vision often produces a lovely appreciation of diversity: wide-ranging interests, different groups of friends, and a willingness to let the children be their own unique selves. On the high side both types enjoy an open-minded investigation of life's possibilities, but the down side of "anything is possible" is an inability to choose.

It may take a long time to finalize decisions. There are too many options and no fixed plan. Sevens hate to be pinned down and can spread themselves so thin that priorities are neglected, while Nines are overwhelmed by choice. The two collude in choosing not to make choices. Choices are limiting, and if everything's possible, why bother? Decision making is complicated by the fact that Nines avoid anger and Sevens avoid pain. Both are determined to eliminate conflict and may simply ignore the hard questions.

Epicures avoid choosing by moving very fast. In the Buddhist maps of consciousness they have been called monkey mind because attention rapidly shifts from thing to thing in an attempt to satisfy the gluttony for experience. Sevens need to limit themselves and to concentrate on what's really possible in the relationship. Nines, on the other hand, can get obsessively attached to a single course of action. They avoid choice by circulating around all the possibilities of the same question without moving on. The Nine state of mind could be likened to that of the proverbial elephant, a mind that never forgets and stays in the same place until it gets tired. Nines need to work toward what is essential in their relationships without getting distracted.

Seven is one of the most self-referencing of the Enneagram types, which means that the focus of attention turns toward self-interest. Nines, by contrast, typically merge with a partner, often losing their own agenda in the process. The result is obvious: Mediators focus on Epicures, and Epicures focus on themselves. It is for this reason that the Seven partner typically introduces new perspectives to the relationship, providing a Nine with choice. The arrangement works well when Nines will try something new. It's also possible that the partners will simply form separate orbits of interest. Nines are creatures of habit, and left to their own devices they can either develop activities that sustain them or fall into an armchair depression. This couple can move through periods in which Nine is depressed while Seven stays busily occupied, and neither notices the dilemma. In the absence of conflict, the relationship can drift until some outside event pulls the two together again.

Once alerted, Sevens can pull a Mediator out of an armchair and back into activity; and once in motion, Nines will follow an energetic routine. It helps to formulate a guiding plan. What are we aiming for as a family? What's essential between us? What's productive, and what can be left behind? Once on track, the couple may fight more because they're more invested. It may be a sign of renewed commitment when Sevens are willing to deal with pain and Nines find a position that's worth defending.

Seven-Nine Partnership at Work

Most Nines are energetic workers, but they typically produce under the pressure of a deadline or with a structured schedule that minimizes decision making. The schedule keeps them mobilized, and they can be very efficient when they get rolling; but rapid changes of plans are disorienting, and decisions can signal a dead halt. Mediators are secure when they wake up in the morning and know exactly what they have to do that day, while Sevens continuously revamp the schedule. Sevens are unusually flexible people, and Nines run on habit. These very different work styles can complement each other, although the two may find themselves communicating only when deadlines pull them together.

The partners can share an illusion of limitless time. Work has an unending sameness to Nines when they labor for someone else's agenda, or when they're not identified with their work, it seems like there's always enough time to fit in something extra. You can tell when Nines are vitally interested because they manage their time by refusing additional commitments. Mediators can become inefficient by taking on more than is humanly possible to accomplish, and Epicures misuse time by doing several projects at once and staying up late so they won't miss out on anything. Time management and project spread can be interrelated problems. Sevens like to explore the whole net of associations that a good project stimulates, and Nines can meander along tributaries and backwaters rather than sticking to the agenda. The partners will get a little bit done on a whole lot of different projects until a deadline creates focus.

Sevens also seem to slide into a good thing without having to earn their way, and that entitlement can easily upstage a low-profile Mediator. Sensitive to being overlooked, and reluctant to present an image that draws attention to themselves, Nines are acutely aware of who does the work and who gets the credit. For example, Steve the Nine gave this story:

SO WHO DID THE WORK?

It was Pete's sixtieth birthday. I thought a lot about what to get and how to give it without embarrassing him. So I bought this incredible lathe for his home shop, got Pete's wife to let me in after he was asleep, and I set it up. Another guy, a Seven, shows up for the party, checks out the present, realizes he doesn't have one, and asks to chip in ten dollars. When Pete arrives, the Seven steps forward, puts his hand on the lathe and gives a little presentation speech. He says it's from both of us.

The thing is, you can't call the guy on this stuff. It wasn't premeditated; he isn't really mean, but he walks in and takes the credit.

An unappreciated Nine can go mute, get stubborn, and begin to think, "I'm not being paid to do someone else's job. This isn't my problem." Stubborn Nines can account for their time, but the work doesn't progress. As managers Sevens will try to rally disaffected employees with half promises and charm, which is the worst possible tactic for Nines, who want something concrete. Rather than raising hope, Sevens need to listen to grievances. Epicures are universally impatient with lengthy sagalike presentations, and Nines hold the floor for a long time when they have something to say. Yet a Seven manager will do well to tap the gold mine of information that Nines have about their environment. It's just the kind of information that Sevens are likely to miss. Nines are remarkably forthcoming when they feel recognized, and they have probably noticed many of the bottlenecks and pro-cedural glitches that slow the system down. Furthermore they are excellent candidates to handle the organizational detail that Sevens dislike, and they would be happy to have the certainty of operating a reliable system.

Seven managers are famous for bare presence. What's the point of dealing with details when other priorities beckon? The agile Epicurean mind parlays a good idea into a vision, and that vision often leads away from practical matters. Seven managers also like to breeze through the office at odd times to boost the excitement level. It's just more interesting when there's a flurry. Unfortunately Mediators like predictable assignments and dislike altering course on short notice. Nines slow down when they feel uncertain about the direction, and they can get very slow when they feel used.

As managers Nines place great value on harmony in the workplace and will find comfort in routine. Decision making and departures from the known are difficult, which counters the Epicurean belief that routine stifles creativity. Secure in their own abilities, Seven employees continue to invent a job that works to their own advantage. They frequently navigate around authority while assuming that management will agree with choices that they find appealing.

Mediators must be willing to supervise clearly, even if it means confrontation. This is a sticking point because both types avoid anger. The two will collude to let things slide, which can reengage the cycle of Seven evasion and the entrenched passive aggressive stance of Nine. Scheduled check-ins are a must, or an Epicure will carry on without noticing difficulty and a Mediator will begin to keep score. Consistent communication eases the fact that Sevens don't notice and Nines don't speak, and scheduled check-ins keep Nines from falling behind while holding Sevens accountable.

Double Eight: A Double Boss Couple

Eights are literal about going for it. They have a dead-ahead orientation to very simple chores, which makes them seem oblivious to anything else in the room. Focused on what they want at any given moment, Eights sometimes act as if other people have disappeared. If you're standing in front of the sink, they may literally pick you up and move you aside to fish out one of the dishes. If you're cutting vegetables, they may reach around and open the cutlery drawer against your stomach. "Where's my paring knife? Where did you hide the spoons?" It feels like you exist as a movable object in an Eight's line of sight when they're after something they want, and double Eight is especially prone to dead-ahead focus on personal needs.

Double Eight usually draws an "Oh, wow!" response in Enneagram classes. There's a look of amazement that quickly shifts to puzzled brows and something like, "Did they both survive?" From an outsider's perspective, this combination is going to look combative. The planted body language, the assertiveness, and the directive tone of voice lead people to think that an argument is impending. In actuality Eights may be assertive just to get each other's attention. There are plenty of double Boss stories on panels, but they're usually history. "When I dated this Eight" is a common opening line.

Eights enjoy high-decibel contact. Someone who laughs from deep in the belly, who can push the energy throttle up high. Constantly told to hold their presence back, they find relief in letting it all hang out. One memorable pair who spoke on a couples panel described their relationship in ways that sounded like two Titans about to clash. It made the audience squirm because it sounded like they were escalating toward a brawl. Would this turn ugly? Was someone going to get hurt?

In actuality the couple enjoyed the attention. Neither of them felt out of control. What stirred the audience was hearing that two people could have a big fight, go to bed, make love, and wake up still not on speaking terms. As the panel progressed, it became clear that the problems that particular double Eight couple had did not include abuse; but they did enact their attraction through sexuality and fighting.

For most of us, argument arises from anger or passionate feeling. It may not be that way for double Eight. They like to argue because it's high-intensity contact, and discharging energy feels physically pleasurable. Eights engage their energy in argument but may not be terribly invested in the outcome. Argumentation is their way of trying other people out. It has less to do with winning than with stirring up enough energy to feel vibrant and alive. Double Eight understands that fights can be a way to get closer. Anger doesn't necessarily mean that your feelings are hurt, and you're not breaking up just because you're not on speaking terms.

The stereotype of double Eight romance pictures a highly volatile mix of anger and sexuality. This can be true, but like all couples, each double number partnership has a unique configuration. I've seen couples in which one of the Eights leaned to a wing and seemed strongly Nine-like or Seven-like, lending a very different dynamic to their life together. The most common combination shows one of the partners with all of the extroverted, flamboyant attributes of the type, while the other is more withdrawn and Five-ish. There can be only one real Boss in any household, or the action would periodically escalate beyond the point of return.

Long-term relationships seem to have an obvious Eight, either male or female, coupled with an Eight who is strongly positioned in either Five or the Two-like pleasing stance. Eights "at home" are often mistaken for Twos. They go toward people, they're comforting, and they like to draw people out. Eights in love look very different from the aggressive "masculine" style that we are used to seeing in the workplace. For any of us, affection quite naturally elicits the receptive, surrendered aspects of our type.

It helps when either partner begins to focus inward. Eights lose track of how they come across to others. They usually look outward to challenge what angers them rather than inward to their own motives and needs. If either Eight becomes self-observing, the other can take on the role of protector. Eights rarely go first when they are unsure of the outcome. They find it easier to be a strong supporter than to expose themselves in unexplored emotional territory.

Double Eight Partnership at Work

Eights are focused on winning rather than on looking good as a winner, and that attitude makes them both respected and feared in the workplace. They typically gravitate to positions of power, simply because they dislike being controlled, and they are often successful as a founder. Their quality of energy is especially valued during periods of growth in the business cycle, times when people naturally fall in behind a figure who can handle confrontation and keep moving ahead under fire.

Double Eight combinations almost guarantee a power struggle. Each represents a strong territorial force unless both happen to be on the same side and need each other's assistance. An exchange of favors is the usual way to ensure cooperation. Eights like to respond in kind. A fair offer has a good chance of an honest response, but unfairness stimulates open resistance.

Vengeance is often covert in civilized, high-rise business circles, but I do remember the story of a young Eight entrepreneur who was betrayed and responded by having a large marble tombstone engraved with his ex-partner's name. The stone was delivered, noisily uncrated, and left standing in the front office while dissolution meetings were in progress. The whole point of revenge is to even the score so that you don't feel disadvantaged.

At the very least, Eights are impelled to write an "informative" letter or withhold a piece of useful information. The trick with double Eight is to make the boundaries so clear, and the advantages of cooperation so obvious, that the two wind up supporting each other.

As managers Eights often respect the ambitions that make employees organize a power base. Expecting to be challenged, this manager uses benefits to align employees with the company or against a rival faction. It's a tactic that allows management to control the action rather than leaving a power vacuum for employees to fill, and it's congruent with Eight's tendency to be either protective or adversarial. When the manager has an exaggerated lean toward the stress point of Five, a stingy quality of controlled generosity becomes evident. Giving with one hand (Eight) and taking back with the other (Five).

Eights are less comfortable in the employee position, especially if the boss isn't fair. Fair means room for advancement, and unfair is being kept in your place. Managers should listen to the early warning signs of an Eight employee's thinking, because an Eight often becomes a spokesperson for disaffected factions. Eights become a natural rallying point for dissension because they are willing to handle confrontation and are able to extend a protective mantle over the workspace. Mistrustful Eights want to punish. It's difficult for them to tell the difference between the issue itself and the person who holds that point of view. In a confrontation they may lose track of the issue and simply focus on taking out an opponent by whatever means necessary. If they feel betrayed, then anything goes as long as it can be defended in court.

Most Eights are quite aware that an all-out fight equals being fired, but escalating power struggles can be conducted within the letter of the law and still polarize the workplace. Personnel will feel pressured into taking sides when an Eight wants to know where they stand. It helps to acknowledge difficulty immediately and to be willing to talk face-to-face. Eights have little awareness of their impact on others and will simply turn up the volume until they feel heard. Third-party referees work very well, because discussion stays on track rather than spilling over into personality conflicts. Do not assume that problems will disappear of their own accord, and remember that withholding information is a red flag for Eights.

Eight with Nine: A Boss-Mediator Couple

A stereotype of this relationship pictures the dynamic Boss followed by a docile mate. The actual story, however, seldom fits that picture. Both partners acknowledge Eight's dominant character, and both agree that Nines seldom say no. But those factors don't often produce a dominant-compliant partnership. Questions like, "Who initiates?" or "Who's the follower?" draw an exchange of baffled smiles. What does happen when an irresistible force meets an immovable object? In a meeting of colossal powers, both sides have to give.

The sense of wonder that this pair can develop about each other originates in seeing that a radically different style of relating actually works. Eights chronically overpower their environment, and Nines contain their energy. Eights push through obstacles, and Nines try to forget. It can be enlightening when a Boss learns to defer, and it can be equally educational when Mediators witness the positive effects of rage. This relationship unites the energies of impulse and inertia, which either cancel out each other or produce a distinctive blend.

In the cycles of nature, the irresistible force of a storm barely affects the immovable structure of a mountain. Mountains in turn do not initiate and can only react to what the weather brings. Likewise a relationship depends on both excitement and acceptance. Like Eights, we all call up our force when something matters deeply, and, Nine-like, we have to contain excitement to produce appropriate results. Eights bring an excitement to relationship that sparks a partner's energies. In return, like mountains standing fast during emotional storms, Nines are suited to weather periodic rage.

Because both are placed as wing points on the diagram, we can expect their outlook to coincide slightly. The juncture of lust with self-forgetting (sloth) commonly produces an attraction to creature comforts. The couple settles into a steady domestic routine, and each matches the other's energy level. On the high side they make a good home together and are generous to each other and with friends. On the low side "comfort passions" drain time and energy. During a low-functioning phase, inertia sets in, and the partners do very little for each other. Eights like to control resources, and Nines have a strong appetite for ease. If the activity level drops, either type is prone to not-giving and not-doing. Decisions are made by default. Energy settles into a holding pattern, and very little gets done.

The Eight usually takes action, either constructively or by stirring up trouble. In trying to break out of boredom, Eights can disrupt relationships beyond the point of repair. It helps when either partner can focus on moving ahead in his or her own sphere, without pushing the other to go first. When either falls into self-forgetting, attention wanders from real needs to lesser agendas, and both are likely to think, "Why should I change when you don't make the effort?" The task is to find a personal priority by turning attention inward rather than falling into a cycle where Eight controls and Nine resists.

Eight-Nine Partnership at Work

This partnership can either move rapidly forward or turn into a test of wills. Each has a distinctive way of expressing anger. Eights anger easily and assert control directly, whereas Nines express anger indirectly through passive aggressive resistance. Both types are part of the Enneagram's anger triad (Eight, Nine, and One), which means that anger is crucial in the formation of their passions. Eight's lust is a passionate demand for satisfaction that develops from angry frustration, and anger is also at the root of sloth or a Nine's impulse to forget. The combined energies are highly constructive, with Eight initiating action and handling conflict, leaving Nine to mediate and provide support.

As managers Eights set comprehensive and complicated guidelines that ensure top-down control. Rules will be erratically enforced depending on the Boss's changing level of interest. All rules are off when the manager feels expansive, and the same rules are enforced when an Eight wants to tighten the reins. As managers Eights are likely to make the rules and then break them. They delegate power and then change their minds. There may be unannounced site visits and ominous beetle-browed inquiries followed by a sudden shift to permissiveness. Control lies in ignoring the regulations that other people have to obey and in personally administering the system of rewards and punishment.

Nine employees appreciate firm leadership but can't endure personal confrontation. A best-case scenario shows the decisive Eight rallying employees for a massive push that benefits everyone. Nines can be swept up in the momentum of group action and will line up behind aggressive leadership in a go-ahead stance. Once the goal is accomplished, a Nine's interest easily turns to consolidating gains, and a wise manager will keep the momentum going by letting Mediators set a reasonable pace that can last over time.

If the manager can't shift from combat mode and begins to pressure employees to take on more responsibility than they want to, then Nines can entrench for a war of wills. The manager enforces, and the employee shifts blame. The manager argues, and the Nine goes mute. Stubborn Nines are a match for assertive managers—they can shield themselves from direct confrontation and wait it out for years. They may look amiable and they may not oppose openly, but they can become impossible to supervise.

It's difficult to control passive aggression with a system of rewards and punishments. Rules aren't effective unless people either obey or disobey. An Eight manager will typically tighten control to forestall feeling helpless, while the Nine employee resists and ducks confrontation. Eventually the employee's digressions will trigger an explosion. Open anger is far more comfortable to an Eight than covert passivity, and anger may serve to bring Nine's grievances to the surface. This pair can do well once both come to the table. Eights want to know the truth, and Nines are relieved when they can tell it.

Both types have a tendency to blame. Eights blame others before they question themselves, and Nines blame because they feel dragged along by other people's ideas. It helps when an Eight manager can periodically reaffirm the high points of the partnership. Committed to harmony in the workplace, Mediators avoid conflict and will not take center stage for themselves. However, they appreciate unsolicited recognition and can be drawn out by other people's needs. Eights, on the other hand, can be oblivious to relationship dynamics. They often act without consultation, do not offer compliments easily, and are seldom interested in drawing other people out. If an Eight manager can remember to affirm the employee's actual contributions, a Nine can see the good intentions behind the intimidating Eight persona and learn to hold ground under fire. There is a danger that this partnership can end with Nine being driven out after "the last straw"; but if Nine holds ground then Eight can listen, and when Eight can listen Nine will stay.

Nine managers who digress or become distracted will frighten their Eight employees. It looks like incompetent leadership, which invites a full-out challenge intended to test management's capability. Staff people may feel pressured to take sides as an uneasy Eight tries to separate office enemies from friends. Eights want clear communication coupled with objective rewards and penalties, but Nines often favor a consensus management style. In consensus everybody gets a little bit of the action, often just enough to maintain the status quo. The little-pieces approach makes Eights want to lobby for attention, and the manager will find that indecisiveness leads to open revolt. Eights want certainty, and if they can't get it, they exert influence by making enough noise to get management's ear.

Double Nine: A Double Mediator Couple

A double Nine couple gives the appearance of being merged with each other. It's not that the partners physically look the same, it's more a similarity of resonance and a way of speaking that seems to reaffirm an ongoing agreement. This is a seemingly settled couple, with few divisive questions or jagged emotions to disturb the peace. It's a live-and-let-live way of being. A willingness to accept each other unconditionally, without forcing change, and a mutual desire to stay comfortable.

The inside story is described quite differently. Roiled by a sense of conflicting inner forces, each looks to the other to stimulate personal identity, standing either for or against a partner's priority rather than for herself or himself. Nines say that they can merge into a symbiotic relationship as long as there's no conflict. But with full commitment, the pressure begins to mount: "Am I doing this for myself of for others? Did I chose to be here, or is this someone else's idea?" Problems with initiating priorities are magnified with a double Nine couple: "Who's choosing here?" There is no fixed reference point to agree with or to oppose. The options all begin to seem similar, and there's a crosscurrent of conflicting needs: "Should we or shouldn't we? Is it worth fighting about? Probably not." Merged in their mutual desire to avoid conflict, the partners can collude in not-doing, as they conspire to build a harmonious lifestyle that will keep distress away. The catch-22 of this preoccupation with comfort is that keeping discomfort away requires a lot of energy.

The low side of this relationship shows each enmeshed in routine interests, unessential undertakings that keep the status quo afloat. A little bit of everything gets done, but nothing seems finalized, for the energy that could force a wake-up call to essential activity might also create conflict. Better to spend energy on familiar, less important matters and preserve the peace.

The high side of double Nine shows the couple in nonverbal, unified accord. If either partner engages a personal reason for being, the other will merge and give support. It helps when each partner can separate from the other's interests, go deeply within, and find that personal reason for being. This couple is ideally suited to help each other, but the partners will have to stand up for themselves, rather than being for or against the other's priority.

Double Nine Partnership at Work

Of the twenty or so double Nine couples I have interviewed, sixteen also work together. It is as if the business provides an external focus that animates the partners, drawing them into a familiar arena every day. There is a mutual desire to rely on the schedule and to avoid complicated decision making; each carries out his or her own duties, refining the system little by little until the business seems to run on its own.

In tough decision-making situations, both Nines will have to be drawn out and encouraged to take a position. Nines often see decisions as matters of convenience, as arbitrary: "Don't all roads eventually lead to the same end?" "Why take this route rather than that one?" Conflicts may appear to be resolved and then erupt at a later date if a real position hasn't been uncovered. Settlement will be delayed until the full story emerges from both sides and each can express her or his resentments.

Nines who feel compromised may "wake up" later and feel sold out. They may have gone along in order to avoid conflict and only later realized what they really felt. Third parties often have to ask Nines to voice all the opinions involved and to discover their own voice by a process of elimination: "Not that, not that," will finally unearth a position.

As managers Nines have to learn to give clear directives. Not wanting to influence others, to say no, or to stir up controversy can produce lethargic leadership. These managers identify with all sides of a question, becoming overburdened by too much input, rather than simply focusing on the best interests of the business. In management, Nines would rather mediate for others than defend a position of their own. Of all the types, they can most easily slip into temporary agreement with an adversary, with the desire to avoid conflict placing them at a disadvantage in negotiating for themselves. It's always easier for Nines to disclose their thinking to neutral parties than for them to go public on their own behalf, which makes them good candidates for arbitration procedures.

As employees Nines are vulnerable to merging with the workplace atmosphere. In interacting with other Nines it may feel too unsettling, too disturbing to push the energy throttle up higher than the requirements of the next job or the next half hour of the day. The message is "don't rock the boat." The path of least resistance lies in repeating a routine. Although the routine can be physically exhausting, it feels secure to be doing something familiar. It's far more attractive to improve a known system with an expected outcome and preset standards of quality control than to initiate an experiment. Known procedures give Nines a feeling of flow, of being into it, of conducting themselves in ways that they can count on. Even though it can be arduous, the exhaustion is familiar, protective, and attractive.

It helps to periodically review grievances and then to come to a resolution in stages. Nines have to feel that they are making the decision on their own, without being pressured into a compromise. Setting a schedule of dates for the stages of a decision—"Can you hand in documents by the end of next month?"—is a far better tactic than pushing for immediate closure. Each piece should be discussed and given time to settle, allowing change to take place in a reasonable, humane manner. If the Nine has anything at all to lose in the situation, resolving a conflict has to be assimilated piece by piece.

IV

Epilogue

I SEE A BIT OF myself in all nine types because each is grounded in an appropriate emotional response. I do not have to be a Nine to merge with a loved one's agenda, nor must I be a Four to share another's pain. Each of these reactions is appropriate and normal. How natural to feel afraid when we are threatened. How human to be angry if we feel misused.

The Enneagram model is a way of organizing the human condition around nine emotional passions, each of which is based in a common emotional concern. The characteristics that form around the nucleus of the passion correlate well with contemporary personality theory, but the Enneagram's power lies in the view that a passion can act as a transformer from ordinary to higher consciousness.

The passions themselves have a long history in sacred tradition. As I pointed out in Part I, they are best known as Christianity's seven capital sins, plus two generic tendencies that all types hold in common. Rather than being a new psychological discovery, it would seem that the Enneagram of personality types is really a modern rediscovery of a very old spiritual tradition.

This jewel of sacred tradition is currently being reset in a framework of contemporary psychological ideas. The Enneagram is a living teaching in the sense that it lives in the self-observations of the people who inhabit the types. Those who embody the nine passions can speak as living authorities about the modern ways in which our own dilemma is acted out.

The "Directory of Relationships," which summarizes the key interactions between the types, is based on information offered by participants in what we call oral tradition classes. Here representatives of the types speak with one another and their significant others on stage. The audience has an opportunity to witness the conversation and to question the couples directly. The couples who produced this material are normal and high-functioning people. Their goals in attending classes were to improve their relationships, to see themselves through the eyes of their loved ones, and to examine their own inner biases. If, as the Enneagram suggests, those same biases are distorted aspects of the human essence, then the couples win twice: first by gaining insight into their own relationships, and, second, by discovering a key to their spiritual nature.

Future Directions

Over the last ten years the Enneagram has moved from the small domain of private classes into a broad public arena. This is a fascinating phase for Enneagram studies. Many authors have put forward their personal views about the system. Each has something unique to offer. I see our emerging differences of opinion as a healthy atmosphere for growth, and I believe the different views will coalesce into a unified teaching in the next few years.

To me the whole model, rather than merely a single piece of the nine-pointed star, is worthy of attention. In looking at the diagram as a whole, I see type as tripartite: each personality represents a dynamic relationship between the concerns of the type proper and the ways in which the type alters in security or under stress and risk.

I conclude this because I see the model as a flow pattern, in which energies descend from essence, or the realm of pure being, into ordinary events. The arrows chart the movement of energy between the types, indicating a normal flow at the security point, which gets bottlenecked at the type point when childhood defenses form. If the system indeed describes energies as well as personality characteristics, the energetic flow is weakest after the bottleneck, in the behaviors attributed to the point of risk. This does not mean that the characteristics of the stress point are necessarily more compulsive; they are simply coping strategies that appear when the psychological defenses of the type proper are inadequate. I also observe a dynamic relationship between the two wing points adjacent to each type point, which I believe contributes to the formation of type.

These theoretical matters are of importance to Enneagram scholarship as the system begins to find its place in psychological literature. My co-teacher, David Daniels, M.D., and I are currently preparing a book about Enneagram theory and the psychological and spiritual strategies for healing that the theory suggests.

Notes

1. The statement is commonly attributed to Freud. His actual formulation has drawn considerable commentary through the years. For example, the *Introductory Lectures (1916–1917)* contains a formal statement of his thinking. "The distinction between nervous health and neurosis is thus reduced to a practical question and is decided by the outcome—by whether the subject is left with a sufficient amount of capacity for enjoyment and of efficiency. . . . I need not tell you that this discovery is the theoretical justification for our conviction that neuroses are in principle curable in spite of their being based on constitutional disposition" (XVI, 457).

Ruben Fine, commenting on the value of the psychoanalytic tradition, sees the criteria of love and work as "a good example of how the analytic ideal evolved in the minds of leading analysts" (Rubin Fine, *Love and Work: The Value System of Psychoanalysis* [New York: Continuum, 1990], 160).

2. *"Lieben und arbeiten"* (to love and to work) is the reported quote as discussed in Erik H. Erikson, *Childhood and Society* (New York: W. W. Norton, 1963), 265.

3. Idries Shah, *The Sufis* (New York: Anchor Books, Doubleday, 1964), 69.

4. Webster defines *consciousness* as an awareness that something was or is happening or existing. The Enneagram system

implies that there are many different orders of consciousness. A classic work on defining states of consciousness is Charles T. Tart, *States of Consciousness* (El Cerrito, CA: Psychological Processes, 1983), originally published in 1975. Another discussion of levels of consciousness from the Gurdjieff point of view can be found in Charles Tart, *Waking Up* (Boston: Shambhala, 1986).

5. Thinley Norbu, *Small Golden Key.* Trans. Lisa Anderson (New York: Jewel Publishing House, 1985), 24.

6. We think of ourselves as the structure of thoughts, feelings, bodily memories, and motivations that were laid down in early life. The combination of these identifications forms a self-concept that in spiritual teachings is sometimes referred to as the false personality. The false-self system arises from the need to cope with physical and emotional life. Sacred tradition points to the "real" as the full spectrum of awareness that lies beyond the private boundaries of thought, feeling, and physical sensation. From this perspective, the real self is far more expanded than the attributes of a type.

7. See the Enneagram Bibliography on page 413 for a list of books in print.

8. The fixed ideas, or cognitive aspect of a passion, are simply the mental preoccupations that are anchored in the emotional bias of the passion. Both the passion and mental ideas are to some extent conscious. Unconscious defense mechanisms exist that also affect both the emotional and the cognitive aspects of a passion.

9. Gurdjieff's concept of chief feature, or vice, continues the teaching that a negative feature of personality can be transformed to its higher opposite. Gurdjieff believed that our chief feature, or chief liability, could be converted to our greatest asset.

10. C. S. Nott, *Journey Through This World: The Second Journal of a Pupil* (New York: Samuel Weiser, 1969), 87. It is useful to note Nott's choice of *vanity* as a generic source of personality

bias in conjunction with the seven capital sins. Vanity was placed as the cognitive aspect of the deceit passion by Oscar Ichazo at the Three point on the diagram. Ichazo also placed the generic characteristic of fear at the Six point, to a total of nine capital tendencies.

11. Gurdjieff Foundation schools are active today and can be found in most major cities. The standard work for Gurdjieff information is by J. Walter Driscoll, *Gurdjieff, An Annotated Bibliography* (New York: Garland Publishing, 1985).

12. Richard Rohr and Andreas Ebert, *Discovering the Enneagram: An Ancient Tool for a New Spiritual Journey* (New York: Crossroad, 1992), 25.

13. Paolo Milano, ed., *The Portable Dante* (New York: Viking, 1947), *Purgatorio* section.

14. John Lilly and Joseph Hart, "The Arica Training," in *Transpersonal Psychologies,* ed. Charles Tart (1975; reprint, El Cerrito, CA: Psychological Processes, 1983).

15. Points Three and Six in the model's central triangle were said to mark the invisible junctures (shock points) between the planes of ordinary awareness and the realms of essence, or pure being. For an introduction to the theory of shock points, see Kathleen Riordan Speeth, *The Gurdjieff Work* (Los Angeles: Jeremy P. Tarcher, 1989), 21–29.

16. For a classic work on this center, see Karlfried Graf Von Durckheim, *Hara: The Vital Centre of Man* (London: Mandala Books, 1977).

17. Claudio Naranjo, M.D., *Ennea-Type Structures: Self-Analysis for the Seeker* (Nevada City, CA: Gateways/IDHHB, 1990), 4.

18. Gurdjieff's model suggests that the rising force of the consolidated abdominal center is fed by three separate "instinctual" energies. In my opinion these energies are mediated by the

physically based subcenters described in the physiology of sacred experience. These subcenters are located in the physical body and can be energized during meditation. When energized, the primary subcenters can be felt at the perinium, the solar plexus, and the base of the spine. Whether Gurdjieff's three "instinctual" centers are in fact related to the stages of psychological growth that depend on maturing instinct is totally open to question by developmental theorists.

19. Gina Price, *Type A Behavior: A Model for Research and Practice* (San Diego: Harcourt Brace Jovanovich, 1982).

Bibliography

BOOKS ABOUT THE ENNEAGRAM

Elbert, Andreas, ed. *Experiencing the Enneagram.* New York: Crossroad, 1992.

Hurley, Kathleen, and Theodore Dobson. *What's My Type?* San Francisco: HarperCollins, 1991.

Keyes, Margaret. *Emotions and the Enneagram.* Berkeley: Wingbow Press, 1989.

Metz, S. N. D. deN, Barbara and John Burchill, O. P. *The Enneagram and Prayer: Discovering Our True Selves Before God.* Denville, NJ: Dimension Books, Inc., 1987.

Naranjo, Claudio. *Ennea-Type Structures.* Nevada City, CA: Gateways/IDHHB, 1990.

Palmer, Helen. *The Enneagram: Understanding Yourself and the Others in Your Life.* San Francisco: Harper & Row, 1988.

Riso, Don Richard. *Personality Types: Using the Enneagram for Self Discovery.* Boston: Houghton Mifflin, 1987.

————. *Understanding the Enneagram.* Boston: Houghton Mifflin, 1990.

————. *Discovering Your Personality Type.* Boston: Houghton Mifflin, 1992.

THE ARICA PERSPECTIVE ON THE ENNEAGRAM

Ichazo, Oscar. *Interviews with Oscar Ichazo.* New York: Arica Institute, Inc., 1982.

————. *Letters to the School.* New York: Arica Institute, Inc., 1988.

Jeffrey, Francis and John C. Lilly, M.D. *John Lilly, So Far . . .* Los Angeles: Jeremy P. Tarcher, Inc., 1990.

Lilly, M.D., John C. *The Center of the Cyclone: An Autobiography of Inner Space.* New York: The Julian Press, Inc., 1972.

HISTORY OF THE SEVEN CAPITAL TENDENCIES

Bloomfield, Morton W. *The Seven Deadly Sins.* Michigan State College Press, 1952.

Cayré, A. A. Fulbert. *Manual of Patrology and History of Theology.* Vol. I. Paris: Desclée & Co., 1897.

Chadwick, Owen. *John Cassian.* Cambridge University Press, 1968.

Fleming, Ian, ed. *The Seven Deadly Sins.* New York: William Morrow, 1962.

Hausherr, Irénée. *Spiritual Direction in the Early Christian East.* Kalamazoo, MI: Cistercian Publications, 1990.

Luibheid, Colm. *John Cassian Conferences.* New York: Paulist Press, 1985.

Luke, Helen M. *Dark Wood to White Rose: Journey and Transformation in Dante's Divine Comedy.* New York: Parabola Books, 1989.

Lyman, Stanford M. *The Seven Deadly Sins: Society and Evil.* New York: St. Martin's Press, Inc., 1978.

Schimmel, Solomon. *The Seven Deadly Sins.* New York: The Free Press, 1992.

Tanquerey, S. S., D. D., Adolphe. *The Spiritual Life: A Treatise on Ascetical and Mystical Theology.* Toutnai, Belgium: Desclée & Co. Publishers, 1938.

A CHRISTIAN PERSPECTIVE ON THE ENNEAGRAM

Beesing, Maria, Robert Nogosek, and Patrick O'Leary. *The Enneagram: A Journey of Self Discovery.* Denville, NJ: Dimension Books, 1984.

Callahan, S. J., William. *The Enneagram for Youth, Student Edition.* Chicago: Loyola Univ. Press, 1992.

————. *The Enneagram for Youth: Counselor's Manual.* Chicago: Loyola Univ. Press, 1992.

Rohr, Richard, and Andreas Ebert. *Discovering the Enneagram.* New York: Crossroad, 1992.

————, et al. *Experiencing the Enneagram.* New York: Crossroad, 1992.

Tickerhoof, Bernard. *Conversion and the Enneagram.* Denville, NJ: Dimension Books, 1991.

Zuercher, Suzanne. *Enneagram Spirituality.* Notre Dame, IN: Ave Maria Press, 1992.

ARTICLES AND CHAPTERS ABOUT THE ENNEAGRAM

Keen, Sam. "A Conversation About Ego Destruction with Oscar Ichazo." In *Psychology Today,* July 1973.

Lilly, John, and Joseph Hart. "The Arica Training." In *Transpersonal Psychologies.* Ed. Charles Tart. New York: Harper & Row, 1975.

Metzner, Ralph. "The Arica Enneagram of Types." In *Know Your Type: Maps of Identity.* New York: Doubleday, 1979.

Wagner, Jerome. "Reliability and Validity Study of a Sufi Personality Typology: The Enneagram." In *Journal of Clinical Psychology.* 39(5), September 1983.

————. "The Enneagram and Myers-Briggs: Two Windows on the Self." In *New Catholic World,* May/June 1986.

DISSERTATIONS ABOUT THE ENNEAGRAM

Beauvais, Phyllis. "Claudio Naranjo and SAT: Modern Manifestation of Sufism." Ph.D., 1973, Hartford Seminary. 35/12-A, P. 8005. GAX 75–13868.

Campbell, Richard. "The Relationship of Arica Training to Self-Actualization and Interpersonal Behavior." Ph.D., 1975, United States International University. 36/03-B. GAX 75–20244.

Gamard, William Sumner. "Interrater Reliability and Validity of Judgements of Enneagram Personality Types." Ph.D., 1986, California Institute of Integral Studies. GAX 86–25584.

Lincoln, Robert. "The Relation Between Depth Psychology and Protoanalysis." Ph.D., 1983, California Institute of Transpersonal Psychology. Research Abstracts International. LD 00676.

Randall, Stephen. "Development of an Inventory to Assess Enneagram Personality Type." Ph.D., 1979, California Institute of Integral Studies. 40/09-B. GAX 80–05160.

Wagner, Jerome. "A Descriptive, Reliability, and Validity Study of the Enneagram Personality Typology." Ph.D., 1981, Loyola University, Chicago. 41/11A. GAX 81–09973.

Wolf, Steven. "Effects of the Arica Training on Adult Development: A Longitudinal Study." Ph.D., 1985, Saybrook Institute. 46/11B GAX 85–28854.

Zinkle, Thomas. "A Pilot Study Toward the Validation of the Sufi Personality Typology." Ph.D., 1975, United States International University. 35/05B. GAX 74–24529.

(To order copies, contact *Dissertation Abstracts International,* Dissertation Publishing, University Microfilm International, 300 N. Zeeb Road, P.O. Box 1764, Ann Arbor, MI 48106. Telephone: 800–521–3042.)

THE GURDJIEFF TRADITION

Bennett, J. G. *Enneagram Studies.* York Beach, ME: Samuel Weiser, 1983.

Campbell, Robert. *Fisherman's Guide.* Boston: Shambhala, 1985.

De Ropp, Robert. *The Master Game.* New York: Dell, 1974.

Driscoll, J. Walter. *Gurdjieff: An Annotated Bibliography.* New York: Garland Publishing, 1985.

Friedlander, Joel. *Body Types: The Enneagram of Essence Types.* New York: Globe Press, 1993.

Moore, James. *Gurdjieff: The Anatomy of a Myth.* Rockport, MA: Element Inc., 1991.

Mouravieff, B. *Gnosis I: Exoteric Cycle.* England: Agora Books/Praxis Institute Press, 1989.

Nicoll, Maurice. *Gurdjieff and Ouspensky Vol. I–V* (Enneagram in Vol. II). Boulder, CO: Shambhala Publications, 1984.

Nott, C. S. *Teachings of Gurdjieff: A Pupil's Journal.* York Beach, ME: Samuel Weiser, 1961.

Ouspensky, P. D. *The Psychology of Man's Possible Evolution.* New York: Vintage, 1974.

Popoff, Irmis B. *The Enneagram of the Man of Unity.* New York: Samuel Weiser, 1978.

Speeth, Kathleen. *The Gurdjieff Work.* Los Angeles: Jeremy P. Tarcher, 1989.

Tart, Charles. *Waking Up.* Boston: Shambhala, 1986.

Webb, James. *The Harmonious Circle.* New York: G.P. Putnam's Sons, 1980.

BOOKS THAT SUPPORT THE ENNEAGRAM CONTEXT

Almaas, A. H. *The Elixir of Enlightenment.* York Beach, ME: Samuel Weiser, 1984.

———. *Essence: The Diamond Approach to Inner Realization.* York Beach, ME: Samuel Weiser, 1986.

———. *The Void.* Berkeley: Diamond Books, 1986.

———. *The Pearl Beyond Price.* Berkeley: Diamond Books, 1988.

Horney, Karen. *Our Inner Conflicts.* New York: W. W. Norton & Company, Inc., 1945.

———. *Neurosis and Human Growth.* New York: W. W. Norton & Company, Inc., 1991.

Shah, Idries. *The Sufis.* New York: Anchor Books, Doubleday, 1964.

Helen Palmer's office will furnish information about all areas of her work. These include oral tradition workshops, professional trainings, and organizational consulting.

Her office will also provide information on Enneagram teaching throughout the United States, with referrals to graduates of her Enneagram Professional Training Program in your area.

Workshops in the Oral Tradition have developed the *Nine Points of View Video Series,* including a companion set to this book: *Men on Relationships* and *Women on Relationships.* Using illustrative graphics and speakers who represent their own types, these videos explicate the themes of love and work. These and other videos are available to the general public. A wide-ranging list of audio cassettes is also available on request.

To have your name added to the mailing list so that you may receive the current teaching schedule, please contact the office:

Workshops in the Oral Tradition with Helen Palmer
1442 A Walnut Street, Suite 377
Berkeley, California 94709
Voice (510) 843–7621
Fax (510) 540-7626